# THE LIVES OF STORIES

### THREE ABORIGINAL–SETTLER FRIENDSHIPS

**Aboriginal History Incorporated**

Aboriginal History Inc. is a part of the Australian Centre for Indigenous History, Research School of Social Sciences, The Australian National University, and gratefully acknowledges the support of the School of History and the National Centre for Indigenous Studies, The Australian National University. Aboriginal History Inc. is administered by an Editorial Board which is responsible for all unsigned material. Views and opinions expressed by the author are not necessarily shared by Board members.

**Contacting Aboriginal History**

All correspondence should be addressed to the Editors, Aboriginal History Inc., ACIH, School of History, RSSS, 9 Fellows Road (Coombs Building), Acton, ANU, 2601, or aboriginal.history@anu.edu.au.

**WARNING:** Readers are notified that this publication may contain names or images of deceased persons.

# THE LIVES OF STORIES

## THREE ABORIGINAL–SETTLER FRIENDSHIPS

EMMA DORTINS

Published by ANU Press and Aboriginal History Inc.
The Australian National University
Acton ACT 2601, Australia
Email: anupress@anu.edu.au

Available to download for free at press.anu.edu.au

ISBN (print): 9781760462406
ISBN (online): 9781760462413

WorldCat (print): 1066258764
WorldCat (online): 1066259271

DOI: 10.22459/LS.12.2018

This title is published under a Creative Commons Attribution-NonCommercial-NoDerivatives 4.0 International (CC BY-NC-ND 4.0).

The full licence terms are available at
creativecommons.org/licenses/by-nc-nd/4.0/legalcode

Cover design and layout by ANU Press

This edition © 2018 ANU Press and Aboriginal History Inc.

# Contents

List of Figures . . . . . . . . . . . . . . . . . . . . . . . . . . . . . . . . . . . . . . . . . vii
Acknowledgements . . . . . . . . . . . . . . . . . . . . . . . . . . . . . . . . . . . ix
Introduction: Ambassadors Between the Present and the Past. . . . . . . 1

## Part 1: The Life and Adventures of James Morrill

1. Crossing There and Back, Living to Tell a Tale. . . . . . . . . . . . . . .13
2. Becoming First White Resident. . . . . . . . . . . . . . . . . . . . . . . . .41
3. Ways of Knowing the Burdekin. . . . . . . . . . . . . . . . . . . . . . . . .67

## Part 2: The Many Truths of Bennelong's Tragedy

4. Bennelong's Rise and Fall. . . . . . . . . . . . . . . . . . . . . . . . . . . . .91
5. History, Tragedy and Truth in Bennelong's Story . . . . . . . . . . . .115
6. Ambassador between the Present and the Past. . . . . . . . . . . . .137

## Part 3: Friendship Beyond the Grave

7. A Family Heirloom . . . . . . . . . . . . . . . . . . . . . . . . . . . . . . . .157
8. At the Confluence of Two Stories . . . . . . . . . . . . . . . . . . . . . .183
9. Friendship and the Grave . . . . . . . . . . . . . . . . . . . . . . . . . . .213

Conclusion: Living Histories, Living Stories . . . . . . . . . . . . . . . . . . . .227
Bibliography . . . . . . . . . . . . . . . . . . . . . . . . . . . . . . . . . . . . . . . . .233

# List of Figures

Figure 1: Morrill's grave in the Bowen Cemetery, marked by the obelisk erected by the Bowen Historical Society in 1963 . . . . . . 68

Figure 2: Mural representing the story of James Morrill in the grounds of Bowen State Primary School, painted by Robert Paul in 1992, and restored by the artist in 2012 . . . . . . . 83

Figure 3: Depiction of Bennelong with the Sydney Opera House, *National Aboriginal Day Magazine*, 1981, artist unidentified . . 100

Figure 4: Bennelong featured in the *Cadi Jam Ora* garden panels, Royal Botanic Garden, Sydney. . . . . . . . . . . . . . . . . . . . . . . . . 107

Figure 5: Memorial dedicated to Windradyne by Mr and Mrs Roy Suttor and the Bathurst Historical Society in 1954, with two burial mounds visible behind. . . . . . . . . . . . . . . . . . . . . . . . . 160

Figure 6: Windradyne's grave conservation area in 2018. . . . . . . . . . 223

# Acknowledgements

This book is based on a thesis I wrote at the University of Sydney between 2007 and 2012, and I wish to express my thanks to the university and its Department of History for supporting much of the research and writing that make up this book. My supervisors Peter Read and Mark McKenna provided intellectual nourishment, guidance and inspiration along the winding path of my thesis, and the book it has become. Richard White acted as sounding board for many of my ideas, and he and Cath Bishop have encouraged me to persist with this book and with my interest in history. Kate Fullagar opened up invaluable opportunities for collaboration around Bennelong's story. John Hirst enlivened the postgraduate history experience with a seminar series that broadened our horizons and enabled us to contribute to each other's work. A warm thanks to members of John's writing groups who did so, especially Rosemary Kerr, Hannah Forsyth, Daniel Fleming, Deborah Beck, Judith Bonzol, Matt Allen, Avril Alba and Alex Cameron-Smith. Thanks to Iain McCalman and Larissa Behrendt for comments on my thesis that have been invaluable in writing this book.

Thanks to those who gave me a home away from home while I undertook research, as well as connecting me with local people, places, events and resources. I would particularly like to thank Glyn and Glenis Davies, Viv and Ian Youngs, Heather and Evan Lawton and my cousin Vivien Keller-Tuberg and her family, Russell McGregor and his colleagues at James Cook University, and Peter Whalley and staff of the Oodgeroo Unit, Queensland University of Technology.

Many generous people shared the results of their hard-won research with me, and their expertise in and passion for history and community, and I would particularly like to thank Anna Clark, Keith Smith, Valerie Cooms, David Roberts, Loftus Dun, Colin Ellis, John and David Suttor, Phillip Murray, Bill Murray, Alex Roberts, Kath Schilling, Gavin Andrews,

Bronwyn Batten, Chanelle Burman, Vanessa Cavanagh, Judy MacGregor Smith and the Bennelong Residents for Reconciliation, and Dilys Maltby and Ann Wills of the Bowen Historical Society. Thanks also to the staff of the Mitchell Library and State Library of New South Wales, the National Library of Australia, Fisher Library, the Australian Institute for Aboriginal and Torres Strait Islander Studies Library and the Office of Environment and Heritage librarians, for your patience and dedication.

Thank you to Aboriginal History Inc. and to Rani Kerin (who has been a welcoming and patient editor) for making it possible to write this book alongside my work, at the same time as being a mother. My colleagues in the former research section of the Country, Culture and Heritage Division, Office of Environment and Heritage, enriched my interpretations of places and people's connections to them, encouraged me to set sail with a book proposal and supported me in seeking a publisher—thanks especially to Caroline Ford, Denis Byrne and Steve Brown.

Sue Rosen taught me how to manage my research, write early and be a persistent historian, skills without which I would never have written this, my first book. Fellow members of the Professional Historians Association have also kept me connected and inspired about making history, especially my friend and neighbour Laila Ellmoos.

Friends and family encouraged me in this project over the past decade, especially Louise and Marita Dortins and Matthew Wallman, who read and commented on my work, and Mum and Dad, and Matt and August, who have supported this project and lived with it.

# Introduction: Ambassadors Between the Present and the Past

Shipwreck survivor James Morrill was re-adopted into frontier settler society in 1863 after spending 17 years living with Birri-gubba people in North Queensland. In researching his story, I wanted to know how he had experienced his Birri-gubba adoption and whether his beliefs and world view had changed as a result. Instead, I found a story about a story: a story Morrill told not once, but repeatedly—to magistrates, journalists and jostling public audiences who shaped it with their questions and with the kind of colony they were making. After his death, Morrill's story lived on, and he became a 'first white resident' of North Queensland. His story became part of the region's pioneer history; however, it also remained apart from it, emerging as well from the profound reservoir of knowledge that Aboriginal peoples of the Burdekin had shared with Morrill, knowledge that is claimed and reclaimed as Birri-gubba people tell his story today.

In this book, I follow the ins and outs of Morrill's story and two others: the story of Bennelong and the personal costs of his relationship with Governor Phillip and the Sydney colonists, and the story of friendship between Wiradjuri leader Windradyne and the Suttor family. Each is an intimate story about people involved in relationships of goodwill, care, adoptive kinship and mutual learning across cultures, and the strains of maintaining or relinquishing these bonds as they took part in the larger events that signified the colonisation of Aboriginal lands by the British and Aboriginal peoples' adaptations in response. This book focuses on the changing meanings of these stories as they have been told and retold by generations of storytellers. It is through histories of storytelling that I seek to reinterpret these three relationships and to shed light on the ways in which cross-cultural bonds and cultural crossings have been understood more generally in Australian engagements with the past.

Regarded from a distance, each of the three stories contributes to a now well-recognised pattern of Australian history-making. A few intriguing and isolated retellings survive from the nineteenth and early twentieth centuries in which Aboriginal histories formed curious historical backwaters or 'melancholy footnotes'—to pluralise John La Nauze's epithet—to memoirs, local histories and stories of empire. A proliferation of versions, stemming from the 1960s and 1970s, reflects both the democratisation of history writing and access to publishing in postwar Australia, including for Indigenous people, and a growing recognition of Indigenous histories that stretch into the deep time of ancient human migrations and continue to be a central part of contemporary Australian histories and lives.[1] Closer examination reveals committed and passionate storytellers telling and retelling each of these stories for reasons of their own, from the lifetimes of Bennelong, Morrill and Windradyne up to the present. Storytellers have told these stories to demonstrate social theories and narratives of local and national progress, or to advance civil rights and land rights activism. Sometimes, even at the same time, they have been told to make family connections, communicate intimate personal reflections and more free-floating musings on human nature, and for the joy of storytelling itself. This book explores the historical, social, cultural and narrative meanings of these three stories as they have been told and retold by storytellers grappling with the realities of their own times and their own place in history.

The form of narrative, or 'genre', is an integral part of the traditions formed by the tellings of these stories. Morrill's story, even from his own lips, is entangled with shipwreck and castaway stories; Bennelong's story has come to be closely associated with features of tragedy and elements of a much larger story of 'cultural collision'; and the friendship of Windradyne and the Suttor family has shifted in emphasis over the decades, and is now understood by many storytellers as a reconciliation story. Critical histories and their public and popular interpretations since the 1970s have multiplied the possibilities for these stories by helping Australians to think about a much greater range of historical relationships between Aboriginal people and settlers. At the same time, genre has generated and transmitted cultural meanings on parallel paths, intersecting at times with

---

1   La Nauze, 'The Study of Australian History 1929–1959', 11. For an account of this change, and how it has been reflected upon by historians and other public thinkers, see Curthoys, 'W. E. H. Stanner and the Historians'.

conscious shifts in Australian history-making, but not at their bidding, making these stories 'ambassadors' between the present and the past on several levels.

Retelling old stories of friendly relationships between Aboriginal people and settlers over the past three decades embodies a fascinating ambivalence. If recognising moral actions in the past helps us move forward in an ethical way in the present, then stories of goodwill might provide a foundation for present and future reconciliation. Yet, this process is riddled with anxiety. Could the course of history have been different? How should we feel about friendly relations in situations in which they did not seem to make a difference, let alone friendships that now seem to have been based in inequality, or even made in the service of invasion?

It was partly the *First Australians* television series—a substantially Indigenous production presenting a history of the past two centuries from an Indigenous perspective—and responses to it, that focused my attention on stories about mutually respectful and caring relationships.[2] Such stories were a central feature of the series, partly because producers Rachel Perkins and Darren Dale wanted to help their viewers maintain a sense of 'salvation and hope' as they contemplated a history that is bleak in so many ways. Perkins and Dale wanted to communicate the moral complexity of Australian history in the face of political forces that had tended to reduce it to a 'goodies and baddies story'.[3] Their aim struck home with some viewers. For example, 'Matthew from North NSW' praised *First Australians* as:

> A beautiful documentary. Seriously brought a tear to my eye. There was friendship in the past, let's not let this war mongering, ignorance that prevailed ruin this nation again. I want our kids to look back to our generation with pride not shame, not hurt.[4]

Past friendship, as much as past violence, engaged this viewer emotionally and sounded a call to better relations in the present, as well as showing him that they might be possible. Stories of friendship showed him that pride in Australian history might be possible too, without denying the dispossession of Aboriginal people. Stories of mutual respect, cultural

---

2   Nowra and Perkins, 'Episode 1: They Have Come to Stay'.
3   Sacha Molitorisz, 'The Story of Black Australia', *The Age*, 9 October 2008, Green Guide, 12; 'Unearthing Our First Voices', *The Canberra Times*, 14 October 2008.
4   'Matthew from North NSW', 16 October 2008, SBS First Australians, Your Comments, accessed 16 December, 2008, www.sbs.com.au/firstaustralians/.

curiosity and the building of trust between people tend to be small-scale, with faces we can focus on and individuals with whom we can identify—the kinds of histories that readily tap into the 'distinctly personal sense of historical subjectivity' that Anna Clark found at the centre of her respondents' engagement with the past when she spoke with diverse groups of Australians about Australian history.[5] The *First Australians* series was firmly based in the activity of *retelling* stories—that is, telling them from an Indigenous perspective to new generations, to broader audiences and on television. The series invited viewers to become part of a community of storytellers and listeners capable of communicating across time and across cultures, engaging in a thoughtful, and personal, re-examination of the national past.

Telling stories of caring and respectful cross-cultural relationships can be uplifting, and can forge connections between people. However, in tracing the stories of Morrill, Bennelong, and Windradyne and the Suttor family, this book finds that it is never straightforward. As much as such stories are founded on cross-cultural understanding, they are also infused with an incompleteness of understanding, as first the participants themselves, and then subsequent storytellers, have sought to apprehend and articulate these relationships from within their own social and cultural realities. The contemporary written sources for Windradyne's friendship with the Suttor family are a pair of letters to the editor of the Sydney papers, in which the foreground is occupied by an imagined relationship between a gentleman writer and his gentlemen readers. The writer positioned himself as a patron to Windradyne and his people, a form of friendship that is hard to conceive of in the early twenty-first century. There is no way of telling how differently he may have thought about his bond with Windradyne when there was no-one listening.

Stories of goodwill and good relations cannot be separated out from broader histories of colonisation, conflict and dispossession. Bennelong's meals with the governor, his exchange of language and customs with the officers and his journey to England were born of kidnap, prolonged by imprisonment, diluted as the colony expanded and became more sure of itself, and were then loudly and enduringly interpreted by the victors. Reaching an understanding of his story that embraces the sincere and open curiosity on both sides, as well as a critical appraisal of the intentions

---

5   Clark, *Private Lives,* 112–13.

and power dynamics of Bennelong's time in and out of the colony, is genuinely difficult. Yet, it has been attempted in so many contexts that those who present Bennelong's relationship with the colony as simply 'friendly' stand out as being both disingenuous and culpable.

It would be disingenuous to celebrate the mutuality of these three stories—as stories that embrace communication, respect and compassion across cultures—unless we also acknowledge the histories of the separation of Aboriginal children from parents, and parents from grandparents, breaking the vital links of oral storytelling between generations of Aboriginal people. A part of all these stories is the suppression of Aboriginal languages and traditions, and the movement of many Aboriginal people—sometimes forced, sometimes times seeking work or refuge—away from the places connected with the stories of ancestors, and even parents and grandparents.[6] Most of the people you will encounter telling stories in this book before about 1960 will be non-Indigenous people. However, flowing from cultural revival over two, three and four generations, Aboriginal people have begun retelling Bennelong's, Windradyne's and Morrill's stories in the public realm as part of the 'histories that matter' to them, connecting up the family traditions and cultural knowledges that were maintained across the generations with the histories documented by non-Indigenous history-makers. As we emerge from the reconciliation era, this book reflects on the role of stories of friendship in sharing histories, and acknowledging the different experiences and different priorities that Aboriginal and non-indigenous storytellers may have in telling these stories.

Australians engage with the past in manifold ways: making family, public, political and media histories popular via commemorative activities, memoir, theatre, art and literature, and in the conversations we have with each other—making history 'at the dinner table, over the back fence, in parliament, in the streets', as Tom Griffiths put it.[7] In this book, I consider each of these three stories of friendship as a living tradition that is maintained (or, after lying dormant, may be revitalised and reclaimed) in the telling. While the objectives and understandings of the people who tell the stories are undeniably diverse—as family historians, academic historians, song-writers and so on—they are brought into conversation, in a sense, in telling the same story.

---

6   See, for example, Read, *A Hundred Years War*; Langford, *Don't Take Your Love to Town*; Goodall, *Invasion to Embassy*; Kijas, *Revival, Renewal and Return*.
7   Griffiths, *Hunters and Collectors,* 1.

My approach to understanding the tellings of each story is inspired by folklorist Linda Dégh, who listens carefully for the 'birth of a new version' of an old story as the storyteller performs a tale that matters to them, reinterpreting traditional material for their audience as they do so. This approach allows me to inquire into the significance of each interpretation on its own terms, characterising rather than categorising it, and trying to explain what its storyteller *does* do, rather than policing 'offences against the truth' or enumerating its failings. Like Dégh, I have come to think of telling a story as an event in its own right—a new 'birth' of meaning—that adds new historical, social and cultural meaning to the wider conversation about the past.[8]

Each time I encountered a new version of an old story, I asked Dégh's question: 'why tell this story now?' I also asked Michel Foucault's question: 'how is it that [this] particular statement appeared rather than another?' In his *Archaeology of Knowledge*, Foucault urged historians to encounter everything as if it was unexpected, and to sift back through the soil of time, finding new knowledge in the placement of even the most mundane items. While a new version of Bennelong's story may look like many others, it is not enough to say it is unremarkable, for it is also a tiny 'monument' to human activity (unceasing meaning-making about the past) that can be examined to see how it was made, what uses it may have had and through whose hands it may have passed.[9] In the layers of storytelling, patterns of enduring and shifting meanings can be read—and this is what I seek to draw out in the three 'lives' or histories of stories examined here. What have these stories meant to storytellers? What kinds of knowledge have they been understood to embody and what kinds of knowledge have they produced? This inquiry is as interested in the social and cultural realities of the storyteller as the 'original' events that the stories are about. I have found, in exploring the telling and retelling of these three stories, that closely examining the lives of the stories reflects insight back onto the events and relationships themselves, thereby potentially creating new knowledge about them.

Neither history nor story is easy to define; the two have run the gamut from deep communion to uneasy truce. Linked to the notion of 'scientific' history, the professionalisation of history from the nineteenth century led those who considered themselves historians to turn their backs on local

---

8   Davison, *The Use and Abuse*, 18–19, 275; Dégh, *Narratives in Society*, 21.
9   Foucault, *The Archaeology of Knowledge*, 6–7, 25–28.

and family stories in favour of archival research that could shine a light on the formation of nations and institutional change. The histories they produced predominantly narrated the progress of civilisation and industry through the efforts of eminent men. From the 1930s, the influential *Annales* school, named after the French scholarly journal *Annales d'histoire économique et sociale*, rejected narratives of important individuals engaged in war, diplomacy and politics as superficial. Instead, they sought to describe human populations, their relationship with geography and climate, and fundamental economic, social and cultural structures beyond the reach of individual change-makers. Taking in far greater scales of time, quantifying large human patterns on the one hand and documenting impressionistic micro-histories on the other, the *Annales* approach threw into doubt the straightforward relationship between history and its narrative vehicle. History did not simply correspond with the past itself—the relationship between the two was not natural; it was cultural or even literary. Since the 1980s, it has been increasingly re-recognised that historical inquiry can take place through story (including local and family stories) and, also, that investigating story is an important part of historical inquiry. However, the debate thrown open in the mid-twentieth century is by no means settled; the most radical view of history as story (i.e. that writing history is more of a poetic act than an empirical one) continues to be rejected by most historians who, to different degrees, maintain that the past can be known, and can, and must, be communicated in ways (including via story) that capture the truth and reality of past events.[10]

Story is a broader stream than history. If history-making is a more or less conscious engagement with the past—an inquiry into the past or an explanation of it—story is, perhaps, one of the fundamental ways of communicating: 'an art deep within human nature … one of the oldest communicative skills that we possess'. Yet, one of story's central roles remains to transmit the 'histories that matter' to successive generations.[11] Graeme Swift examined the relationship at length in his novel *Waterland*; he argued that history seeks to provide an explanation in response to the constant human question 'why?'. Story takes over when life cannot be explained and when explanation is not enough; it reaches towards history again when even ordinary people long for 'presence, for feature, for purpose, for content'. Together, history and story are pervasive modes of

---

10   Griffiths, *Hunters and Collectors,* 5, 25–26, 214–16; O'Malley, *Making History New,* 184–87.
11   Binney, *Stories without End,* 21.

human reality, only occasionally interrupted by the naked, non-narrative 'here and now'. Swift found history and story mingling at different orders of magnitude: the histories of progress in mastering a landscape, or the changes wrought by war, intertwined with stories of people's lives—both set against the long, slow story of the formation of sands and rivers, and the rise and fall of seas.[12] I do not seek to define or separate history and story. Instead, I aim to make a purposeful inquiry into the past that is immersed in story. I use narrative to coalesce and communicate my own meanings; I use the three stories I have chosen as a way of defining my field of interest. In the event, I often find stories making history and histories embracing stories.

For Aboriginal people, 'history'—as an industry, a discipline and a Western cultural tradition—remains a difficult space. Aboriginal people have fought to gain access to the archives that hold traces of their pasts, found that much of the new 'Aboriginal history' written by academic and professional historians does not speak to their own experiences and priorities, and grappled with history as an integral part of the highly divisive process of establishing native title. The recognition and justice that many had hoped would flow from the acknowledgement that 'white Australia has a Black history' have been partial at best.[13] Part of the problem lies with the slippery nature of history itself. Gordon Briscoe observed that 'history' is a word used 'with gay abandon' by Europeans, at once a discipline, a force for progress and a void for forgetting: 'it seems that as soon as Indigenous people gain some appreciation of their own past, Whites shift the goal posts'.[14]

John Maynard described history as central to the wellbeing of Aboriginal people. He argued that a 'scientific', document-based approach to history, which may aspire to global hegemony, is only one way of making history. For Maynard, story is the 'core and soul of history' and can reclaim the past from what he characterised as the deconstructive dead-end of academic history-making. Mudrooroo elaborated on the tension between recognising and championing distinctive Indigenous ways of making history (so that they are not swallowed up by a standardised Western

---

12  Swift, *Waterland*, 35, 51–54.
13  See, for example, Fourmile, 'Who Owns the Past?', 16–27; Peters-Little, 'The Community Game'; Grieves, 'Windschuttle's Fabrication', 194–99.
14  Briscoe, 'Review', 25.3.

narrative), and ensuring that these are recognised as 'history'—because history has come to mean the 'true' past and such a past (with authority and power) is vital to the cultural identity of Aboriginal people.[15]

When I invite Aboriginal history-makers into the story space of this book, it is with great respect for their commitment to truth; the use of the terms 'story' and 'storytelling' are not intended to trivialise their meaning-making about the past.[16] Considering Aboriginal perspectives and the 'popular' history of hobbyists and columnists side by side inevitably creates tension. 'Popular' history-making is often, at least on the surface, about entertainment. Meanwhile, Aboriginal people continue to fight for the recognition of their living heritage. In 1994, Aboriginal and Torres Strait Islander Social Justice Commissioner Michael Dodson found it necessary to argue that a people's right to self-definition:

> must include the right to inherit the collective identity of one's people, and to transform that identity creatively according to the self-defined aspirations of one's people and one's own generation.[17]

The 'gap' in recognition is perhaps akin to the socio-economic gap that continues to reproduce affluence for non-Indigenous Australians at the expense of Aboriginal people and their access to country.

In taking all storytellers seriously, I assume that 'history is never bloodless'.[18] As Bain Attwood and Helen Doyle showed in their close examination of the story of Batman's treaty with Kulin leaders at Port Phillip near today's Melbourne, telling a story about the history of land can, itself, be an act of possession; further, it can, in the mouths of non-Indigenous people, continue and be 'continuous with the original work of dispossession'.[19] None of the three stories explored in this book is trivial; whether a storyteller acknowledges it or not, telling Morrill's, Bennelong's or Windradyne's stories, and many others like them, is always about the present as well as the past, and always opens a dialogue with the stories of other parties who make history about the same places.

---

15  Maynard, 'Circles in the Sand', 117–20; Mudrooroo, *Us Mob*, 178.
16  Birch, 'History is Never Bloodless', 48. Birch argued that the term 'stories' was being used as a dismissive appellation for Aboriginal testimony.
17  Dodson, 'The End in the Beginning', 5.
18  Birch, 'History is Never Bloodless'. Birch adopted this title from Birmingham, *Leviathan*, 509.
19  Attwood with Doyle, *Possession*, 105.

My intention in tracing the telling and retelling of these three stories of cross-cultural adoption, care, curiosity and respect is to show how rich in meaning the lives of these stories are. Rather than tell an authoritative version, or arbitrate between versions, I aim to do as Maria Nugent did in exploring stories of Cook's landing at Botany Bay—that is, to draw out their 'open-ended quality, to reflect upon the lively and constant interplay between past and present' and to be part of the ongoing conversation between storytellers, proposing 'yet more possibilities for interpreting this particular past'.[20] At the same time, I want to reflect on my involvement—as observer historian and storyteller—and encourage other historians to continue working at how we do this, as stories are part of our cultural inheritance. A better understanding of how they have been passed down to us, the meanings that they had when told by previous generations and what they have to do with 'history', can help us to be more conscious of our own effect as history-makers as we retell old stories with new meanings in the present, and pass them on to new generations.

---

20  Nugent, *Captain Cook Was Here*, x–xi.

# Part 1: The Life and Adventures of James Morrill

# 1

# Crossing There and Back, Living to Tell a Tale

Karckynjib Wombil Moony approached the hut with caution. A friend's wife had come with him (perhaps to help convey that the approach was friendly), but when she caught sight of the sheep, she fled. Moony bent down to a small waterhole and washed himself as white as possible. Then, climbing onto the fence above the snapping guard dogs, he took a deep breath and called out: 'What cheer, shipmates'. A man emerged and, surprised, withdrew again. His hearing sharp with anxiety, Moony heard the man say, 'come out Bill here is a red or yellow man standing on the rails, naked, he is not a black man, and bring the gun'.

Moony knew there would be a gun. A friend had been shot dead a few months earlier approaching strangers who had landed on the coast near the mountain Bibbiringda. Just a few days before, a message had arrived from the clan on Mal Mal (now the Burdekin River): a group of men on horseback had shot a number of their kin. These were not the clumsy single-shot arms that Moony remembered; report had it they could fire over and over again. At least now he knew these men spoke English.[1]

---

1   Morrill told Thomas Murray-Prior that he had had difficulty understanding reports of firearms that could produce multiple shots. It was an innovation that had entered general use since Morrill had departed the industrialising world in 1846. He told C. S. Rowe he was worried that the white intruders might have been Spanish or Portuguese. Thomas Lodge Murray-Prior, Private Letter Book ('Journal of Tour of Inspection' [1863]), Mitchell Library (hereafter ML), MS 3117, CY Reel 495, 18; Rowe, 'Rowe's Memoranda', 113.

The two stockmen came back out of the hut aiming the gun at Moony's chest. 'Do not shoot me. I am a British object—a shipwrecked sailor.'[2] The gun was lowered (but not put away).

James Morrill had been about 22 years old, an able seaman on the *Peruvian*, when it was wrecked in 1846. He was one of only four to survive the wreck, a long drift to shore on an improvised raft and a fortnight scavenging shellfish from the rocks. The four were taken in and nursed back to health by two of the Birri-gubba clans based around Mount Elliott and Cape Cleveland near today's Townsville. The other survivors died after two or three years, but Morrill lived, worked and loved as an adopted Birri-gubba man.[3] A correspondent to *The Courier* reported that Morrill had been named Karckynjib Wombil Moony 'after one of their chiefs'.[4] When the two stockmen, Hatch and Wilson, informed him that the date was 26 January 1863, Morrill was astounded; he had lived among the Birri-gubba people for 17 years.

Queensland was declared a separate colony in 1859 and settlers and their flocks of sheep streamed northward by sea and overland.[5] Like hundreds of others, C. S. Rowe travelled north from Melbourne to take up land near the Burdekin River. He later recalled the attitude, and the armoury, with which he and his companions set out, saying:

> We looked on the North of Queensland, as a terra incognita inhabited by fierce tribes of Cannibals and all sorts—so that thorough preparations were made for our defence. The arms procured were, six Tranter revolver rifles, six revolvers of the same make, two shot guns, one Ferry's rifle, six cutlasses and no end of ammunition.[6]

It was men not unlike Rowe who had terrified and, in some cases, mortally wounded Morrill's adoptive kin. These men would go on doing so, attempting to expel the Birri-gubba people and their neighbours from

---

2   Morrill, *Sketch of a Residence*, 14–21.
3   I follow the advice of Eddie Smallwood, Chairman of the Gudjuda Corporation, in referring to Morrill's adoptive people by their language-group name. Others have attempted to chart his association with Birri-gubba clan groups, particularly the Bindal and Juru people, but this is not necessary for the story I wish to tell.
4   *The Courier*, 11 March 1863.
5   Evans, *A History of Queensland*, 82–83.
6   Rowe, 'Rowe's Memoranda', 104–05. Noel Loos found that the Aboriginal peoples of North Queensland had gained a formidable reputation for ferocity by the 1860s. The first settlers set out for Port Denison from Rockhampton to meet a 'strong party of Queensland Native Police' who it was intended would keep the peace and protect their interests. Loos, 'Frontier Conflict in the Bowen District', 113–17.

pastoral leases that, on paper, allowed them to stay.[7] Rowe later claimed not to have had any trouble from the 'blacks'; he attributed the calm to the activities of the native police, the official war machine of this invasion of the north.[8]

Rowe encountered Morrill as he travelled from the stockman's hut into the fledgling town of Bowen to report to the authorities. He noted that Morrill carried rather than wore his trousers and that:

> There was no mistaking him for any but a white man … he had the manner of an aboriginal. From some feeling of uncertainty about his new friends, he had a wild stare about him, and his eyes constantly shifted from place to place.[9]

This wary, troubled man had found a home far from home. He was now faced with a sudden re-adoption. He travelled south, under escort, telling his story at Bowen, Rockhampton and Brisbane. It was neither an easy nor a safe story to tell, and his listeners were so voracious that their (often sharp) questions, as well as their tacit expectations, were imprinted deeply into the shape of his story.

Morrill returned to Bowen, which is where he died just two years and nine months after making himself known to the two stockmen, Hatch and Wilson. He had found work with the customs service and married Eliza Ann Ross, who was pregnant with their son when he passed away. North Queensland was still being drawn into the influence of the colony. The sporadic, diffuse war between the settlers and the Birri-gubba and their neighbours wore on, and ambitious commercial ventures prepared to set out for Cape York and the Gulf country, men and their stock ready to claim what they could. Morrill's story continued after his death, developing a life of its own that is imprinted on the history and history-making of North Queensland. Morrill's story, as it survives today, was not a product of leisurely reminiscence; it was a story of survival, and a story told *to survive* as he made two dangerous crossings. Morrill's story was his raft.

---

7   The Queensland Land Act of 1860 allowed Aboriginal people access to pastoral leases, but they were denied access to food and water by pastoralists. Breslin, *Exterminate with Pride,* 82–83. See also Loos, 'Frontier Conflict in the Bowen District', 142–44, 171.
8   Rowe, 'Rowe's Memoranda', 105; Breslin, *Exterminate with Pride,* 82; Evans, *A History of Queensland,* 96–97.
9   Rowe, 'Rowe's Memoranda', 115.

After 42 days drifting at sea, catching rain in a sail canvas and baiting sharks with the limbs of their dead companions, James Morrill and six other survivors finally beached their raft. They had buried 14 souls at sea. Three men had wandered off in separate directions seeking food and water and had perished; Morrill had stayed on the beach with Captain and Mrs Pitkethly and the cabin boy, eating oysters from the rocks.

Two weeks later, these four were discovered by a party of Birri-gubba men. As they later explained to Morrill, shooting stars had been seen over the coast several nights in a row—a clear sign that something was amiss in that direction—and had led them right to the rocks where the survivors struggled for life. Investigation under the damp rags confirmed that these bedraggled strangers were human beings, male and female. After some debate, the Aboriginal men extended an invitation to their camp. When the strangers agreed to go with them, the men performed a 'corroboree'. The survivors felt they could not participate, perhaps through exhaustion, and instead sang a hymn, 'God moves in a mysterious way/his wonders to perform',[10] in a spirit of reciprocity.

The men gave the hungry four some tasty, starchy roots to eat and, carrying the exhausted cabin boy on their backs, led the way to their camp. Another small Birri-gubba group was soon encountered, and the party paused to repeat the previous night's corroboree for their benefit. When the main camp was reached, Morrill remembered:

> The first thing that they did was to lay us down and cover us over with dried grass, to prevent our being seen [until] the appointed time. They then collected together to the number of about 50 or 60—men, women and children—and sat down in a circle; then those who discovered us went into the middle, dressed up in the things that they had taken from us ... and danced a corroboree, in which they explained ... what they had discovered, from whence they had brought us, and all they knew about us ... That being over, we were led into the middle in triumph.[11]

This performance was repeated for the 'near tribes' the following evening, and then night after night for a seemingly endless stream of visitors. On one of these evenings, when the survivors dragged their feet, it was gently but firmly indicated that participation was compulsory.[12] This

---

10  First published in Newton and Cowper, *Olney Hymns in Three Books*.
11  Morrill, *Sketch of a Residence*, 8–12.
12  Ibid., 11.

process of identification and introduction was apparently essential to the survival and prosperity of Morrill and his companions in their new community.

Seventeen years later, another process of storytelling began. Morrill's plea to the two stockmen—'do not shoot me. I am a British object'—was his initial passport. He needed to negotiate a new place in the world. When he spoke positively about his experiences among Aboriginal people, perhaps wanting nothing more than to soften the effect of this sudden invasion, he found he might be despised by association with his adoptive people. Yet, at the same time, as soon as he opened his mouth, he was expected to add to geographic, ethnographic and botanical knowledge about the region. He was also expected to entertain. Audiences crowded around him to hear his story of survival, appetites whetted by a popular literature about shipwreck victims, escaped convicts, renegades and captives. This time he was on his own. The four survivors of the wreck of the *Peruvian* had been nursed back to health by the Birri-gubba people, and they gradually learned how to work, live and speak anew. However, after two or three years, the cabin boy, then the captain and his wife, died one after the other in quick succession. Morrill was the only one left to tell their story.

Stumbling over his forgotten first language, Morrill was 'cross-questioned' by the stockmen, Hatch and Wilson, about his wreck and survival. His life hung on his story as he spent one more night with his Birri-gubba kin, returning to the stockyard in the morning. Hatch and Wilson had apparently told him 'that if I did not come back in the morning they should conclude that I had told them a lie, and that they would put the black trackers on our track and shoot us'.[13] After a fortnight at this outpost of Mr Anthill's Inkerman Station, Morrill was washed, clad and passed along a line of settlers to the commissioner's orderly, who escorted him into Bowen (known then as Port Denison), a journey of over 100 kilometres.[14]

Morrill made a statement at the Bowen Court House on 23 February 1863 in which he explained how the *Peruvian* had been overcome by high winds and driven onto a reef, and how he had come to be the sole survivor. He testified to his desire to make contact, 'which I had always been trying

---

13  Ibid., 15–16.
14  *The Courier*, 11 March 1863, 2.

to do, from the time I heard there were white men settled near me', and tried to ward off suspicions that he may have acted in aggression from the Birri-gubba side. Though he admitted that he had heard that a white man had been killed by Birri-gubba men, and although he acknowledged that the town of Bowen had been in existence for some time, he professed not to have laid eyes on a white person between his last contact with his fellow shipwreck survivors and his deliberate encounter with Mr Anthill's stockmen.[15]

Morrill was interviewed in a less formal manner too as a 'white-blackfellow'. His incredible story of shipwreck and 'exile amongst the blacks', given credence by a crocodile bite on one leg and impressive rheumatic holes in his forehead, arms and body, would put Port Denison on the map. One of his interlocutors, under the pseudonym 'Advance Australia', supplied a report to the newspapers that enlivened the courthouse statement with sufferings 'impossible to describe', including an account of the virile frontier dialogue exchanged by Morrill and Hatch and Wilson as they had faced each other across the outstation yard a month earlier. This account, which narrated the four survivors' adoption by one of the Birri-gubba clans and emphasised their kindness over the years, nevertheless concluded with confirmation of their cannibalism and the strange statement that Morrill would 'not trust them generally'.[16]

Trust was surely a pressing issue for Morrill as he was passed from pillar to post, from courtroom to drawing room, and as he saw in the colonists' attentive faces curiosity mixed with aggression. He needed to explain himself, promptly. From the perspective of the colony, he was a man of fighting age living as part of an Aboriginal group at a time when the native police and the settlers themselves aimed to clear away the Aboriginal presence to facilitate British exploitation of the land.[17] What was he doing

---

15   Copy of a statement made by James (Jimmy) Morrell before one of Her Majesty's justices of the peace for Queensland in the Court House, Bowen, 23 February 1863, State Library of Queensland, Heritage Collections, James Morrell Papers, Box 8923, Reference Code OM74-92, typescript viewed courtesy of Phillip Murray.

16   'Advance Australia's' report, dated 25 February 1863, appeared in *The Courier*, 11 March 1863, 2; *Queensland Guardian*, 12 March 1863.

17   The *Port Denison Times* provided candid reportage of conflicts from its first issue in March 1864, and a thorough local assessment of the policies pursued up to 1869 as the 'letting in' of Aboriginal groups was debated. The 1861 Select Committee enquiring into the native police force included open debate on the effectiveness of the force employed in the region to that point. The native police 'dispersed' (i.e., shot at any large group of Aboriginal people encountered), but this alone could not ensure the protection of the settlers and their interests—settlers also needed armed stockmen to patrol their own runs. Loos, 'Frontier Conflict in the Bowen District', 120–38, 157–68.

on the wrong side of the frontier? Was he a renegade or criminal? C. S. Rowe accounted for the nervousness of Hatch and Wilson by explaining that 'they suspected he might be a bushranger'. Several escapees from the Moreton Bay penal settlement had set precedents for such a career. One of the more famous was John Graham, known as 'Moilow' to his adoptive people, who escaped in 1827, took part in the rescue of Eliza Fraser and then disappeared from the colony again. As an escaped convict who had joined an Aboriginal group for survival's sake, he would still have had cause to make an account of himself. William Buckley escaped from the short-lived penal settlement at Port Phillip in 1803 and, after 32 years living on and off with the Wathaurong people, approached the fledgling second settlement with great trepidation, anticipating that his sentence would be resumed.[18] Even known shipwreck victim and captain's wife Eliza Fraser struggled to provide an account of the wreck of the *Stirling Castle* and her interactions with the Butchulla people of Fraser Island that met with the satisfaction of the Crown and the public and preserved her own and her husband's reputation.[19] Morrill's claim that he had not even seen a white man, let alone been party to any hostile action from the Birri-gubba side, did not stop contemporaries from speculating, as Rowe did, that 'Morrill knew more about some affrays between blacks and whites than ever he cared to relate'.[20]

Morrill was bundled onto the *Murray* steamer bound for Rockhampton, where his arrival was awaited with 'considerable excitement'. Onlookers waited on the wharf, craning their necks for a glimpse of this 'new Robinson Crusoe' (as the *Queensland Guardian* would style him).[21] Here, he was interviewed by Police Magistrate John Jardine and a select audience of gentlemen who anticipated that 'much valuable information could be extracted from this man'.[22] The questions put to him ranged from the curious (had he heard report of the camels accompanying exploring parties?) to the downright hazardous (how much did he know of the numerous murders that had occurred in the district?).[23] At least some of those in attendance were left frustrated. Despite Jardine's 'unwearied

---

18   Morgan, *The Life and Adventures of William Buckley*, 86, 89–90.
19   Rowe, 'Rowe's Memoranda', 114; Mulvaney, 'John Graham', 109–45; Morgan, *The Life and Adventures of William Buckley*, 86, 89–90; Schaffer, *In the Wake of First Contact*, 34–39.
20   Rowe, 'Rowe's Memoranda', 115.
21   *Queensland Guardian*, 17 March 1863. A crowd also awaited his arrival on the wharf at Brisbane, *The Courier*, 16 March 1863, 2.
22   *Queensland Guardian*, 17 March 1863.
23   *The Argus*, 18 March 1863, 6 (quoting correspondence from the *Rockhampton Bulletin*).

patience and ... exemplary desire to confine his examination to matters of public interest', Morrill furnished 'monosyllabic replies ... [that] augmented rather than satisfied the thirst of his audience for information', one correspondent complained.[24] Part of this thirst was for information that would lead to wealth; though Morrill had never knowingly seen gold-bearing rock, and was somewhat baffled that he should be expected to recognise it, he was repeatedly asked whether the country he knew so well was 'gold-bearing country'.[25]

A second steamship conveyed Morrill to Brisbane, where he met with Governor George Bowen and Mayor George Edmonstone. Several correspondents to *The Courier* anticipated that Morrill must be lacking funds, and offered their assistance in generating a subscription for him if only he would appear in public in Brisbane, as he had in Bowen and Rockhampton.[26] All along this journey south, Morrill was 'besieged' by the curious.[27] As Marcus Clark later put it, 'snatched from barbarism, he ran the usual round of tea parties. People were eager to hear this newly caught lion roar'.[28]

In Brisbane, Morrill told his story to journalist Edmund Gregory at *The Courier* newspaper office. It was published under the title *Sketch of a Residence among the Aboriginals of Northern Queensland for Seventeen Years; Being a Narrative of My Life, Shipwreck, Landing on the Coast, Residence among the Aboriginals, with an Account of Their Manners and Customs and Mode of Living; Together with Notices of Many of the Natural Productions, and of the Nature of the Country, by James Morrill*. This slim pamphlet was advertised in *The Courier*'s classifieds from mid-April 1863 (with a second thousand in print within a month), promptly reached readers in Victoria and South Australia, and had apparently travelled as far afield as Boston by 1864.[29] Morrill hoped that the booklet, as well as bringing in a small income, would alleviate the pressure to 'wait on persons for the purpose of narrating my past sufferings ... day after day'.[30]

---

24 Ibid.
25 Dortins, 'James Morrill: Shipwreck Survivor', 65–86.
26 *The Courier*, 21 March 1863, 2; 13 April 1863, 2; 29 April 1863, 3.
27 Edmund Gregory used this phrase in his second edition of *Sketch of a Residence,* published in 1865–66, 16–17.
28 Clarke, *Old Tales of a Young Country*, 194.
29 *The Courier*, 18 April 1863, 8; 16 May 1863, 6; *The South Australian Advertiser*, 6 October 1863; Welch, *17 Years Wandering*.
30 Morrill, *Sketch of a Residence*, 2.

Indeed, when the curious sought Morrill out in Bowen over the following two years, they seemed to have read it. Thomas Lodge Murray-Prior visited Morrill in the closing months of 1863 and questioned him on, among other things, his marital status as a Birri-gubba man, telling him 'that it was all humbug to try and make me think that a man would be 17 years with the natives without a lady love', as Morrill's published account would have him believe.[31] Although something can be learned from the writings and reminiscences of these curious visitors, as well as the newspaper reports of Morrill's appearance and travels, *Sketch of a Residence* remains the most detailed account of Morrill's life.[32] In fact, the curious among Morrill's contemporaries often short-change today's curious by leaning on the booklet and neglecting their own memories of other accounts. E. B. Kennedy, writing a version of Morrill's story for a popular magazine, stated that, although he had heard parts of the story from Morrill's own lips 50 years earlier, Morrill had also given him a copy of the story printed at the Brisbane *Courier* office. Kennedy's story is an abridged version of *Sketch of a Residence*, adding only a few details from his own recollection. Tantalisingly, William Robertson, speaking on 2BL radio in the 1920s, claimed to have talked to several men of the 'Mal Mal' clan who had adopted Morrill at Cleveland Bay in the 1880s; however, Robertson described the published booklet as 'the real history' and proceeded to paraphrase it.[33]

As I waited, one of the curious, for *Sketch of a Residence* to emerge from the depths of the Mitchell Library into the light of the reading room, my expectations of this definitive account were enormous. I wanted the 24-page pamphlet to provide a key to understanding Morrill's life as a Birri-gubba man. Did he adopt Birri-gubba ways of thinking? Did he marry in and bring up children? Did he remain on the outer edge of their society, or was he part of his clan's most important decisions and conflicts? Was he happy? Would he have chosen to remain part of the Birri-gubba world if the choice had been open to him? The title of the book suggests that it is about Morrill's 'residence' with his adoptive community. However, I soon found that Morrill's Birri-gubba life is very

---

31  Murray-Prior, Private Letter Book, 19.
32  It is possible that he was working with E. J. Byrne towards a more extensive account of his experiences when he passed away in 1865; however, it would seem that no such account was published. *Port Denison Times*, 1 November 1865, 2; 3 September 1902.
33  E. B. Kennedy, *Seventeen Years amongst Queensland Blacks*; Robertson, *Coo-ee Talks*, 143.

little *lived* in its pages. The middle years of Morrill's life as a Birri-gubba man are summed up in a single, pregnant sentence: 'I lived on year after year in the tribe as one of themselves—nothing particularly happening'.[34]

I am not the only reader who has been disappointed. Scholars have been apologetic about how little *Sketch of a Residence* illuminates Birri-gubba life and Morrill's part in it. Here he was, in the perfect situation for cultural observation—complete social immersion; yet, his account barely touches on so many vital aspects of Birri-gubba life. Historian Noel Loos, working on his master's thesis in the late 1960s, wondered how Morrill could be so 'exasperatingly reticent'. Was he a little dim or lacking in curiosity? Was his interviewer, impatient to publish, a poor listener?[35]

The context in which Morrill told his story raises questions that touch on the relationship between Morrill and his interviewer, Gregory; however, it also raises questions that are much broader than the character and intelligence of these two men. Why did Morrill's story focus on his departure from and return to civilisation, rather than his life as a Birri-gubba man? Did Morrill deliberately shut off difficult questions about love, loyalty, power and happiness as he wrote *Sketch of a Residence* with Gregory? Was the day-to-day life of Morrill as a Birri-gubba man a story that could be told in Queensland in 1863? Indeed, can such story be told today? These are some of the questions that fuel this 'life' of Morrill's story.

*Sketch of a Residence* is a slender account; it is not difficult to say what it lacks. This makes it all the more important to ask what it *does not* lack— that is, what it contains and emphasises, and why. *Sketch of a Residence* tells Morrill's story in three parts. The first part provides a vivid account of the wreck of the *Peruvian*, the adoption of the castaways by Birri-gubba people, and the deaths of the cabin boy and Captain and Mrs Pitkethly. The second furnishes a rather more reserved account of Morrill's experience of the rapid entry of settlers and their flocks into Birri-gubba country and his 'return to civilisation'. The third and final chapter presents information about Aboriginal life and local natural resources in response to the interests of his anticipated readers. The statement resulting from Morrill's appearance at the Bowen courthouse and several newspaper

---

34 Morrill, *Sketch of a Residence*, 13.
35 Brayshaw, *Well Beaten Paths*, 20; Breslin, *Exterminate with Pride*, 47; Reynolds, *The Other Side of the Frontier*, 24; Moore, *Islanders and Aborigines at Cape York*, 10; Loos, 'Frontier Conflict in the Bowen District', 23–24, 37.

reports of his appearances at Bowen and Rockhampton also favoured a three-part narrative: Morrill's departure from civilisation and his return, followed by a smattering of information about his adoptive people and their country. Though *Sketch of a Residence* added much to these shorter reports, it followed a similar pattern.

As Morrill told his story, this time with the help of the colonists, there was a superfluity of reasons for it to focus on the story of his crossing out of, and crossing back into, civilisation. Like the corroborees that had facilitated his adoption by the Birri-gubba 17 years earlier, Morrill's storytelling was a vital part of his re-adoption. British historian Linda Colley, making a study of the narratives of British captives and renegades in Morocco, southern India and Canada from the sixteenth to the nineteenth centuries, found that, for those absent without leave from European civilisation, publishing a first person account of their experiences played a significant role in their re-admission into the fold of Empire as moral, social and intellectual beings. Accounts of the events of 'capture' by, and 'escape' from, the natives were essential ingredients that had become part of a lively literary tradition.[36] In stories like Morrill's, then, the conceptual centre was 'civilisation'—the British Empire or Europe more broadly—being the shared home of the storyteller and audience. Amid the ongoing warlike situation in the region, the interest in Morrill's journey out of and back to civilisation had an urgency about it, but one that was admixed with fascination.

The first task of *Sketch of a Residence* is to locate Morrill as an Englishman.[37] The reader is presented with a portrait of Morrill as a young man in Essex with a 'restless disposition', who found his father's engineering workshop 'too confining'. The Blackwater River, passing close by his home, offered continual temptation to 'get amongst the shipping'. Short voyages around the British Isles did not sate his appetite, and he sought employment on the open ocean.[38] Morrill's own adventuresome thoughts as he breathed the salt air may have been fanned by the burgeoning genre of seagoing adventure, inspired and typified by Daniel Defoe's story of

---

36  Colley, 'Going Native, Telling Tales', 170–74.
37  Corroboration of Morrill's identity and story was to come later; the account of his family, situation of birth, childhood and career as a sailor that was printed in 1863 was reliant on his own recall and the trust of his readers. The 1865–66 edition of the pamphlet corrected the spelling of Morrill's remembered name; apparently his real name had been Murrells. Gregory, *Sketch of the Residence of James Morrill*, 3.
38  Morrill, *Sketch of a Residence*, 3.

Robinson Crusoe, as truly popular literature began to take off in the mid-nineteenth century.[39] Certainly, contemporaries saw in Morrill something of a Crusoe. Morrill was of the 'middle state' of life, with prospects for a comfortable existence if he was willing to apply himself, as Crusoe's father prudently counselled his son. However, like Crusoe, Morrill's head was 'filled very early with rambling thoughts' and he would be 'satisfied with nothing but going to sea', signing up to a seagoing vessel on the spur of the moment without informing his mother or father.[40] By the time Morrill was telling his story in the mid-nineteenth century, De Foe's 150-year-old story was both a 'charming book of [one's] childhood' as well as the story of a wanderer whose moral fibre would be put to the test.[41] Knowing something of his class and family life, and his route into the unknown, was essential background information for this test: how would Morrill measure up?

The possibility of mismanagement hung over shipwrecks and their aftermath, and so did a suspicion of selfish acts on the part of those who may have survived at the expense of others; in particular, the humanity of survivors who stooped to eat the flesh of their dead companions.[42] Morrill's accounts of the wreck of the *Peruvian* were, in part, a testament to honourable conduct: the captain's, the Birri-gubba people's and his own. *Sketch of a Residence* gives a powerful rendition of the wreck and the long, soul-destroying voyage on the raft, not only provoking sympathy, but also attesting to the durability of the survivors' morality. The dead are accounted for as far as Morrill's memory can stretch, and he describes good government on the raft via the democratic division of provisions and the respectful sea burials of the perished (with some flesh taken as bait to catch sharks).[43] This was of acute interest to families of the other crew and passengers. The story quickly reached Perthshire, Scotland, where

---

39   Phillips, *Mapping Men and Empire*, 10–12, 23–28.
40   *The South Australian Advertiser*, 6 October 1863. At least one northern newspaper story was headed 'The New Robinson Crusoe', *Queensland Guardian*, 17 March 1863; De Foe, *The Life and Adventures of Robinson Crusoe*, 2–5. Colley noted that British narratives of captivity and return became 'coloured' by the novels of Defoe, Swift and others. See Colley, 'Going Native, Telling Tales', 174.
41   *The South Australian Advertiser*, 6 October 1863; Phillips, *Mapping Men and Empire*, 25–26; Green, *The Robinson Crusoe Story*, 22.
42   An unwise and 'apathetic' captain might bear much of the blame, as in the wreck of the *All Serene* en route to Sydney from Vancouver. See *Empire*, 21 June 1864, 2. The survivors of the wreck of the *Elvina* were apparently driven to eat those who had died as they drifted. See *Geelong Advertiser*, 6 October 1864, 2. Kay Schaffer understood Eliza Fraser's initial testimonies as centring on her role as captain's wife, defending the integrity of her husband's good government. Schaffer, *In the Wake of First Contact*, 34–39.
43   Morrill, *Sketch of a Residence*, 7.

Captain and Mrs Pitkethly had left family behind. It was also read by the friends and family of the distinguished Mr and Mrs Wilmot, and Mr Quarry, passengers of the *Peruvian* who had departed Melbourne for India never to be heard from again.[44] On adoption by the Birri-gubba clan, the narrating voice is equally concerned to vouch for the courage and dignity of the captain and his wife, and the kindness and generosity of their Aboriginal rescuers. Morrill's anticipated readership had particular concerns about the fate of white women among savages; for example, Eugene Fitzalan, botanist and early resident of Bowen, versified about the 'bitter feelings' in Mrs Pitkethly's breast as she was forced to 'herd with human beings / Little raised above the beast'.[45] The narrating voice in *Sketch of a Residence* assured the reader that his Aboriginal rescuers respected the privacy (after establishing her gender) and married status of this sole white woman survivor.[46]

After several months, just as the four survivors had begun to pick up the local language, a large event was hosted by their adoptive clans. When visitors from the south returned home, the four slunk away with them, apparently hoping they might make contact with ships or a settlement of some kind. It was there, away from Mt Elliot, that the cabin boy and Captain and Mrs Pitkethly died. Morrill stated that he had ensured a Christian-style burial for the couple (according to this narrative, the usual Birri-gubba practice was to cremate the dead). Feeling 'lonely', he then decided to return to his original adoptive clan on Mt Elliot, 'thinking they would take more care of me'. Whereas, in the eyes of those who had adopted the other three castaways, Morrill was responsible for their deaths, Morrill's own adoptive clan protected him from the 'crack on the head' that the other clan felt he deserved.[47] With the strongly Christian gaze of Captain and Mrs Pitkethly extinguished, *Sketch of a Residence* leaves off its conscientious account of Morrill's movements, and the reader loses sight of him for more than a decade. Morrill had acquitted his responsibilities to the dead as best he was able. More broadly, in the moral courtroom

---

44  *Queensland Guardian*, 17 March 1863.
45  Eugene Fitzalan, 'Lines', as reproduced in Bowen Historical Society, *James Morrill: His Life and Adventures*, 1–3. Fitzalan wrote this verse some time before his death in 1911. See also *Queensland Guardian*, 17 March 1863, in which Morrill seems to have been asked about the preservation of Mrs Pitkethly's dignity.
46  Darian-Smith, '"Rescuing" Barbara Thompson'. The reader is assured that Mrs Pitkethly died uncorrupted, very soon after her husband, Morrill, *Sketch of a Residence,* 10, 12–13.
47  Morrill, *Sketch of a Residence*, 12–13.

of the British Empire of the mid-nineteenth century, the narrative had established that Morrill's defection from civilisation was not deliberate, but was the result of catastrophe.[48]

When the account resumed, a fresh project was at hand. Surveys of the coast around Cape Cleveland had begun in the late 1850s, and settlers and native police detachments had begun to venture into the hinterland soon after the establishment of Bowen in 1861. Why was it that Morrill had not 'given himself up' until more than a year later? Under cross-examination at Bowen, Morrill insisted that he had known of white men in the region for only one month before his appearance.[49] In the interview at Rockhampton, he was more vocal about the dangers involved in his position. He was highly cautious about approaching white men as he expected to be recognised as an Aboriginal man and shot summarily, for 'that is the ordinary salutation an Aboriginal gets from a white man'. Openly seeking information from the Birri-gubba about the settlers in this warlike situation also had its dangers, and Morrill said that he felt it necessary to maintain a semblance of indifference about the possibility of meeting the colonists.[50] The second chapter of *Sketch of a Residence* gives a careful account of Morrill's near misses with reconnaissance and settlement parties, his attempts to catch up with them and his explanations to Aboriginal associates of his desire to meet with the newcomers.[51] Most significantly, an encounter between a government schooner, the *Spitfire*, and a Birri-gubba group had been officially reported as an attack repulsed, followed by a subhuman cacophony on shore as the boat retreated. Morrill provided another side to the story. According to him, the Birri-gubba approached the *Spitfire* party to tell them about Morrill, as he had asked them to do whenever they encountered white men; yet:

---

48   Kay Schaffer found that John Curtis constructed a courtroom-like narrative in his *Shipwreck of the Stirling Castle* (1837–38)—the narrator is the counsel and judge and the reader part of the jury, sitting in judgment on Eliza Fraser's negotiation of the civilised and the savage. Schaffer, *In the Wake of First Contact*, 66–67.
49   *The Courier*, 11 March 1863, 2.
50   *Queensland Guardian*, 17 March 1863.
51   For example, on one occasion, Morrill spied a ship, but 'she was too far out for me to attract her attention'. On another occasion, his people came in contact with a party that landed near Cape Cleveland, but Morrill himself was on Mt Elliot. Morrill, *Sketch of a Residence*, 13–14.

Nothing is said in the report about shooting the natives, but one … stout, able-bodied blackfellow, a friend of mine, was shot dead by some one in the boat, and another was wounded; and the hideous yelling was the noise they usually make over their dead.[52]

Morrill's counter-reportage was subversive, suggesting that even government parties were not honest about their dealings with Aboriginal people, and that they might shoot too readily. It was also subversive in that it vouched for the gentleness and goodwill of the Aboriginal men involved. At the same time, it formed part of Morrill's defence against the potential accusation that he had participated in attacks on British parties, or that he had known about the settlements and could have made himself known to colonists sooner than he had. In Ross Gibson's view, this was the key to the colonists' nervousness about Morrill; his story provided a glimpse of Aboriginal meetings, movements and trade in knowledge. There was no simple, silent wilderness occupying the spaces beyond settlement; instead, there was a 'cogent confederacy of Aboriginal intelligence' abuzz with information.[53] Morrill was able to live as a respected, married man in Bowen for the short time left to him. *Sketch of a Residence* perhaps helped to form a foundation for this new life by ascribing humane, yet non-partisan, motives to Morrill and giving an account of the uses to which he put his knowledge of the colonists as he watched them from the other side of the frontier (if, indeed, that is what he did).

Morrill had already answered to representatives of the Crown at Bowen, Rockhampton and Brisbane. By the time he was retelling his story with Gregory, the need to testify, and to demonstrate his own integrity and innocence, was less urgent; however, it may have been significant on another level. The rituals that might be necessary to ensure a man's re-adoption following an extended period in 'savage' society are exemplified by the experience of Narcisse Pelletier, a young French castaway who lived with the Sandbeach people of Cape York for 17 years. According to local tradition, Pelletier was subject to exorcism by a priest at Saint-Gilles; despite his return to France, his family wished to return him more completely to the Catholic beliefs of his childhood. Morrill's rebirth into

---

52  Morrill, *Sketch of a Residence*, 14. *Sketch of a Residence* includes an extract from the Spitfire's official report, 15–16 September 1860, presumably located and copied by the journalist or his assistants. Morrill, *Sketch of a Residence*, 13–14.
53  Gibson, *Seven Versions*, 88. For a closer examination of what can be known about Birri-gubba knowledge networks in that period, and how Morrill may have participated in them, see Breslin, *James Morrill*.

the Christian universe was less extreme, but no less significant; he gave a public profession of his faith in Christ and was re-baptised.[54] He also returned to the world of science via an excursion into the forest with a visiting French botanist, and translating some of the knowledge he had learned from Birri-gubba teachers into Latin plant names and points of interest for the scientific reader.[55] No less important was his rebirth into the republic of letters, the rational and commercial world of the press, and the reconstitution of his British self under the gaze of the reading public—something that Morrill achieved with Gregory's assistance through *Sketch of a Residence*. Certainly, he 'became something of a celebrity', as the Bowen Historical Society observed in 2002. Yet, his repeated storytelling was not simply a matter of responding to the invitations of the interested; it was also a complex cultural and social process, no less vital to Morrill's survival and prosperity than the assimilative 'corroborees' had been 17 years earlier.

If there were reasons for Morrill's narrative to focus closely on his crossings out of and back into civilisation, there are also possible reasons why his story of life as a Birri-gubba man could *not* be told. First, Gregory published a story of a 'residence' centred on a narrative void: 'I lived on year after year in the tribe as one of themselves—nothing particularly happening'. Second, bringing to life in story form any of the desires of his Birri-gubba life may have been inimical to his published narrative's main objective: his reassimilation into the British world.

Day-to-day life is not the stuff of adventure, no matter where it is lived. In J. M. Coetzee's novel *Foe*, the narrator is a female companion to Crusoe and Friday who realises the narrative failure of their story while the trio are still marooned on the island. She worries: 'let it not … come to pass that Cruso [sic] is saved … for the world expects stories from its adventurers'. The problem was a lack of willpower resulting from a contentment of sorts:

> There was too little desire in Cruso and Friday: too little desire to escape, too little desire for a new life. Without desire, how is it possible to make a story?[56]

---

54 Anderson, *Pelletier*, 171–72. Rev. B. G. Wilson, a Baptist Minister, apparently performed the service. Gregory, *Sketch of the Residence of James Morrill*, 17.
55 Dortins, 'James Morrill: Shipwreck Survivor', 67–88.
56 Coetzee, *Foe*, 34, 88.

Part of Coetzee's irony is, perhaps, that most versions of Robinson Crusoe's story are replete with utterly tedious detail about day-to-day survival. Constant Merland, presenting the story of Narcisse Pelletier to the French public in 1876, grappled with a similar problem. He wrote that 'although their tribe is constantly on the move, the life of the savages is generally uniform and monotonous', and that Pelletier, like Crusoe and Morrill, had settled into these new patterns of life.[57] Merland attempted to solve this literary problem by moving quickly from castaway narrative to ethnography. Once his subject's clothes had rotted away, he relinquished Pelletier's personal story and allowed it to merge with the textures of Sandbeach life:

> It is no longer the cabin boy Narcisse Pelletier who will be the subject of our discussion but Amglo, citizen of the tribe of Ohantaala. His personality will often recede into the background as we turn to the description of the customs, habits and beliefs of tribes among whom civilisation has not yet penetrated.[58]

He was no longer present in Merland's story as someone with his own desires; in fact, as Merland's translator Stephanie Anderson observes, it was 'as if Pelletier [was] in suspended animation as his years of residence with the Sandbeach people' passed.[59]

Morrill and Gregory solved this same problem of narrative by creating a there-and-back story linked to the desire to survive—first the shipwreck and later the coming of the colonists to the north. Commentary on day-to-day Birri-gubba life was largely left to a separate chapter at the end. This problem of narrative, and its solution, was tied up with what sorts of desires could be spoken of, and heard, as Morrill (and, of course, Pelletier too) told his story. In *Sketch of a Residence,* there are glimpses of Morrill acting on Birri-gubba motivations. For example, in responding to a question about whether the country might be gold bearing, Morrill recalled that 'once when out, looking for coloured earths to paint myself with', he found an interesting, heavy piece of rock. Likewise, while summarising the knowledge he had of white settlement in the area, he explained: 'four stray cattle were seen in our district, but I was on the coast with … my brother-in-law, making a possum skin rug'.[60] Like

---

57   Anderson, *Pelletier*, 182.
58   Ibid., 156.
59   Ibid., 41.
60   Morrill, *Sketch of a Residence*, 14, 24.

Morrill's brush with Birri-gubba justice after Captain Pitkethly's death, these asides give a fleeting glimpse of his negotiation of kin relationships and his participation in the economic and ceremonial happenings of his adoptive people. This was a life no doubt full of 'desires' capable of driving interesting stories during the course of his 17 years residence; however, since these stories did not find a place in *Sketch of a Residence*, we can only reach towards them via imagination and empathy.

As he prepared to return to Inkerman Station on 26 January 1863, Morrill's adoptive family wept; they did not believe they would ever see him again. *Sketch of a Residence* recounts, in Morrill's first person narrating voice:

> The remembrance of their past kindness came full upon me and quite overpowered me. There was a short struggle between the feeling of love I had for my old friends and companions and the desire once more to live a civilized life, which can be better imagined than described.[61]

The outcome of this struggle was Morrill's return to colonial life. According to Linda Colley, this was the 'imperially correct' outcome.[62] Yet, it was not enough that Morrill had made this decision; his audiences were also listening out for his *desire*. In fact, his contemporaries had difficulty understanding how it had been suspended for so long. A correspondent to *The Sydney Morning Herald*, though he acknowledged that it would have been almost impossible for Morrill to reach the southern colonies, marvelled that 'he does not seem to have been ever inspired with a desire to force his way on foot down to the settled districts'. The question of why his fellow survivors had not lived long after their adoption by Birri-gubba people was readily answered; they had died from 'sickness of the heart, and hope deferred'—they could not reconcile themselves to life away from civilisation. Inexplicably, Morrill survived.[63]

Morrill's published narrative is not unlike the waterfowl he liked to snare in the Burdekin wetlands; above the waterline, it seems to make its way without effort, yet, beneath the surface, webbed feet paddle furiously (though not necessarily consciously) working on Morrill's disentanglement from Birri-gubba kin and lifeways. In *Sketch of a Residence*, the physical and social processes of his passage out of 'civilisation' are reversed as he is restored to it. Discovering Morrill on the beach, the Birri-gubba men had

---

61 Ibid., 16.
62 Colley, 'Going Native, Telling Tales', 176.
63 *The Sydney Morning Herald*, 21 March 1863, 6.

transcended mutual fearfulness and begun to assimilate him by making him naked, sleeping alongside him and providing him with food. The first impulses of Hatch and Wilson, after they lowered their guns, were to offer him bread, tea and clothing. In both cases, Morrill then began the hard work of overcoming a language barrier and integrating himself into the community's economy.[64] *Sketch of a Residence* invites us to think that our protagonist is arriving, as he speaks, back at 'square one', an uncomplicated English sailor. However, we should not be lulled into forgetting how culturally complicated an English sailor might be, how he might find resonances in Aboriginal ways of thinking, and how peculiar the culture and language of the colonists was. Novelist Alan Garner instructively imagined William Buckley travelling along an intriguing cultural and linguistic spiral as his world view as a Cheshireman, re-wrought via shipboard and convict life, became shot through with Wathaurong ideas via the warp and weft of his 32 years living around Port Phillip Bay.[65]

In the most literal sense, Morrill was 'restored' to a frontier town that was not even dreamed of when he crawled onto the beach in 1846, a town full of strangers. Yet, as Morrill himself anticipated by announcing himself a 'British object', *Sketch of a Residence* presumed that readers near and far would understand that Port Denison, Rockhampton and Brisbane represented the bosom of empire. It was this home, rather than his family in Essex or the familiar shipboard life, to which this narrative safely delivered him.[66]

At the opening of the third chapter, Morrill's narrating voice proclaimed:

> The aboriginals among whom I have been living are a fine race of people, as to strength, size and general appearance; but like those of other parts of this colony, they are treacherous, jealous and cunning.[67]

This lofty comparative perspective is hardly one that Morrill himself could have gained. His Australian experience, apart from Birri-gubba life, consisted of a few days in Sydney, a short stop in Rockhampton and

---

64  Morrill, *Sketch of a Residence,* 2. Morrill was at first dependent on his Birri-gubba adopters to feed and care for him, but, once he recovered, he began to pull his weight by working, finding the snaring of waterfowl particularly satisfying. When he wrote *Sketch of a Residence,* Morrill was not yet financially independent; he hoped his published account 'may yield me what I much need—the means of living'. Morrill, *Sketch of a Residence,* 12.
65  Garner, *Strandloper.*
66  Morrill, *Sketch of a Residence,* 10. Morrill's family in Essex were amazed to hear that he was alive and expressed a desire to be reunited with him. *The Courier,* 19 August 1863, 2.
67  Morrill, *Sketch of a Residence,* 17.

a few weeks in Brisbane, and he had had little leisure time for reading the papers or comparing notes with others. With this statement, Morrill became a civilised man looking down on savages. As much as his journey into Bowen, this statement returned him to civilisation.

The third chapter presents a brief account of the Birri-gubba people. It is arranged according to ethnographic categories (e.g., familial structures, language and diet) and attempts to provide information of interest to pastoralists and miners.[68] Looking back, Morrill's involvement in Birri-gubba life is converted into information. As the narrating voice explains how fire is made, how children are raised and how the dead are honoured, we can no longer see Morrill participating. All his adoptive kin—the brother-in-law with whom he made a possum skin rug, his friend shot dead by the *Spitfire* party—are absorbed into a 'race' and into the collective third person: 'they have sunken eyes, broad noses … they get their living by fishing, hunting, digging … they think they have power over the rain'. Morrill's own role as kin to the dead and, possibly, a father to children, is not acknowledged. If he had once partaken of ceremony to make the rain (durgun) come or go, the third chapter of *Sketch of a Residence* gives the impression that he, as a Christian and civilised man, had never considered these beliefs plausible.[69] His observations are generally sympathetic, but they are just that, observations. Morrill's 17 years 'residence', advertised in the title, becomes a mere 'sojourn' in a British life, as James Bonwick put it. He becomes something of an explorer-in-retrospect, returned from an expedition from which he was always destined to return, and on which he was always destined to report.[70]

History-makers have continued to disentangle Morrill's information from his Birri-gubba experiences. A local history published in 1988 remarked that 'as is understandable in one who lived off the land for such a long time, Morrill's knowledge of the vegetation and indeed the fauna, was, by the layman's standards, prolific'. The author cited botanist M. Thozet's observation that 'had explorers Burke and Wills had the benefit of Morrill's knowledge of indigenous foods, their own safe return would have been more than a probability'.[71] It is well known that Burke rejected

---

68   Ibid., 18–20.
69   Ibid., 21–23.
70   Bonwick, *The Wild White Man*, 17.
71   London, *The Burdekin*, 72–73. See also Kerr, *Black Snow*, 15. Thozet accompanied Morrill on a tour of local food and medicinal plants in March 1863.

Aboriginal assistance when it may well have saved his life.⁷² Morrill was neither scientist nor layman (and he was certainly no Crusoe inventing knowledge in isolation); instead, he learned from Birri-gubba teachers within adoptive relationships. Noel Loos found *Sketch of a Residence* a valuable source for his account of the Aboriginal people of the Burdekin region, along with the accounts of coastal surveyor Joseph Beete Jukes and Curr, a sympathetic pastoralist. However, to show how much more might have been documented, Loos assessed the value and nature of Morrill and Gregory's third chapter against the thorough, methodical anthropological work of Ronald and Catherine Berndt and other twentieth-century authorities on Aboriginal life. In this light, Loos found Morrill's account lacking in detail and neglectful of important matters, such as the governing structures of his Birri-gubba clan.⁷³ Yet, it must be remembered that Morrill's participation in ethnography was quite different from that of his contemporaries Jukes and Curr (and, most certainly, from that of professional anthropologists more than a century later). Whereas for them, ethnography involved documenting what they gleaned from the exercise of curiosity, sympathy and cross-cultural communication, for Morrill, it signalled the transformation of his Birri-gubba knowledge into something that could be understood, and used, by his re-adoptive community.

Morrill told his story as conflict continued around him and as he became further embroiled in it. In the interview reported in the *Rockhampton Bulletin*, he had offered to act as an interpreter and to share his knowledge of the country with the settlers.⁷⁴ He apparently set off for Brisbane intent on dialogue with the government about the best way in which he could act both to 'protect the aboriginal blacks' and 'make the white settler feel secure'.⁷⁵ Morrill's survival and his testimony to Aboriginal kindness did kindle hope in some breasts that conciliation might be possible in the north, a hope that many had seen as vain after the killing of settlers who had shown friendliness and compassion towards Aboriginal people at Hornet Bank and Cullin-la-ringo in 1857 and 1861.⁷⁶ In some readers, his story inspired a sense of obligation to prevent unnecessary violence against the Birri-gubba and their neighbours, as these same people had succoured

---

72   Fitzpatrick, 'Burke, Robert O'Hara (1821–1861)'.
73   Loos, 'Frontier Conflict in the Bowen District', 16–17, 23–24, 37.
74   *Queensland Guardian*, 17 March 1863.
75   *The Argus*, 18 March 1863, 6, printing correspondence from the *Rockhampton Bulletin* office.
76   Loos, 'Frontier Conflict in the Bowen District', 78, 80.

a white man for so many years.[77] Yet, others cautioned against being lulled into a false sense of security by Morrill's testimonies while Aboriginal groups continued to perpetrate 'outrages' on an almost daily basis. One pastoralist promised to shoot Morrill if he attempted friendly intercourse with the Aboriginal people anywhere near his property.[78] In the midst of an extended discussion of the native police in the Queensland Legislative Assembly, Member for West Moreton, Dr Henry Challinor, suggested that Morrill might do good employed as an interpreter explaining British law to Aboriginal people in the north; however, the discussion quickly returned to the remuneration of the native police and the most effective way of 'dispersing' Aboriginal groups on pastoral runs.[79]

In the event, Morrill's potential as a go-between appears to have been little utilised. The *Rockhampton Bulletin* implied that authorities had deliberately hobbled Morrill by putting him in 'charge of colonial candles and dispensation of official soap' in the customs service; the reporter hoped that Morrill would be able to exceed those responsibilities.[80] Having carefully considered the economics of the region's settlement, Loos suggested that government's lack of interest in Morrill's potential as a negotiator reflected its unwillingness to make a change that would incur any additional costs.[81] On one occasion, Morrill acted as a guide on an exploratory mission that resulted in the founding of Cardwell (a port town about 360 kilometres north of Bowen). Among the exploration party was George Elphinstone Dalrymple, founder of Bowen. Dalrymple was among those published letter writers refuting Morrill's positive accounts of Aboriginal character. Morrill's central role in the undertaking was to explain to the Aboriginal people of the envisioned port that Europeans were taking their land and that they should vacate it.[82] Given these circumstances, the experience must have been highly ambivalent for Morrill; yet, his diary records a conference just prior to the return of the

---

77  See, for example, *Empire*, 19 March 1863, 2; *The Sydney Morning Herald*, 21 March 1863, 2; *The Courier*, 23 March 1863, 3; 31 March 1863, 3; 15 July 1863, 2; *Port Denison Times*, 4 October 1865, 2. Several of these correspondents were writing from Sydney.
78  *The Courier*, 20 March 1863, 3;19 June 1863, 2.
79  *The Courier*, 7 August 1863, 2–3.
80  *The Courier*, 15 May 1863, 3, quoting from the *Rockhampton Bulletin*, 6 May 1863.
81  Loos, 'Frontier Conflict in the Bowen District', 154–55.
82  See Maynard and Haskins, *Living with the Locals,* 188–89.

exploring party in which a petition to the governor was mooted asking that 'the land occupied by the present inhabitants' (i.e., the Aboriginal inhabitants) be withdrawn from the first land sale.[83]

Not all of Morrill's contemporaries were convinced that the struggle over his loyalties had been as short, or as readily resolved, as it appeared in *Sketch of a Residence*. Indeed, even within that narrative, his desire to return to civilisation was tepid, an ambivalent mixture of 'hope' and 'unease'. Morrill's palate betrayed him; the roots he was offered on first meeting the Birri-gubba were described as enjoyable and nutty, whereas the bread he was given by Hatch and Wilson stuck in his throat and the tea was too sweet. The bread and tea were also redundant, as Morrill and his group 'had caught 20 small grey wallabies' that day.[84] Gregory, preparing a new edition of *Sketch of a Residence* in 1896, apparently felt that Morrill's joy on returning to British cuisine required augmentation. He embellished Morrill's first meal with the stockmen with the jubilant ejaculation: 'Oh, for that supreme moment of my life, with knife and fork in hand once more, and that salt and pepper, can I ever forget it!'[85]

The report of Morrill's interview at Rockhampton described his life with the Birri-gubba as a state of 'captivity' and regarded his meeting with Hatch and Wilson as an escape 'by strategem [sic]'.[86] However, some of those who met and conversed with Morrill at Bowen were convinced neither that he had 'come in' to the settlement of his own accord, nor that he wished to stay. Thomas Lodge Murray-Prior speculated:

> My own impression is that Morrill knew about the whites being in the neighbourhood long before he came in and was either detained forcibly or had become reconciled to his savage life and attachments and only came in when he was afraid of being shot by his own countrymen.[87]

Had he 'returned' not (or not only) because he wished to leave his Birri-gubba clan and live once more a British life, but because he meant to intercede on their behalf or because he was sent by a council of Elders? A correspondent to the *Port Denison Times* considered Morrill a 'deputation to the whites' sent by the Aboriginal people of the Kennedy

---

83  James Morrill's diary, Monday 14 January 1864, quoted in Bowen Historical Society, *The Story of James Morrill*.
84  Morrill, *Sketch of a Residence*, 10, 14, 16.
85  Gregory, *Narrative of James Murrell's*, 31.
86  *Queensland Guardian*, 17 March 1863.
87  Murray-Prior, Private Letter Book, 21. See also Carrington, *Colonial Adventures*, 165–66.

District to offer an agreement about a division of land. On his way back north, Morrill left the *Rockhampton Bulletin* office with the impression that he was en route to see his Birri-gubba clan, not only to deliver presents from the government, but also to report back to them more generally. His obituary in the *Port Denison Times* suggested that he may not have been entirely trusted by colonial authorities, as there was some fear that he 'might again join the natives and act, perhaps, in unison with them'.[88]

Morrill was about 20 years old when he began his Birri-gubba life and, despite occasional sightings of ships, for the most part he must have resigned himself to living out his life in his adoptive community, committing himself to Birri-gubba lifeways and connections. Historian and Worimi man John Maynard and historian Victoria Haskins, looking at adoptive relationships partly from the point of view of the structure of Aboriginal communities, estimated that Morrill was well integrated into Birri-gubba life (after all, he spoke no less than eight dialects of the local language); however, they wondered about his position of 'acceptance' as a Birri-gubba man. As noted by Maynard and Haskins, there was no indication that Morrill bore the ceremonial cicatrices on his body that would have signified initiation, and thus full manhood status, among his adoptive people.[89]

In the minds of Morrill's colonial contemporaries, the question of his status as a Birri-gubba man was closely connected with the question of whether he had had a wife or female companion and, in turn, with his ongoing loyalties. At Rockhampton, Morrill explained the polygamous practices of his adoptive people, and the early age at which girls were often married. Rather coyly, it was reported that he had 'fought shy of the seductions of female blandishments' (i.e., the flattery and persuasion of Birri-gubba women).[90] In *Sketch of a Residence,* Morrill is said to have told his adoptive people 'from the first that I had a wife and two children, knowing they would not think it so strange at my wanting to get away'. Later editions added: 'and because I could the better excuse myself from being too closely linked in with them by taking a wife, which I knew

---

88   *Port Denison Times*, 4 October 1865, 2; *The Courier*, 15 May 1863, 3, with a report taken from the *Rockhampton Bulletin*, 6 May 1863; *Port Denison Times*, 1 November 1865, 2. For further examination of the clues to Morrill's movements and interactions with locals after his return to Bowen in mid-1863, see Breslin, *James Morrill*.
89   Maynard and Haskins, *Living with the Locals*, 191–92.
90   *Queensland Guardian*, 17 March 1863.

would be dangerous in many ways'.⁹¹ This danger may well have been a real one. Morrill stated elsewhere that the 'wars, fights and feuds' of his adoptive people were typically waged over wives.⁹² However, it is equally possible that he felt a sense of danger around this issue as he told his story. One of the returned British subjects Linda Colley discussed, Thomas Pellow, claimed in his memoirs that, after being allocated a wife from the Moroccan sultan's harem, he rejected seven black women and seven 'mulattos' before being offered the white-skinned woman he took as his wife. Colley saw this as 'a concession to opinion in England, where Pellow was by then desperately trying to reintegrate himself'.⁹³

As we have seen, Thomas Murray-Prior pressed Morrill on this point, telling him he could not believe that he would not have had a 'lady love' among the Birri-gubba. Morrill replied that his claim in *Sketch of a Residence* was that he had had no wife. However, he had frequently been loaned the wives of others, a convention that caused no ill feeling between men. Murray-Prior posited that he had been 'a greater favourite than was good for his constitution'.⁹⁴ Attestations to the presence of Morrill's Aboriginal descendants in the region today are sometimes accompanied by similar suggestions that his sexual involvement in Birri-gubba life was notable. Henry Young, a local historian residing in Bowen, told me that he knows about eight people locally who believe they are descended from Morrill's children with Birri-gubba women and that he 'wasn't a bad old bull'.⁹⁵

Speculations about Morrill's allegiances were not unconnected with the settlers' own feelings about their part in the violence of the frontier. George Carrington wrote about his experiences in North Queensland in the mid-1860s on his return to London, and was frank about the violence involved in staking claim to this country. He let his reader in on the true meaning of the colonising verb 'to disperse (i.e. to shoot) the blacks'. With a heavy sense of irony, he discussed the virtues of the native police

---

91  Gregory, *Sketch of the Residence of James Morrill*, 14.
92  Morrill, *Sketch of a Residence*, 18.
93  Colley, 'Going Native, Telling Tales', 170.
94  Murray-Prior, Private Letter Book, 19. Their conversation appears to have been a cordial one. It is not known whether Morrill would have been aware of Murray-Prior's involvement in the retaliatory action that followed the killing of the Fraser family by Aboriginal people at Hornet Bank in 1857. McKay, 'Writing From the Contact Zone', 57–58.
95  Henry Young, in conversation with the author, 23 November 2010.

who were not 'wanting in zeal, and are not likely to err on the side of injudicious mercy'. He implied that Aboriginal women were killed as the surest way of eliminating the race.[96]

Carrington, who had been tramping along the coast looking for shepherding work, recalled stopping at one station where he was offered a job, only to discover that he was to replace a shepherd killed days before by the 'blacks'; no-one had gone out to look for the body.[97] He took a similar job at the next station. One day, out alone with the sheep, his horse and his gun, Carrington spied movement in a nearby patch of grass and, without thinking, shot twice. He had shot a man. He approached and the man was still alive but seemed fatally wounded, so he shot him again, in the head. He asked the reader what else he could have done; was this not the kindest—the only—course of action? Carrington turned almost immediately to Morrill's story. He recalled, from talking to Morrill, that 'he had several wives, and, I suppose, would have spent the rest of his life with them had it not been for an accident'. This 'accident' was his meeting with the stockmen Hatch and Wilson. 'After talking a while he wished to re-join his companions, but his new friends prevented him, and he was sent down to Port Denison.' Carrington's Morrill 'did not live long, and would much have preferred going back to his wild life with the blacks, but one of his wives came to inform him that, should he return, the blacks would kill him'.[98] Morrill's story seemed to speak to Carrington as he recalled his own part in the larger 'accident' that was the beginnings of pastoralism in North Queensland. His Morrill was caught up in a personal tragedy, its push and pull meshed with the tensions of a warlike situation, but also strongly hitched to a universal humanity, as Carrington felt he was.[99]

The reported visit to Morrill by his wife, which apparently closed his relations with the Birri-gubba, had a melancholic resonance for Carrington as he remembered his own experiences; yet, this does not foreclose the

---

96   Carrington, *Colonial Adventures*, 151–53.
97   Ibid., 156–57.
98   Ibid., 163–65.
99   With some similarity, W. Robertson, in his 'Coo-ee' talks of the 1920s, concluded Morrill's story with the account of the fate of a friend with whom he had once visited 'the remnants of Murrell's tribe', and who was always on 'good terms with the aborigines'. The friend's unrelated family tragedy evokes feelings similar to those Robertson and his listeners might have felt towards Morrill's kin (but displaced from them). Robertson, *Coo-ee Talks*, 147. Frank Reid reported in 1929 that some of the old-timers in Bowen remembered how Morrill 'used to relate some very touching incidents concerning that race, which often brought tears to their eyes'. *Townsville Daily Bulletin*, 2 October 1929, 9.

possibility of Morrill receiving such a message of renouncement. For Bruce Breslin, writing in 1992, Morrill's story formed a window onto the dangers and uncertainties of the North Queensland frontier. He believed that news of Morrill's involvement in the colonising activities of the settlers, including the founding of Cardwell, which did involve some conflict, would have travelled fast among the Aboriginal peoples of the Herbert–Burdekin region. Breslin understood Carrington's story of the final spousal visit as reflecting Morrill's own anguish, the open 'psychological wounds' that would lead to his early death in 1865.[100] Morrill's story, even as he told it himself, became an entanglement of history and feeling, allegory and aspiration, laid over with shifting patterns of the said, the unsaid and the unsayable.

---

100  Breslin, *Exterminate with Pride*, 81–82. It is not clear whether the wife's visit is held by Breslin to be an occurrence in fact that *caused* Morrill's anguish, or a story told by him to Carrington that *expressed* his feelings. In *Sketch of a Residence*, the Birri-gubba and their southern neighbours seemed to keep a close eye on Morrill once they realised the extent of his intimacy with the ways of the newcomers; on his departure, some apparently told him to 'go and get drowned with the other white men' in the context of their belief that a great flood was approaching. Morrill, *Sketch of a Residence*, 14–15. Today, although several Birri-gubba clans tell positive stories about Morrill, the Wulgurukaba are apparently hostile to his memory. Russell McGregor, associate professor in history, James Cook University, in conversation with the author, 29 November 2010 (information from Dorothy Savage).

# 2
# Becoming First White Resident

Barbara Thompson was a young Scottish woman who had migrated to Sydney with her parents and then eloped to Moreton Bay at the age of 16. With her sailor husband and a few others, Thompson took a small vessel to the Torres Strait, aiming to salvage material from a wrecked ship, but they were driven onto rocks by a storm and wrecked themselves. Her husband and their other companions drowned, but Thompson was pulled from the water by a man named Boroto who was part of an islander turtling party also caught in the storm. Thompson was adopted as the returned granddaughter of a man named Pequi and his eldest wife, and lived with his extended family among the Kaurareg people of Morolug (today known as Price of Wales Island).[1] In 1848 and 1849, a scientific ship named the *Rattlesnake* made two visits to the Torres Strait; on the second of these visits, Thompson introduced herself, having spent about five years living in the strait. Some members of the *Rattlesnake* party had met some of the same islanders the previous year and were already on familiar and friendly terms (Thompson had been ill with a fever on this occasion).[2] The ship remained alongside the island for several weeks and Thompson lived on board, spending much of her time talking with the young naturalist Oswald Brierly, who made a detailed record of their conversations. Thompson's adoptive kin wanted her to stay with them, but she decided to return to Sydney with the *Rattlesnake*, stating simply, 'I am a Christian'.[3]

---

1  Moore, *Islanders and Aborigines at Cape York*, 7–8.
2  Ibid., 160. She had also attempted to make contact with another ship, but hesitated, thinking that her adoptive family might try to stop her, and then had failed in leaving her attempt too late.
3  Ibid., 80.

Brierly had arrived in Australia in 1842 to help Benjamin Boyd establish his whaling station at Twofold Bay on the south coast of New South Wales. Brierly expected to be terrified of the Aboriginal people there, but soon learned to enjoy being in the bush sketching and painting, and began to interact with the Aboriginal people who moved around Twofold Bay. He made a particularly strong friendship with a man he called Toby from whom he learned some of the local language, and with whom he travelled inland and mixed with groups of Aboriginal people up into the Monaro region. An active colonist, Brierly saw himself as engaged in a process of civilising a new land and integrating it with the economy of the British Empire, but he was also sensitive, open-minded and respectful towards Aboriginal people.[4] When he decided to join the survey expedition, Brierly was already well prepared to be a sympathetic, interested and skilled listener for Barbara Thompson and the many Kaurareg people who added to the story of her rescue and residence with them.

Brierly's notes on his conversations with Thompson, together with his daily journal in which he recorded the frequent visits of the islanders to the *Rattlesnake*, provide an intimate account of Thompson's adoption, some of the ways in which she navigated her new life, and her prolonged farewell. He recorded Thompson's words as far as he was able (whether he understood her meaning or not), as she spoke a combination of working-class Scottish English and Kaurareg language. Thompson's speech often erupts from Brierly's commentary in his journal, her voice heard more and less directly. On 23 October 1849, Thompson told Brierly: 'Since I left them, one of the gins has taken my *pota* out of my *lie* and wears it round her neck and at night they have a cry for me in the camp as if I were dead'. In this and other cases, clarification and confirmation came from Thompson's Kaurareg kin. About a month later, a group of women came by canoe to visit Thompson (whose Kaurareg name was 'Giom'); one of them took hold of her hand and showed her a shell that had belonged to her, which the other woman now wore around her neck as a memento, saying '"Giom, ye noosa eena"—"Giom this is yours"'.[5]

The situation of mutual friendship and trust created an island between the shores of Thompson's two lives. She was not abruptly thrust into someone else's chafing clothes, as Morrill was, but made her own dress out of the *Rattlesnake* party's spare handkerchiefs, which she proudly showed to her

---

4   McKenna, *Looking for Blackfellas' Point*, 120–24.
5   Moore, *Islanders and Aborigines at Cape York,* 121, 169 (original emphasis).

Kaurareg kin.[6] The ship seems to have been a culturally 'safe' space, if humour and discussion of good-natured disagreement are anything to go by. Brierly was given a Kaurareg name, 'Tarrka', that, like Thompson's name, 'Giom', belonged to someone who had died; he recorded in his journal being teased by the islanders about whether he intended to return to them as well.[7] Thompson felt able to talk about her maintenance of cultural difference from her adoptive people; she laughed at the Kaurareg rules about women not speaking to their father-in-law and men to their mother-in-law, and told everyone 'that we always spoke to our father and mother-in-law in our country'. She had given the Kaurareg women an opportunity to express horror over Thompson's birth culture—they had apparently exclaimed, 'the white people: they have no mother-in-law and no shame', but their affection for her was not diminished.[8] There was no haste to make public an account of her experiences. Brierly's notes were not made with a view to publication, and it seems he never sought to bind this record of her story into the corset of an orderly narrative. Although his journals were very much a part of his identity and activity as a scientific man and colonist, his now published notes remain full of meanings far richer than colonising narratives or scientific classifications.[9]

*Sketch of a Residence* is written in the first person, commencing: 'I, James Morrill, was born on the 20$^{th}$ May, 1824 … near Maldon … where my mother and father were also brought up from childhood before me'. Yet, his was not the only voice in his account. Compared with Brierly's journals, *Sketch of a Residence* is an opaque text; the processes of recollection, communication, misunderstanding and revision are smoothed over within the closely woven published narrative. Brierly noted where each conversation took place, the parties present, what the atmosphere was like, and often wrote down his own questions as well as Thompson's answers. By contrast, in the case of Morrill's collaboration with Edmund Gregory, we have no idea how many times the two men met, how formal or otherwise their meetings were, how they went about their task, and to what extent they established a rapport.

---

6   Ibid., 90.
7   Ibid., 87, 92.
8   Ibid., 172.
9   McKenna, *Looking for Blackfellas' Point*, 130.

Morrill was literate and, in ideal circumstances, may have been able to be an active collaborator, reading over drafts and suggesting corrections. However, he may have found it difficult to make himself understood. Without expressly referring to their interviews, Gregory recalled that when he arrived in Brisbane Morrill was 'shy, especially at first, and was not communicative … the knowledge of his own language came back to him very slowly'.[10] Pelletier, after placing his French at the back of his mind for the same interval, conversed with the French consul in Sydney with the greatest difficulty:

> Putting his hands to his ear like a horn when trying to understand, and when trying to respond 'he put one hand above his eyes and looked into the distance, as if he would have liked to discover the person to whom he had to reply'.[11]

A comparable gulf of understanding between Morrill and Gregory can be glimpsed in the third chapter of *Sketch of a Residence*, in which a sense of frustration is almost palpable in their characterisation of Birri-gubba language:

> [It] is very guttural in sound and extremely limited in power of expression. Of course they have no means of teaching [it] but by imitation and memory, assisted by their wants … The language is very irregular, and seems to me totally impossible to systematise … in any way.

A vocabulary of about 75 words is offered. After naming the elements, parts of the body and a number of animals, it ends abruptly with 'Enugedy—enough, that will do'.[12]

Speaking in Rockhampton, Morrill had apparently named his clan or tribe 'Baeaberuggedy' and claimed that 'every peak or mountain has its own particular name … I could give the names of many places which I learn have been recently discovered by the whites'.[13] Yet, *Sketch of a Residence* includes very few place names; further, in his Cardwell journal of the following year, Morrill referred very generally to 'natives' and 'blacks' in the parlance of his re-adoptive community. It is possible that

---

10  Morrill's diary or journal remains in the private collection of the Jack family, Morrill's descendants via his marriage with Eliza Ann Ross. It was reproduced in the Bowen Historical Society's 1964 publication. Gregory, *Sketch of the Residence of James Morrill*, 17.
11  Anderson, *Pelletier*, 62.
12  Morrill, *Sketch of a Residence*, 20–22.
13  *Queensland Guardian*, 17 March 1863. He also claimed to have been able to speak eight dialects of the local language. Morrill, *Sketch of a Residence*, 14, 24.

Morrill's interviews with Gregory had persuaded him that the specific local vocabulary that he had used during his Birri-gubba adoption was neither useful nor useable for a re-adopted colonist.

The first person narrating voice in *Sketch of a Residence* is seductive; it is tempting to think we can hear Morrill speaking more or less freely to us.[14] It seduced Noel Loos, who understood Morrill to be speaking through *Sketch of a Residence* with 'naive candour'. It also seduced Bruce Breslin who, even as he brought to life the precariousness and complexity of Morrill's situation, did not seem to think it would constrain Morrill's ability to express himself. Breslin cited Morrill's 'short struggle between the feeling of love I had for my old friends and companions and the desire once more to live a civilized life', as if these, unquestionably, were the words Morrill himself had chosen to represent his feelings.[15] Yet, we must ask: how did this 'struggle' find expression in such an economical sentence? We might imagine that Morrill told Gregory of this farewell in a more awkward way, perhaps attempting to translate the impassioned dialogue that had taken place on that hillside or, perhaps guardedly, with a stoicism behind which Gregory glimpsed a deep sadness.

When Morrill's narrative voice describes 'the aboriginals among whom I have been living' as 'a fine race of people … [but] treacherous, jealous and cunning',[16] there are numerous possible relationships between these words and Morrill and Gregory, all of which are tied up with Morrill's loyalties and allegiances as he told his story. Did Gregory contribute these unflattering adjectives to fit in with his anticipated readers' prejudices? Did Gregory extract these words or sentiments from Morrill by asking

---

14  Breslin, *Exterminate with Pride*, 73, 76. Breslin discussed Morrill's adoption into Birri-gubba society alongside the narrative of Jukes's, *Narrative of the Fly* (1847), the latter being a leisurely exploratory drift up the coast, during which the officers interacted closely, and mostly on friendly terms, with Aboriginal people of the Burdekin region. No distinction was drawn between the different manner in which the two men arrived on that coast and the significance of Jukes's ability to depart at will. Loos, 'Frontier Conflict in the Bowen District', 16–17.

15  Morrill, *Sketch of a Residence*, 16. Breslin has since produced a new edition of *Sketch of a Residence* with a critical introduction, which considers with more subtlety how the contemporary reader might hear what Morrill meant to say in his narrative. Breslin, *James Morrill*. Iain McCalman, who sought to listen to Morrill through his published narrative, sheds some light on his experiences. McCalman, *The Reef*.

16  Morrill, *Sketch of a Residence*, 17. In the second edition, Gregory altered this statement to one that more plausibly reflected Morrill's experience in southern Queensland: 'The aboriginals among whom James Murrells had been living so long, he describes as a vastly superior race of people to any he had seen in the southern part of the colony, physically, and as to general appearance. Nevertheless, they are treacherous, jealous and exceedingly cunning'. Gregory, *Sketch of the Residence of James Morrill*, 18.

whether he had always understood Birri-gubba politics, or whether he had not felt safe to take a Birri-gubba wife? Did Morrill himself realise that his status as a re-adopted colonist would be enhanced by separating himself from the Birri-gubba? If he had been reviving his reading skills on recent back issues of Brisbane's chief newspaper, *The Courier*, he may have encountered discussion inspired by Charles Darwin's *The Origin of Species* that could easily have prompted a disavowal of his own Aboriginality. One jocular article proposed an experiment in which certain Sydney gentlemen might be stripped of the 'advantages of the tailor and hatter' and left in the wilds of Africa for 10 or 15 years—what would a naturalist say 'as to their exultation above the inferior races of mankind, or even above the gorilla'?[17] The newspaper report of the interview at Rockhampton cited Morrill describing his adoptive people as 'cunning, thievish, and treacherous'. This time, the claim was connected with Morrill's offers to mediate, guide and interpret, and he may have uttered these words in an effort to make himself indispensable, carving a niche for employment and bargaining power by claiming that the Aboriginal people and politics of the region would be incomprehensible to anyone but himself.[18]

William Buckley, living in the new settlement at Port Phillip in circumstances similar to Morrill's, was described by writer and historian Barry Hill as a:

> Desperate defender of [his] indigenous affiliations … as a go-between on the frontier of the sheep run that would destroy his clan … What happened next? Buckley, faced with the tragedy of white invasion, fled to Hobart, to live a quiet life as a white man.[19]

The fullest account of Buckley's experiences living with the Wathaurong people was produced in Hobart in 1852, 20 years after his 'return to civilisation', in collaboration with a long-time friend, John Morgan. While the narrative is partly shaped by Morgan's concerns,[20] Morgan played a vital role in assisting Buckley to weave a rich tapestry of memory around the relationships, imperatives, satisfactions and fears of his time with (and, at times, avoiding) his adoptive people as they moved across their

---

17   *The Courier*, 28 January 1863; 5 January 1863. For an account of these debates see Griffiths, *Hunters and Collectors*, 22–25, 39–46.
18   *The Courier*, 11 March 1863, 2; *Queensland Guardian*, 17 March 1863.
19   Hill, 'Crossing Cultures', 116–20.
20   McDonald, *The Extraordinary Tale of William Buckley*.

country around Port Phillip.[21] Buckley had been much less forthcoming in earlier interviews. The Reverend Langhorn described Buckley as 'difficult' and did not bother to publish the results of his interviews with him; several others decided that Buckley was simply a dunce with nothing worthwhile to say.[22]

As Morrill conversed with Gregory, they were establishing a level of trust. Surprise attacks and brutal reprisals continued in and around Birri-gubba country, and the Birri-gubba crowded into 'safe' areas away from the settlements, all movements rendered strategic.[23] From his first appearance, Morrill was expected to participate in the thrust of colonisation by divulging information. One of the earliest reports of his appearance in *The Courier* was confident that:

> This happily reclaimed savage should, if possessed of ordinary intelligence, and not brutalised by protracted association with the blacks, be an invaluable assistant to parties opening up the terra incognita of the north to the … historian of the customs and manners, and to the scientific world in general … to learn the secrets of native unhallowed rites and procure an all-authentic memorial of a race rapidly disappearing from the face of the world.[24]

E. B. Kennedy, an adventurer and writer who met Morrill in 1864, later recalled that Morrill seemed shy and unable to express himself clearly. However, Kennedy, who was serving in the native police force at the time, had just returned from a patrol of Birri-gubba country. His eagerness to learn more about the region may well have seemed predatory.[25] We can hardly imagine that Morrill spoke entirely freely in any of his interviews, amid the clamour of questions. Are they cannibals? Do they

---

21  Buckley many times separated from and reunited with the Aboriginal people who adopted him, living a lonely existence for many weeks or months before once again being thoroughly bound up in the affairs of the community. At one stage, he made his escape with a heavy heart, as many of his closest friends and 'protectors' were killed by another group. Alone, he moved to a place on the Karaaf River where he had previously built a small hut and, without means to hunt for kangaroo on his own, started to make a weir to catch fish as the tides turned; he also continued to harvest roots as his adoptive people had taught him. After an interval, some people approached who he soon found 'belonged to the tribe of my old friend: my tribe, I may say', who congratulated him on his fish traps, and with whom he camped and travelled again until the killing of a young man by another group who had joined them. Buckley was sent as a messenger to inform the kin of the deceased and remained with them until he found their mourning practices too alienating, at which point he returned to the Karaaf River. Morgan, *The Life and Adventures of William Buckley*, 60–70.
22  Sayers, 'Introduction', ix–xi.
23  Breslin, *Exterminate with Pride*, 71–72.
24  *The Courier*, 27 February 1863.
25  Kennedy, *Seventeen Years amongst Queensland Blacks*, 353.

practice polygamy? Have they any permanent residences at all? Do they have any beliefs or superstitions? These are the kinds of questions that Morrill seems to have faced, each interested in measuring the *difference* of the Birri-gubba—their savagery—in a way that was intertwined with the colonists' lust for their land. Loos observed that the question of religion emerged strongly in the 1861 Select Committee inquiry into the native police force, the apparent lack of 'religious susceptibilities' among Aboriginal people justifying the suspension of 'normal European standards of behaviour' in dealing with them.[26]

On the question of religion, Morrill was quoted, somewhat contradictorily, as stating that 'they observe no religious ceremonies. When their children arrive at puberty, or perhaps before, they mark them with the symbols of their tribe'.[27] The question of religion seems to have been one that was difficult to answer. *Sketch of a Residence* created a similar contradiction; it stated that 'they have no written language whatever, and very little tradition', before relating the Birri-gubba understanding of the moon as a human being, sometimes encountered on fishing expeditions, whom the tribes caught and threw into the sky to save from harm.[28] If Morrill self-edited his account of Birri-gubba life ways according to concerns about his own and his adoptive people's safety, he perhaps did so according to Birri-gubba obligations surrounding knowledge. With an eye to the secret and sacred dimensions of Indigenous knowledge, Stéphanie Andersen asked whether Barbara Thompson's very frankness with Brierly indicated a lack of appreciation of the authority structures surrounding Kaurareg teachings. Conversely, Morrill's apparently selective rendition of Birri-gubba traditions and beliefs may be interpreted as a commitment to maintaining significant knowledge conventions.[29]

The newspaper report of Morrill's interview at Rockhampton claimed to be 'nearly verbatim … indeed, our readers will have here the *ipsissima verba* of the narrator'—that is, his precise words, the only difference being

---

26  Loos, 'Frontier Conflict in the Bowen District', 84–86.
27  *Queensland Guardian*, 17 March 1863.
28  Morrill, *Sketch of a Residence*, 20.
29  Anderson, *Pelletier*, 54–55. For example, Martin Nakata discussed the tensions involved in contemporary efforts to integrate Indigenous knowledge into scientific practice. Scientific capitalism remains, in some respects, predatory with Indigenous knowledge 'merely another resource for potential profit'. Even the most sincere efforts can result in separating Indigenous knowledge from its context in collective ownership, regulated by oral conventions and, in some cases, laws of sacred and secret knowledge, and in the detachment of this knowledge from holistic concepts, instead, separating it into components delineated by the categories of Western science. Nakata, *Savaging the Disciplines*, 182–88.

## 2. BECOMING FIRST WHITE RESIDENT

their presentation in the form of a narrative rather than the free-flowing conversation in which they were uttered.[30] Gregory may have taken a similar line of liberty with, and fidelity to, the spoken word in presenting *Sketch of a Residence*. Certainly, hesitation and ambivalence were erased, and suggestion and interpolation were kneaded to create a coherent, smooth whole. We could accuse Gregory of having created a barrier to more genuine insights into Morrill's Aboriginal life, or his feelings on leaving it, by engaging in this activity. Yet, the pamphlet that the two men produced was, perhaps, largely a coagulation of what Morrill did want Gregory, and the world, to know. Arguably, it was a 'tactical' collaboration in which Gregory helped Morrill to say what could be said (i.e., what it was possible to say) about his experiences.[31] In any case, it helped Morrill to create a dignified, reasonable persona through which he could make a plea on behalf of the Aboriginal people of the region that might be heard by readers:

> It will perhaps be pardonable in me if I refer to a suggestion thrown out by a correspondent in the *Courier* newspaper, to the effect that the natives who were so kind to me should be dealt with in a similar manner, as those who succoured Burke, Wills and King … almost their last wish to me was with tears in their eyes that I would ask the white men to let them have *some* of their *own* ground to live on. They agreed to give up all on the south of the Burdekin River, but asked that they might be *allowed* to retain that on the other, at all events that which was no good to anybody but them, the low swampy grounds near the sea coast.[32]

Morrill died in October 1865 at the age of 41. Gregory wasted no time in releasing a second edition of *Sketch of a Residence*, in which he bumped Morrill aside as author. *Sketch of the Residence of James Morrill among the Aboriginals of Northern Queensland for Seventeen Years … by Edmund*

---

30  *Queensland Guardian*, 17 March 1863. Similarly, John Morgan noted in his preface to William Buckley's story: 'In giving the history of a life in the first person … I have endeavoured to express the thoughts of a humble, unlearned man, in that language of simplicity and truth which, in my mind, is best suited to the subject'. Morgan, *The Life and Adventures of William Buckley*, xx.
31  Penny van Toorn identified 'tactical' advantages for contemporary Indigenous storytellers in collaborating with sympathetic non-Indigenous writers in terms of control and in getting their messages across to an audience; such advantages must be acknowledged alongside any concerns about the 'authenticity' of the results of collaborative endeavour. van Toorn, 'Indigenous Australian Life Writing', 17.
32  Morrill, *Sketch of a Residence*, 24 (original emphasis). The letter to *The Courier* he refers to may have been the one by 'Reader', published 12 March 1863, 2. It may have been Gregory's idea to appeal to it as a way of linking Morrill's proposal with respectable public opinion. It is notable, though, that 'Reader' seemed to be suggesting that the Birri-gubba people be compensated with a consignment of useful items, rather than with an agreement about land.

*Gregory*, seems to have rolled off the press barely a month after Morrill's last breath.[33] In his new preface, Gregory claimed that the story had 'long' been out of print, and that it had been 'necessary to re-write it'. His rewriting was slight but not without significance. He began with the correction of Morrill's name: 'James Murrells, not Morrill, was born on the 20th May 1824'; apparently, 'seventeen years' isolation in the bush, had taken from him the power to re-call his own name with accuracy'. Communications from Essex, or from the customs officials in Sydney, had evidently corroborated Morrill's correct identity too late for inclusion in the first edition. Gregory then rewrote the brief first chapter in the third person, before resuming the original narrative, claiming 'the rest ... will be read with greater interest in [Morrill's] own words'.[34]

In translating part of the story into the third person, Gregory may have been reclaiming a text he felt *he* had written in the first place. The boundary between first and third person, at least in this second edition, was closely related to marketability—a yarn such as this owed much of its appeal to the 'I'. Gregory's 'authority' resurfaced at the end of the second chapter, at which point he provided an account of the final years of Morrill's life, concluding with the obituary that had appeared in the *Port Denison Times*.[35] Morrill 'the man' was dead, and now, symbolically, so was the Morrill 'the author'.

Castaway stories have been understood as a genre providing the 'mythic fuel' of the 'expansive imperialist thrust of the white race', reflecting, inspiring and legitimising the possession and control of new lands.[36] Morrill himself may only have participated in one exploratory expedition and helped the townsfolk of Bowen to feel at home in their new environment by making its features seem familiar.[37] However, his story has had a long life after his death. In his 1865 edition, Gregory omitted

---

33   Advertisements for a new volume on 'the life and experience of James Morrill' that could be purchased direct from the Courier General Printing office appeared under the heading 'Published This Day' in the classifieds pages of *The Brisbane Courier*, 27–29 November 1865. My references to this second version are to the 1866 edition. Ferguson indicates that the 1865 and 1866 editions were very similar. The 1866 edition was most likely a reprinting (perhaps indicating a high level of demand). Ferguson, *Bibliography of Australia*, 779–81.
34   Gregory, *Sketch of the Residence of James Morrill*, 3, 5.
35   Ibid., 16–18.
36   Green, *The Robinson Crusoe Story*, 1–3.
37   His obituary anticipates that the people of Bowen would feel the loss of him as one 'who was always ready to explain the use of a blackfellow's mysterious weapon, or the qualities ... of the various roots and plants found in the neighbourhood'. Gregory, *Sketch of the Residence of James Morrill*, 18.

Morrill's closing plea on behalf of the Birri-gubba and their neighbours for reciprocal good treatment and for a division of land. Instead, the second edition concluded with the formerly penultimate paragraph narrating the 'extinction' of the Birri-gubba people through 'destruction by the settlers and black police' and 'natural deterioration'.[38] In the first edition, this narrative of decline was tempered by an image of Mount Elliott as a place of 'safe asylum' for Aboriginal people, with an abundance of fresh water and food—a foothold in a future that may have given rise to ambivalent feelings in its readers. Some may have found it rather Arcadian, others may have lobbied for an intensified native police patrol of those nurturing slopes. In the second edition, Mount Elliott was no longer a refuge, and the descriptors 'thick scrub' and 'low and swampy' were removed, leaving the mountain simply 'well grassed and watered' like an inviting sheep run. The first edition's tentative references to gold were replaced by the statement 'he thinks it a gold bearing country'.[39]

In producing a new edition, Gregory may have been responding to local readers who wanted a volume to remember Morrill by, enquiries from overseas and interest from other colonies. In his preface, Gregory remarked on the importance of the story for posterity: 'the narrative of the sufferings and strange incidents here recorded will be read with interest as long as Queensland is in existence'.[40] At this stage, though, the future of North Queensland was perhaps not so assured. In 1865, Governor Bowen compared the combat against Aboriginal forces in North Queensland to the Maori War in which 10,000 imperial troops were just then engaged.[41] Loos and Breslin have shown how relentless Aboriginal attacks on stock, outlying stations and station workers drove pastoralism to its knees in the mid to late 1860s. A radical (if uneven) change in policy was necessary: the 'letting in' of Aboriginal groups to stations and towns to hunt, fish and camp from about 1868.[42] The colony's government saw massive British and European immigration as the key to success; however, after a few

---

38   Morrill, *Sketch of a Residence*, 24; Gregory, *Sketch of the Residence of James Morrill*, 23.
39   Morrill, *Sketch of a Residence*, 24; Gregory, *Sketch of the Residence of James Morrill*, 23. The references to gold may have sparked a minor gold rush. 'The Sad, Bad, Mad but Sometimes Glad Old Days by A Survivor', *Truth* (Brisbane), 21 May 1916.
40   Gregory, *Sketch of the Residence of James Morrill*, 2.
41   Evans, *A History of Queensland*, 94–95.
42   Breslin, *Exterminate with Pride*, 82–84, 88–90. The native police detachments were moved to more newly settled areas, leaving the Burdekin settlers alone to defend their properties, families and employees. From a thorough perusal of the *Port Denison Times* from March 1864 to December 1874, Loos concluded that conflict in the region peaked between 1864 and 1868. Loos, 'Frontier Conflict in the Bowen District', 157–64.

sharp cycles of boom and bust, things seemed to be going backwards. As the decade rolled on, colonists fled drought and economic depression in the tens of thousands.[43] E. B. Kennedy, having himself departed the north after crossing paths with Morrill, implored readers of his London-published *Four Years in Queensland* to see a future for this colony:

> Queensland is *bound* to advance, *cannot* be held back ... She will become a land not only flowing with milk and honey, but with wine also, and all the fruits of the earth. She has passed through a period of severe distress, but her present prospects point to a more prosperous state resting on a more secure basis.[44]

If Morrill had been cautious about sharing his knowledge of the Birri-gubba with Kennedy and others for fear that his knowledge might be used against them, his reservations were well founded. Kennedy's representation of the Aboriginal peoples of North Queensland in this volume was damning: 'there is not a redeeming point in their whole character ... there is no savage in the world so thoroughly low and degraded'. Kennedy supported this thesis by citing *Sketch of a Residence* at length.[45]

As Gregory published his second edition, compromise with Aboriginal groups may have begun to look like a rational as well as humane option in Bowen; however, it is doubtful that compromise would have inspired, either among local or international readers, the migration, labour and investment that would ensure the progress of the colony. From his comfortable position in Brisbane, Gregory had the leisure to assume the 'imperially correct' outcome for the settlement of North Queensland—that is, that it would grow and prosper. His second edition of Morrill's story, like Kennedy's book, functioned as a weapon in this war, attracting more investors, and more fortune seekers, as it helped them to imagine this new and wild land under their possession.[46]

---

43  Evans, *A History of Queensland*, 83–90.
44  Along with unsuitable land laws and unsuitable men, part of the problem was depredations on stock by Aboriginal groups. He goes on to call on men of 'moderate capital and moderate tastes' to try their hand at agriculture in this land of promise. Kennedy, *Four Years in Queensland*, 1–2, 6, 70–71 (original emphasis).
45  Ibid., 67, 82–87.
46  Richard Phillips characterised the writing activities of Ernest Favenc as bound up in the colonising process. Phillips, *Mapping Men and Empire*, 68.

As the nineteenth century wore on, the age of steam reduced the travel time between London and Brisbane to 45 days, and took explorers to what was widely perceived as the last frontier, Antarctica. People started to wonder whether the age of adventure had passed; maps of the world's continents had been filled up with names, and Australia, like Africa and Canada, had 'ceased to be a blank space of delightful mystery'.[47] Was there anywhere in the world where one could still be truly lost? While Jules Verne turned to the fantastic in search of new *terra incognita*, the demand for true stories of adventure boiled over. In 1888, Ernest Favenc wrote a history of exploration in which the Australian interior was a known, mapped space; less than a decade later, he penned a boys' adventure story in which the same space was shrouded in mystery.[48] Impostor Louis de Rougemont appeared in London in 1898, claiming to have lived as a savage chief for over 30 years in the north-western corner of Queensland. He found a British public so insatiable for his story that he stole the limelight from *bona fide* explorers who wished to jump on the same bandwagon, a popular tour combining geographical, ethnographic and zoological revelation with sensationalism.[49] Sir George Bowen wrote to *The Chronicle* in support of the plausibility of de Rougemont's claims on the grounds that he had met James Morrill, who had lived with Aboriginal people for 17 years in his very own colony of Queensland.[50] Sir John Henniker Heaton, who was to set de Rougemont on the path to fame, had included Morrill's story in his *Australian Dictionary of Dates and Men of the Time*, published in 1879, and Marcus Clark had included it back to back with William Buckley's in *Old Tales of a Young Country* (1871).[51] Although, in life, Morrill had barely entered this imperial circus ring as a 'wild white man', later in the century his story joined the ranks of adventurers, castaways and the strange and remarkable.

---

47  Phillips, *Mapping Men and Empire*, 3–7, citing Conrad, *Heart of Darkness*.
48  Phillips, *Mapping Men and Empire*, 6–7, 71, 77–79.
49  The dizzying career of de Rougemont and its propulsion by popular print media and scientific and entertainment tours is brought to life by Rod Howard in *The Fabulist*. According to Robert Dixon, Hurley and his multimedia travel circus entered (in the 1920s) a well-established arena of educational entertainment, in which maximum exposure via print media was combined with 'self-promotion and opportunistic contrivance'. Dixon, 'What Was Travel Writing?', 60.
50  Howard, *The Fabulist*, 95.
51  Heaton, *Australian Dictionary of Dates*, 7; Clarke, *Old Tales of a Young Country*, 185–95. Ironically, as Iain McCalman showed, it was access to these true stories that allowed de Rougemont to create a sensation at a scale unimaginable for either Morrill or Narcisse Pelletier. McCalman, *The Reef*.

Gregory, now 64 years of age and overseer of the Government Printing Office at Brisbane, offered a third edition of Morrill's story to the public in 1896. He reminded readers that he had been involved in Morrill's 'return to civilisation' in no small way; he had raised a 'considerable sum' through the sale of the first edition of Morrill's narrative and had assisted Morrill in finding employment by drawing attention to his plight.[52] The new title bristled with peril and adventure—*Narrative of James Murrell's ('Jemmy Morrill') Seventeen Years' Exile among the Wild Blacks of North Queensland, and His Life and Shipwreck and Terrible Adventures Among Savage Tribes; their Manners, Customs, Languages, and Superstitions; Also Murrells' Rescue and Return to Civilisation, by Edmund Gregory*. It had all the appearance of a shameless marketing strategy (though Gregory demurred that the new pamphlet was intended for 'private circulation').[53] Most significantly, it suggested that Morrill had been captured by the 'Wild Blacks' and then rescued from them.

Europeans had been writing and reading captivity narratives for centuries. Linda Colley estimated that thousands of men and women from Great Britain and Ireland alone had been captured on the shores of North Africa, on the Canadian frontier by the French or their American Indian auxiliaries, or in 'Black Holes' in Bengal, Mysore and elsewhere in India from the late seventeenth century. Those who returned, some after willingly converting to the captors' religion and marrying-in, produced an unknown number of narratives; captivity had become a convention.[54] Even as Morrill made his first appearances among the colonial public, the language of captivity readily mingled with acknowledgements of the kindness of his 'captors'.[55] It was almost as if the state of savagery itself had taken him captive—cruelty was not a precondition. The notion of captivity was convenient

---

52   Gibbney and Smith, *A Biographical Register*, 283–84; Gregory, *Narrative of James Murrell's*, iii. He was perhaps also prompted by the reflections of *The Brisbane Courier*, with which he continued to have an intimate connection, on historical matters in its jubilee year. *The Brisbane Courier*, 20 June 1896, 7–8.
53   Phillips, *Mapping Men and Empire*, 3–10; *The Brisbane Courier*, 18 September 1896, 5. He had sent copies to George Bowen, former governor, among others. *The Brisbane Courier*, 8 December 1896, 4. Public circulation was certainly achieved through the printing of the new edition in serial form in the 'Queenslander' columns of *The Brisbane Courier* between October and December 1896. *The Brisbane Courier*, 16 October 1896, 4.
54   Colley, 'Going Native, Telling Tales', 71–74.
55   See, for example, *Queensland Guardian*, 17 March 1863; *The Courier*, 29 April 1863, 3; *The Sydney Morning Herald*, 21 March 1863, 6. Similarly, Oswald Brierly and his companions, though they knew Barbara Thompson had been rescued by the Kaurareg and had seen first-hand how she had been adopted as part of the community, had difficulty avoiding the vocabulary of savage capture and civilised rescue when writing about her experiences. Darian-Smith, '"Rescuing" Barbara Thompson', 102–05.

in a number of ways. On the one hand, it absolved the captive, who could not be blamed for collaborating with the enemy or assimilating willingly into their society. At the same time, it projected violence and barbarism onto the native captors, helping to justify their extirpation.[56] Gregory addressed a 'new generation … born and grown to manhood and womanhood' since Queensland was first 'excited' by this story.[57] This reading public was no longer the insecure settler population that Morrill's story had first appealed to, grappling daily with the realities of their war on the Aboriginal peoples of the region. However, as Henry Reynolds has observed, for continued colonial success there was an ongoing need to 'keep down' Aboriginal people, even as their labour and knowledge of the country became essential to many pastoral operations, and as they worked side by side with settlers and Pacific Islanders ('kanakas'), fishing, hunting, herding and farming in North Queensland.[58]

Gregory thanked Archibald Meston for his assistance in preparing the new edition, observing that 'any work on the aborigines of this Colony would … be wanting' without his stamp of approval. Meston was in Gregory's office at the time because his *Report on the Aboriginals of Queensland* was in print there. The report, based on four months travel, mostly in far North Queensland, provided a patchy account of the state of Aboriginal contact with white settlers, the native police, and the largely Indonesian operators of the bêche de mer and pearl shell industries.[59] His recommendations fed directly into the *Aboriginals Protection and Restriction of the Sale of Opium Act 1897*. This Act established a protectorate over the Aboriginal population of Queensland, and endowed the government with extraordinary power over

---

56  Schaffer, *In the Wake of First Contact*, 78–80. Eliza Fraser's story had quickly become a 'captivity narrative in which she was subjected to torture and bondage at the hands of savage barbarians', a familiar story with widespread appeal across 'the high-minded Tory press and the sensational stories of the chap-books, ballads and fly-sheets'. Schaffer, *In the Wake of First Contact*, 22; Hoorn, 'Julie Dowling's Melbin', 201–12.
57  Gregory, *Narrative of James Murrell's*, iii.
58  Reynolds, *Frontier*, 63–71. Carl Lumholtz, a Norwegian zoologist touring Queensland in 1880, became interested in Aboriginal people partly through a visit to the farm of a Mr Gardiner on the Herbert River. He understood Gardiner to be one of the 'protectors of the blacks' in a context of continued bad relations in the 'uncivilised districts', and a benefactor in the exchange of Aboriginal labour for foodstuffs, utensils and the like. He depicted Gardiner as generally permissive, allowing Aboriginal people into the kitchen and allowing them to leave and enter his land at will, but also as maintaining a necessary level of control, drawing the line at them entering the living room, shooting over their heads to 'maintain discipline' at times, and instructing them in the rights and wrongs of civilised life. Lumholtz, *Among Cannibals*, 76–78.
59  Gregory, *Narrative of James Murrell's*, iii; Meston, *Report on the Aboriginals of Queensland*. Gregory had also printed Meston's *Geographic History of Queensland*, and *Queensland Aboriginals: Proposed System for their Improvement and Preservation* the previous year.

Aboriginal lives—only gradually lifted from the 1960s. Gregory's preface to *James Murrells' Seventeen Years' Exile* represented the Aboriginal peoples of coastal Queensland as at once extinct and dangerous. He observed of Morrill's rescue and adoption by Birri-gubba people:

> There is now no possibility of such an experience being repeated. The Burdekin blacks have been civilised out of existence, and on no other part of the Queensland coast could a wrecked person remain among any native tribe without being killed, or speedily restored to his own people.[60]

Indeed, under the terms of the 1897 Act, close relationships and cultural exchange would have been impossible. White–Aboriginal relationships were to be closely supervised by a new bureaucracy. The legitimate relation was to be one of employer with indentured labourer, with the state as the controlling third party. Aboriginal people who were not compliant, able-bodied workers would be relocated to a reserve. No unauthorised person classified as non-Aboriginal under the Act was permitted to enter those reserves.[61] Although Meston emphasised the protection of Aboriginal people from exploitation and abuse (both by whites and unscrupulous men of the various 'coloured' races), and the Act itself exempted Aboriginal women lawfully married to non-Aboriginal men from its provisions, the Act was administered in the spirit of keeping the races 'clean' by keeping Aboriginal people away from whites and preventing miscegenation. Gregory, in his return to North Queensland's moment of 'first contact' as the 1897 Act was drafted, provided a fascinating true story of entanglement and disentanglement, as the Act itself attempted to separate the lives of Indigenous and white Queenslanders.[62] Of course, the aspirations of the Act were never fully achieved. Near the Burdekin River's mouth, Aboriginal people lived around Airdale and Clare, supplementing traditional foods with payments for seasonal agricultural and domestic work and collecting blankets at the annual distributions at Ayr and Cape Bowling Green through the 1880s and 1890s. Though there was change around the turn of the century, partly because of the Act, many of these

---

60   Gregory, *Narrative of James Murrell's*, iii.
61   *Aboriginals Protection and Restriction of the Sale of Opium Act 1897*, s11, 13–16, accessed 14 June 2018, aiatsis.gov.au/sites/default/files/catalogue_resources/54692.pdf; Evans, '"Steal Away": The Fundamentals', 83–95; Blake, 'Deported ... at the Sweet Will', 52–53.
62   *Aboriginals Protection and Restriction of the Sale of Opium Act 1897*, s10; Blake, 'Deported ... at the Sweet Will', 53. I borrow the terms 'entanglement' and 'disentanglement' from Byrne, 'The Ethos of Return', 82–83.

people continued to live on the flats by Plantation Creek and at the local rifle range for decades to come, often together with members of the Melanesian community.[63]

Meston documented the sad state of Aboriginal workers being paid in opium for their efforts, who were rendered 'a mere semblance of humanity' by the drug. Yet, he felt that contact with civilisation itself was no less deleterious to the Aboriginal constitution. He admired the strength and purity of Aboriginal men who had 'held no intercourse whatever with white men' and recommended they be left alone (pending the discovery of mineral resources on their land). However, those in the 'settled districts' seemed to have lost both integrity and resolve; in Meston's view, they seemed to be collectively wasting away and so needed to be 'collected' onto reserves and treated 'kindly'.[64] The Act was driven by the same strongly paternalist, and fundamentally racist, humanism that gave nineteenth-century middle-class readers an appetite for captivity stories.[65] *James Murrell's Seventeen Years' Exile* is tinted by a new admixture of racism and regret. Gregory grafted an expression of triumphant regret onto the first edition's account of the *Spitfire* incident, in which two Aboriginal men were shot while apparently trying to tell the surveying party about Morrill:

> Alas how much mischief may have been occasioned by similar attempts of our dusky friends trying to make themselves understood for the good of those to whom they wished to communicate![66]

Gregory would have had to turn Morrill's story inside out to create a scenario of captivity; therefore, he did not attempt this. Contradicting the new title, in the body of the third edition, the narrator continued to express his gratitude to Aboriginal people for rescuing him and his fellow castaways from exposure and starvation, as he had in 1863.[67] Observant readers refused to accept captivity as a framework for the story. Matthew Fox, in his 1921 history of Queensland, protested that the relationship 'between [Morrill] and his sable hosts was not that of captor and captive but was friendly to affection'.[68] It was this very friendliness that compelled Fox, Meston and others to continue to grapple with the question of

---

63   Kerr, *Black Snow*, 185–87.
64   Meston, *Report on the Aboriginals of Queensland*, 2, 5.
65   *A Mother's Offering to Her Children* (1841), quoted in Schaffer, *In the Wake of First Contact*, 23–24.
66   Gregory, *Narrative of James Murrell's*, 24.
67   Ibid., v.
68   Fox, *The History of Queensland*, 70.

Morrill's integrity as a white man. Was it possible for him to make a full return to civilisation after such a long association with a savage people and landscape?

According to Martin Green, Robinson Crusoe is put to a test with which his readers identify: 'Can he survive without the protections of his homeland culture … And how can he imagine living with [savages], doing both them and himself good?'[69] Washed up on a deserted island, Crusoe furnished and fortified a cave. He kept a journal, domesticated wild goats and, when he finally encountered a savage, rescued him and taught him English and Christian virtues.[70] Morrill did not have a chance to become a 'castaway colonist' as so many fictional castaways did in Crusoe's wake, for he was washed up on a populous continent. Before he could take possession of the land, he was already being assimilated himself.[71] After his near-death experience, Crusoe, the restless adventurer, was reborn in the mould of a responsible, sedentary, small-scale agriculturalist with a formidable petit bourgeois work ethic.[72] Morrill was reborn a Birri-gubba man. That he failed to civilise or 'elevate' his adoptive people was noted during his lifetime. Murray-Prior wrote disapprovingly that 'many a white man in his position would have gained more influence over the savage, he would at least have manufactured the Bow and arrow'.[73] Nevertheless, Morrill's obituary referred to its subject as 'the pioneer white man in the North', and Carrington described him as the 'first resident in the district'. The adjectives 'white' and 'civilised' are clearly implied by Carrington; he had encountered many Aboriginal people who had lived in the area long before Morrill, but they did not qualify as 'residents' to his way of thinking. As Lorenzo Veracini demonstrated, settler historiography begins when industrious explorers, pastoralists and capitalists arrive and begin to possess the land through struggle. If the settler departs, or 'goes

---

69  Green, *The Robinson Crusoe Story*, 22.
70  De Foe, *The Life and Adventures of Robinson Crusoe*, 47–48, 56–62, 119–22, 167–81. Despite the endless variations in versions of the Crusoe story, Richard Phillips found Christian self-discipline and exertion in rational labour constant elements in the story. Phillips, *Mapping Men and Empire*, 31–33.
71  Weaver-Hightower, *Empire Islands*, xviii–xxi.
72  Phillips, *Mapping Men and Empire*, 31–33.
73  Murray-Prior, Private Letter Book, 19–20. James Bonwick judged William Buckley harshly on these grounds. Searching for Buckley's 'elevating influence' on the Wathaurong in the form of permanent housing, clothing and the like that he believed could have been fashioned from local resources, he exclaimed: 'alas! we see nothing of the kind … the bricklayer sunk rapidly into the savage'. Bonwick, *The Wild White Man*, 3.

native', history ceases and the land plunges back into the 'Stone Age'.[74] The ongoing paradox of Morrill's 'residency' was that he lived as an adopted Aboriginal man for the greater part of his life in the region.

Some of the colonists who met Morrill thought they could detect a 'very faint taint which hangs about him, after so long a solitary association with savages'. Expecting signs, they scrutinised his appearance. A Rockhampton journalist gained a mixed impression of this 'black-white man': 'The man's face is not blacker than those of many men whose lives are spent in the bush under ordinary circumstances; but his body is very dark and much disfigured'.[75] In his second edition, Gregory provided a post-mortem description of Morrill: 'exposure to a tropical sun and climate had made his skin dark', and 'his eyes were sunken and he had a very wide mouth'. This description echoes the same account's physical characterisation of the Aboriginal people of Mount Elliott. Via verbal craniology, Gregory invited the reader to examine Morrill's head as a gauge of his assimilation to Birri-gubba society, and of his ability to recover from it.[76] In his third edition, 30 years later, Gregory added a scattering of interjections pointing out Morrill's loss of 'likeness to a civilised being' as he survived to live as an adopted Aboriginal man.[77] A late nineteenth-century theory about Australia's Aboriginal peoples posited that they themselves were castaways who, in finding little in the way of arable lands and useful tools where they washed up, had *become* hunters and nomads, or, finding nothing on this primeval continent that would encourage their advance out of this state, had simply remained that way while other races progressed to agriculture and industry.[78] How could their company do a lone white man any good?

This question remained pressing in the new century. Writing for an international audience in 1923, and informed by the frightening prospect of racial 'degeneration' (as well as the very incomplete results of his Aboriginals Protection Act after 25 years), Meston felt Morrill's story

---

74  Carrington, *Colonial Adventures*, 165; Veracini, 'Historylessness', 173–75.
75  *The Argus*, 18 May 1863, 6; *The Courier*, 11 March 1863, 3.
76  Gregory, *Sketch of the Residence of James Morrill*, 17. For the 'sunken eyes' and 'broad mouths' of the Mount Elliott people, see p. 18. It is as if Morrill had been subject to a process of regression and evolution within his own lifetime. Griffiths, *Hunters and Collectors*, 39–45.
77  Gregory, *Narrative of James Murrell's*, 1, 27.
78  A columnist for *The Courier* suggested that *Sketch of a Residence*, in providing details of the local language and customs, might support the belief that 'their forefathers had attained to a high state of civilisation and enlightenment when our own were steeped in ignorance and barbarism'. *The Courier*, 21 April 1863, 2. Edward Palmer, one of North Queensland's honoured pioneers, canvassed this possibility as he deliberated the question of the origins of the Aboriginal peoples in the 1890s. Palmer, *Early Days in North Queensland*, 215–16.

provided 'sure proof that the primeval savage wild man in all of us is terribly near the surface'. Combining Social Darwinism with snobbery, Meston declared William Buckley and four escaped convicts who had lived with Aboriginal people in southern Queensland to have been of the 'lowest type'—their failure was to avoid being *improved* by their association with Aboriginal society. By contrast, Morrill, an 'honest English yeoman', was made of the sort of dependable stuff that might be hoped to endure immutably; yet, it had not. The rather muted good news was that, along with these lesser men, Morrill appeared able to 'resume' the 'veneer of civilization' once re-adopted.[79] If civilisation depended on whiteness, then its veneer remained thin in North Queensland through the 1920s and 1930s, maintained via strenuous lobbying of the labour movement for an end to Aboriginal work on sheep and cattle stations, and unremitting legal discrimination against Aboriginal and Melanesian populations. Ray Evans found that, by the 1930s, as much as a third of the state's Aboriginal population was confined on reserves and missions in a kind of 'eugenic quarantine'. Many Birri-gubba families were moved away from Bowen and Ayr at this time, including people who may have been Morrill's descendants.[80]

It is difficult to judge how firmly Marcus Clark's tongue was planted in his cheek when he titled his rather humorous account of Morrill's story 'The First Queensland Explorer', for its protagonist had not set out to know a territory or route, and had not mapped, measured or claimed any new lands for the Crown.[81] Morrill's status as 'first resident' was, perhaps, tinged with irony, suspicion or even contempt in the eyes of his contemporaries and later biographers as they put his story to the test. Yet, this repeated interlocution also offered him an opportunity to become an explorer-in-retrospect. He had, after all, returned to civilisation and reported on his discoveries, as the purposeful explorer Leichhardt failed to do, having disappeared, never to complete his second mission beyond the Darling Downs.[82] Regardless of whether Morrill's civilised attributes

---

79  Meston, 'Wild White Men: Australian Instances', *World's News*, 27 October 1923. Stern traces the development of these notions into the inter-war years. Stern, *Eugenic Nation*, 14.
80  The recruitment of Melanesian labour for the sugar industry had ceased in 1904 and many Melanesians had been deported. Evans, *A History of Queensland*, 145, 170–71. Eddie Smallwood, in conversation with the author, 1 December 2010.
81  Clarke, *Old Tales of a Young Country*, 185–95; Phillips, *Mapping Men and Empire*, 74–75.
82  Erdos, 'Leichhardt, Friedrich Wilhelm Ludwig (1813–1848)'. Morrill's survival raised hopes that Leichhardt or some of his party may have also survived among Aboriginal people. Morrill himself promoted this view, and offered to accompany a search party. *Port Denison Times*, 10 June 1865, 2; Gregory, *Sketch of the Residence of James Morrill*, 17.

had been dormant or dulled during his 17 years with the Birri-gubba, he was the 'first white resident' because he could 'see' the country in a way that the Birri-gubba could not. Even if he did not satisfy the expectations of those who interviewed him at Rockhampton and elsewhere, Morrill could, to some extent (under cross-examination), translate the country and its people into the language of science, thereby bringing it into the realm of progress and the legal language of possession.[83]

In the local landscape today, Morrill stands alongside the official explorers and discoverers of the region. Sinclair Place and Dalrymple Plaza occupy the central part of the foreshore at Bowen, commemorating the 'discovery' of Port Denison by the former, and the official founding of the town by the latter. At the north-eastern end of this landscaped foreshore sits Morrill Plaza, a small open space alongside the skateboard park. At the Flagstaff Hill interpretive centre, Morrill appears as a seafarer alongside captains Cook and Sinclair, and as one of the 'early European observers' of the Birri-gubba people.[84]

In the light of truly essentialist ideas about racial difference, Morrill was not required to perform any pioneering act other than to *be* where he was. The *Townsville Daily Bulletin*, marking the death of Morrill and Eliza Jane Ross's son in 1907, observed that the wreck of the *Peruvian* had brought white eyes to this coastline for the first time since Cook had named Cape Upstart from the deck of the passing *Endeavour*—that is, after an interval of precisely 76 years. Morrill had only to look on the country and it was claimed for his race.[85] Morrill held a pivotal place in Matthew Fox's 1921 *History of Queensland* and his vision of North Queensland as a modern agricultural and industrial landscape. Fox imagined that, 'hopeless of regaining civilization', Morrill had given himself over to the rhythms of Aboriginal life, little knowing that progress was 'bringing the advancing tide of pastoral settlement' and the 'reign of a superior race' nearer. News of stray cattle and men on horses raised 'the white man in Murrells [Morrill], and caused him to take command of the primeval

---

83 Weaver-Hightower, *Empire Islands*, 2–3. For an in-depth analysis of this aspect of Morrill's story, see Dortins, 'James Morrill: Shipwreck Survivor', 67–88.
84 The Flagstaff Hill Interpretation Centre was built in about 2008, and the foreshore landscaping dates to 2009 or 2010. Volunteers at the Bowen Museum, in conversation with the author, 1 March 2012. The story is certainly seen as a defining story for the town. When part of Baz Luhrman's *Australia* was being filmed nearby, the idea that a film might soon be made about James Morrill began to circulate. Henry Young, in conversation with the author, 23 November 2010; Robert Paul, in conversation with the author, 19 November 2010.
85 *Townsville Daily Bulletin*, 28 November 1907, 2.

being he had been for so long'. According to this account, Morrill's whiteness may have slumbered during his life with the Birri-gubba, but it slumbered like a seed ready to blossom with the arrival of the colonists; his cultural outlook may have changed in Birri-gubba company, but his biology continued to assert itself. An important part of Fox's story is that Morrill arrived at Bowen in 1863 to find a town on the spot where he had once built a gunyah.[86] The significance of this is not entirely clear. Fox may have meant that Morrill's gunyah-building was like the laying of a foundation stone or the raising of a flag; alternatively, it may simply have provided a satisfying end to Morrill's story, illustrating how far progress had taken the region. In any case, Morrill's presence in Fox's story lent a naturalness and inevitability to the advance of the pastoralists; in return, Morrill was able to bask in the retrospective glory of progress.[87]

In an address to the Royal Historical Society of Queensland to mark Queensland's centenary in 1959, Sir Raphael Cilento and Clem Lack again conferred on Morrill the title of 'first white resident'. They also acknowledged '"Boraltchou" Baker … the first white man to see the Darling Downs; "Moilow" Graham the first white man to live in the Tewantin area', and so on. Against the lingering doubt that Europeans could remain physically, mentally and morally vigorous in latitudes nearing the equator, one of Cilento's lifelong projects as a doctor was to establish the supremacy of white men in the tropics. In his mind, each of these pioneers-in-retrospect, regardless of whether they were castaways or escapees, had marked out new territory for their race. Morrill's one-man 'triumph in the tropics' was that he had not only endured full initiation, but also, Cilento and Lack fantasised further, exerted supremacy over his companions, 'having the virtual authority … of a chief'.[88]

To borrow a concept from Attwood and Doyle's analysis of stories about Batman's treaty with the Kulin peoples of Victoria, these supremacist histories can be understood as 'fictive' in two ways. First, the details

---

86  Fox, *The History of Queensland*, 69–70.
87  Weaver-Hightower found that castaway stories assist 'imperial expansion and control' by making it 'seem unproblematic and natural, like the innate processes of the human body'. Weaver-Hightower, *Empire Islands*, ix–xi. See also Doherty, *The Townsville Book*; Doherty, *The Bowen Book*.
88  Cilento and Lack, *Wild White Men of Queensland*, 25; Cilento and Lack, *Triumph in the Tropics*, xiii. Frank Reid, writing a highly sensationalised account of North Queensland a few years earlier, found Morrill a fully integrated part of the 'tribe', but did not suggest any form of 'chiefdom'. However, writing about Wini of Badu (a 'wild white man' of the Torres Strait who Barbara Thompson came in contact with), he developed a full-blown fantasy of malevolent overlordship, with Wini dominating the politics of the region until slain by the (in this account) heroic Frank Jardine. Reid, *The Romance of the Great Barrier Reef*, 54–59, 63–66.

they embroidered onto Morrill's story appear to have no basis in historical sources. Second, they created a myth that sought to reconcile a central contradiction within settler history in North Queensland—namely, that European settlers were the rightful possessors of land that very clearly belonged to the Indigenous inhabitants.[89] However, these histories were not only myth-making or legend-making, they were also bringing an immensely powerful (if not total) reality into being through Morrill's story.

Cilento's project was deadly serious; the integrity of the White Australia Policy depended on it. His work perpetuated a view of Aboriginal people as barely human.[90] Probably because he and Lack held the view that Morrill's very biology was different—superior—to that of the Birri-gubba people who adopted him, they did not have to worry about whether he had *become* savage via cultural assimilation, or stayed that way. This had deeply concerned Murray-Prior who feared that, despite consistent denial, Morrill had, in fact, tasted true barbarity during his time with the 'natives'; he suspected that Morrill had not only participated in the ritual cannibalism he described so vividly, but also that he had been irretrievably altered by it.[91] Unperturbed by such fears, Cilento and Lack were free to indulge a rather steamy fascination with the ins and outs of 'going native'. They pictured Morrill's 'brawny torso burnt black by … the hot northern sun', and imagined that he continued to participate in corroborees on the outskirts of town and that he died 'amid the grief-stricken wailing of a mob of blacks'. (Both would have been impossible given the campaign to keep Aboriginal people out of settled districts that continued for some years after Morrill's death; indeed, his obituary had speculated that 'could the Mount Elliot blacks learn that their pale-faced brother was dead, what howling and woe there would be'.)[92]

Somewhat contradictorily, Cilento and Lack imagined that Morrill never relaxed his will to return to civilisation. In an act of mastery over the landscape that forms a typical feature of castaway stories, in their narrative,

---

89  Attwood with Doyle, *Possession*, 5–6.
90  Understanding Aboriginal people to have more in common with the 'local animals' than with other human beings, they argued that a comparison between Aboriginal society and culture and 'primitive civilisation' would be completely erroneous. Cilento and Lack, *Triumph in the Tropics*, 178–79.
91  Murray-Prior, Private Letter Book, 19–20.
92  Cilento and Lack, *Wild White Men of Queensland*, 25. Geoffrey Bolton also imagined that 'Aboriginals for many miles around came into town for a memorable mourning ceremony'. Bolton, 'Morrill, James (1824–1865)'. *Port Denison Times*, 1 November 1865, 2.

Morrill repeatedly climbed a mountain near Townsville in the hope of signalling a passing ship. Likewise, in a popular history of Townsville, published in 1952, Morrill also maintained a mountain-top 'vigil' on Townsville's bluff, Castle Hill.[93] Morrill did not claim to have done so in *Sketch of a Residence*, nor do reports of his other interviews suggest that he frequently climbed a mountain to look out for ships. In fact, he suggested in his Rockhampton interview that his adoptive people often kept a close watch over him, preventing such individual investigative travel.[94] As locals point out today, Castle Hill would be an awkward place from which to spot a ship, unless it was to sail on the landward side of Magnetic Island. Instead (or nevertheless), a local yarn connects a nearby feature known as Jimmy's Lookout to Morrill for the same purpose.[95]

Locally, the bare essentials of the story seem to have circulated through the middle decades of last century. Loftus Dun, who grew up in Ayr, recalled hearing the story for the first time in about 1936, when he was in his teens working at the Kalamia sugar mill:

> All I knew about it was there was a man who had lived with the Aboriginals for some time, and got back with the white people, and that he had some connection with Ayr.[96]

In 1937, the *Bowen Independent*'s 'Early Bowen Memories' column featured a story by Alex Miller who recalled being shown a 'historical relic' by a local pioneer in the early 1880s—the corner post of the outstation stockyard where Morrill had 'made himself known as a white man'.[97] The burial place of Captain and Mrs Pitkethly had also begun to command some interest in connection with a number of possible graves about which locals were curious.[98] A story circulated too around a block of land that Morrill had purchased in Bowen. Apparently, when he went to bid on this lot, the other bidders stepped back, and they and the auctioneer allowed him to take it for the minimum price. Like Fox's story about Morrill's return to find a town where he once shared

---

93   Weaver-Hightower, *Empire Islands*, xviii–xix; Cilento and Lack, *Wild White Men of Queensland*, 25; Rapier and Watson, *The Townsville Story*, 6.
94   *Queensland Guardian*, 17 March 1863; *The Courier*, 11 March 1863, 2.
95   Russell McGregor, in conversation with the author, 29 November 2010; Phillip Murray, in conversation with the author, 3 December 2010.
96   Loftus Dun, in conversation with the author, 16 February 2011.
97   *Bowen Independent*, 11 August 1937.
98   George Turner, 'Is it the Grave of Captain Pitkethly and Mrs Pitkethly of the Barque "Peruvian"?', *Cummings and Campbell's Monthly Magazine*, March 1931, 53.

a gunyah, the purchase converted this place of loss into a landmark of Morrill's resocialisation with his own kind, and saw Morrill's landscape of exile from civilisation transformed into a place that he and his white descendants would experience as a land of security and plenty.[99] A sense of satisfaction or justice is still palpable when this story is told today; not only was it a block of land in his 'own country', now owned as private property, but it is said to be where Morrill was (chopping a possum out of a tree) when he heard that Captain and Mrs Pitkethly had died.[100] More than 150 years later, local history-makers are still bringing Morrill home.

---

99  J. E. Lott, 'Recollections', *Bowen Independent*, 10 September 1937. In July 1863, Morrill purchased a Bowen town lot for just over ten pounds. *The Courier*, 24 July 1863, 2. In the final chapter of *The Townsville Story*, Morrill returns triumphantly to buy a quarter-acre lot in the new settlement, huddled under the bulk of Castle Hill where he had kept his lookout. Rapier and Watson, *The Townsville Story*. As Ann Curthoys observed, in the Australian context, narratives based in the biblical tropes of Exile, Exodus and the Promised Land can be strangely entangled. Curthoys, 'Expulsion, Exodus and Exile', 5.
100  Dilys Maltby, in conversation with the author, 2 December 2010; Phillip Murray, in conversation with the author, 3 December 2010.

# 3

# Ways of Knowing the Burdekin

When the Bowen Historical Society convened for its first meeting in August 1963, members faced the problem of where to begin; civic pride inspired its formation rather than an immersion in history.[1] During deliberations about a suitable first project:

> Someone mentioned 'James Morrill', a very happy suggestion. No one knew very much more than that he had lived for 17 years with the blacks and said on presenting himself to some white stockmen 'Don't shoot—I'm a British object'. What could be more appropriate than to begin with Queensland's first known white resident?[2]

On 26 January 1964, as part of its Australia Day celebration, the society unveiled an obelisk atop Morrill's grave in the Bowen Cemetery.[3] The brass plaque commemorated Morrill as: 'Shipwrecked mariner, who lived 17 years with the aborigines and thus is the first known white resident of North Queensland'. As local dignitaries lined up to speak, and the municipal band played 'Advance Australia Fair', the history of the Bowen Historical Society became part of Morrill's story, and vice versa. The society adopted Morrill; it represented itself as having rescued his story from the wilds of 'obscurity' and honoured him for the first time.[4]

---

1   The society's first meeting had been called by Victor Jones, long-time chairman of the Bowen Regional Research and Promotion Bureau. *Bowen Historical Society Bulletin* 21 (August 1979): 14–15.
2   *Bowen Historical Society Bulletin* 1 (August 1964): 2.
3   The grave was unmarked, but Frederick Raynor, founder of the *Port Denison Times*, had left a record of its location in the cemetery in his papers. *Townsville Daily Bulletin*, 2 October 1929, 9.
4   Bowen Historical Society, *The Story of James Morrill*, n.p.; *Bowen Independent*, 31 January 1964; Jones, 'The Saga of James Morrill'.

The society's first publication, *The Story of James Morrill*, reproduced *Sketch of a Residence* with supplementary material. Even as the society has continued to document many other aspects of local history, Morrill's story has remained important.

Figure 1: Morrill's grave in the Bowen Cemetery, marked by the obelisk erected by the Bowen Historical Society in 1963.
Source: Photograph taken by author.

In the beginning, the only account of Morrill's story that society members possessed was Cilento and Lack's rather lively version. In brass, they re-inscribed the epithet that Cilento and Lack had bestowed on Morrill, and that resonated with the narrative of white possession that had made the story so salient for previous generations, labelling Morrill the 'first white resident'. However, in other respects, the society departed from Cilento and Lack's characterisation of Morrill. At the Australia Day ceremony, he was not remembered as 'wild, unkempt' and indistinguishable from 'a ferocious aboriginal warrior', but as a man of 'courage and character'.[5] Although the society had an eye to the value of the region's history for tourism, it placed the emphasis squarely on Morrill's worthiness; speakers at the memorial's dedication marked his courageousness and 'patience in adversity', and his integrity and 'desire to serve' as virtuous examples to their listeners.[6]

Morrill's life as a colonist after 1863 was of acute importance. As founding member of the Bowen Historical Society Dr Peter Delamothe put it, Morrill strove 'for the advancement of his new country once restored to civilisation'. He assisted in the founding of Cardwell, purchased an allotment at the first land sale at Townsville, and worked as a respected member of the Customs and pilot boat service. Another founding member of the society, Victor Jones, observed in 1979 that 'Morrill created history' by delivering the first bonded goods to Townsville.[7] He had also procreated; he and Eliza Jane Ross, housemaid of the police magistrate at Bowen, produced one son, born soon after Morrill's death. The society undertook genealogical research and gathered Morrill's granddaughters around the obelisk in 1964.[8] Thus, Morrill was remembered as a patriarch in the most intimate sense, as well as a pioneer.

At the same time, not even a dash of sensationalism was necessary to make Morrill's story 'stranger than fiction', as his obituary had observed.[9] As historian Geoffrey Bolton put it when he thanked the society for sending him a copy of *The Story of James Morrill*, it was a pleasure to read a 'true adventure story'.[10] The society, reflecting on its achievements from the vantage point of its second year, compared the quotient of romance

---

5   Delamothe soon 'unearthed' the 1863 testimony at the Queensland Parliamentary Library (see *Bowen Independent*, 31 January 1964) and other accounts began to flow in too, once the search was begun. Cilento was highly respected within the organisation—he was president of the Royal Historical Society of Queensland at the time. The Bowen Historical Society was delighted to receive Cilento as a visitor. See *Bowen Historical Society Bulletin* 1 (August 1964): 11. See also Cilento and Lack, *Wild White Men of Queensland*, 25; Bowen Historical Society, *The Story of James Morrill*, n.p.
6   *Bowen Independent*, 31 January 1964.
7   Delamothe, quoted in *Bowen Independent*, 31 January 1964; Jones, 'The Saga of James Morrill', 8.
8   *Bowen Independent*, 31 January 1964.
9   *Port Denison Times*, 1 November 1865, 2.
10  *Bowen Historical Society Bulletin* 2 (January 1965): 2. Bolton probably used it as the main source for his entry on Morrill in the 1967 edition of the *Australian Dictionary of Biography*. The story had also been passed on to Olaf Ruhen so that it could be included in his forthcoming book of adventure stories, *South Pacific Adventures*. See *Bowen Historical Society Bulletin* 4 (February 1966): 2.

and adventure in Morrill's story with that of their second subject, Bowen's founder, Captain Sinclair. It was judged that both surpassed the adventure stories of popular nineteenth-century British children's writers: 'Cooper, Henty or Ballantyne never wrote more exciting stories than these'.[11]

Adventure stories were less likely than they had once been to prompt serious reflection or self-examination. Even while Morrill was telling his own story, their readership was changing. From *Gulliver's Travels* to *Moby Dick,* castaway and captivity stories and travel fiction had formed challenging and invigorating reading for adults in the eighteenth and early nineteenth centuries, but the genre was progressively handed over to children. For example, scholar Richard Phillips showed how Defoe's Robinson Crusoe began life as a controversial marriage of realism and fiction, and included a pointed political statement about the nature of American colonisation. In the nineteenth century, the story of Crusoe was naturalised (partly due to its own influence on literature) as a true story with normative power for boys in particular.[12] Victor Jones closed his Heatley Memorial Lecture of 1979, delivered to young listeners, with a marriage of Morrill's virtues with the writings of one of the British Empire's favourite children's authors, stating:

> May this narrative of the adventurous life of James Morrill, be an inspiration to each of you students here, to strive for excellence in all you do … then, to paraphrase Kipling's 'If', you will be a worthy citizen indeed.[13]

Had Morrill meant to return to civilisation and stay? Had his adoption by Birri-gubba people changed him irreversibly? Did he have relationships with Aboriginal people that continued to have a claim on his heart? By the time the Bowen Historical Society took up the story, these questions, which had been of pressing importance to Morrill's contemporaries, had lost their urgency. When the authors of *The Townsville Story* (1952) closed their rendition of Morrill's life with musings on 'whether his soul was claimed by the aborigines for their celestial happy hunting grounds, or whether he went to white man's heaven', the question was rhetorical. This was chiefly a story of the 'unusual'; indeed, it would be best if his ghostly companions were fellow adventurers. Cilento and Lack had closed their story with a similar sentimental flourish, claiming, 'pathetically enough,

---

11   *Bowen Historical Society Bulletin* 2 (January 1965): 7; Phillips, *Mapping Men and Empire*, 72–73.
12   Phillips, *Mapping Men and Empire*, 3–10, 25–26, 81–83.
13   Jones, 'The Saga of James Morrill', 9.

the last word he uttered was: "corroboree"'.[14] It had become possible to tell Morrill's story without the ambivalence with which his contemporaries had approached the tale, and to tell it without engaging in histories of local violence and responsibility. In 1964, as the Bowen Historical Society embarked on the work of collecting, preserving and disseminating local history and marking places of historical interest, Morrill's case seemed closed. Gathering together the available resources seemed to yield 'the full story'.[15]

However, there were other directions the society's history-making might have taken. Inaugural co–Vice President Dr John Lacon, recently arrived from England, questioned the place of Morrill's story as an 'ancient' point of origin. Fellow committee members Delamothe and Jones had compared Morrill's virtues to those of the ancient Greek heroes who had 'held the pass at Macedon'; in the memorial obelisk itself local granite pieces were disciplined into a classical form associated with the heritage of civilisation.[16] Lacon observed that 'although we do not consider the history of the James Morrill period as being modern, we are in one sense mistaken. Men were living in Australia a million years ago'.[17] He had possibly read (or read of) Manning Clark's acclaimed and controversial *History of Australia* (the first volume was released in 1962) that set an entirely new horizon for Australian history in taking in Aboriginal migrations, Asian interest in the southern continent and Dutch exploration of the seventeenth century. However, within the Bowen Historical Society, there seems to have been little further discussion of the ancient migrations from Asia that Lacon enthusiastically explained.[18] His transnational horizon and interest in the *longue durée* were not shared by other members. Instead, the society took a leading role in the maintenance of a local nationalism. It was at the fore of Australia Day activities each year and brought to Bowen an

---

14  Rapier and Watson, *The Townsville Story*, 6; Cilento and Lack, *Wild White Men of Queensland*, 27.
15  *Bowen Historical Society Bulletin* 1 (August 1964): 2; Bowen Historical Society, *The Story of James Morrill*, n.p.
16  *Bowen Independent*, 31 January 1964. See also Jones, 'The Saga of James Morrill', 1. Jones wished to 'help raise him to his proper niche in Australian History'. Besley, 'At the Intersection of History and Memory', 39; Griffiths, *Hunters and Collectors*, 156–57.
17  *Bowen Historical Society Bulletin* 1 (August 1964): 5–6.
18  Ibid., 6. McKenna, *An Eye for Eternity*, 441–42.

initiative of the Queensland Women's Historical Society: Pioneer Day.[19] The Bowen Historical Society's emphasis on Morrill as a white pioneer was not peculiar; rather, it signalled the contribution of the region to a national history that had increasingly come into focus across the first half of the twentieth century, in which Australia was worthy of historical attention as part of the 'world-wide community of the British race'.[20]

The *Bowen Independent* subtitled its coverage of the 1964 Australia Day ceremony 'Full Recognition After 101 Years' (its proprietor was a founding member of the Bowen Historical Society).[21] This slightly tardy centenary embodied a commemorative gymnastics. The time frame of 101 years was the interval since Morrill's 'return to civilisation'. If his time with the Birri-gubba was counted, he had arrived in North Queensland 118 years earlier. By 1863, of course, Captain Sinclair had discovered Port Denison, and Bowen was coming into its third year; white settlement in North Queensland had begun before Morrill's rebirth into civilisation. If we are to understand Morrill as the first white resident of North Queensland, his residency must predate white settlement, leapfrogging over Sinclair and the first colonists of Bowen. Yet, Sinclair's shoulders were indispensable; Morrill could only become 'first white resident' by virtue of subsequent settlement. Likewise, he was perhaps only a fitting first subject for the society on the proviso that it would go on to chart the region's 'graph of progress', as the Royal Australian Historical Society urged local historians to do. The society next moved on to a more usual beginning, namely, the 'discovery' of Port Denison by Captain Sinclair.[22]

The society recognised Morrill as a peacemaker, 'working unceasingly to bring about better relations between the settlers and the aboriginals', and expressed regret that Morrill's work as a diplomat had not been attended with great success. However, their history-making did not go any further into the conflict that had ensued.[23] As the belated centenary invoked by the *Bowen Independent* suggests, in one sense, Morrill's 'return to civilisation' was the point at which his 'residency' was understood by the society to

---

19   On the same page as Lacon, Vic Jones argued for the Bowen Historical Society's role in taking responsibility for all of Queensland north of Rockhampton, as Bowen had been the base for 'most of the early explorers and pioneers who did so much to discover and settle' the region. *Bowen Historical Society Bulletin* 1 (August 1964): 5. A perusal of the *Bowen Historical Society Bulletin* from this first issue into the 1990s shows these events at the fore of the organisation's yearly calendar.
20   Curthoys, 'Cultural History and the Nation', 24–25.
21   *Bowen Independent*, 31 January 1964; *Bowen Historical Society Bulletin* 1 (August 1964): 1, 11.
22   Geeves, *Local History in Australia*, 4, 14–17. *Bowen Historical Society Bulletin* 1 (August 1964): 2.
23   Bowen Historical Society, *The Story of James Morrill*, n.p.; *Bowen Independent*, 31 January 1964.

have begun. In this way, his years as an adopted Birri-gubba man were part of the *prehistory* of the region, and the society's own history-making (as well as their understanding of Morrill's story) simply did not go back that far.

Of course, there was no guarantee that readers of the society's *The Story of James Morrill* would understand the story as its authors intended. When Noel Loos wrote his masters qualifying thesis at James Cook University in nearby Townsville in 1970, Morrill's story, made available to him by the society's inaugural booklet, provided a valuable window into Birri-gubba life and frontier conflict in the region. His thesis was one of the first forays into a new history that revisited the primary sources to document the dispossession of Aboriginal people.[24] Teaching at the university in the following decades, Loos 'read Morrill's words to students many times … to describe the shattering impact of colonisation'.[25] Through his friendship with Eddie Koiki Mabo, their mutual interest in Indigenous education and teacher training, and joint leadership of the Townsville Treaty Committee, Loos developed a deep respect for Aboriginal and Torres Strait Islander knowledge, culture and history, as well as an appreciation of just how difficult it was to foster such respect in others.[26] In 2004, in an article printed in the *Townsville Bulletin,* Loos called attention to the 'treaty' that Birri-gubba people had sought to make through Morrill, acknowledging that the white presence would be ongoing and asking for 'the swamps along the coast north of the Burdekin, the rivers to fish in, and any other land whites did not want'. While the colonists were not prepared to consider this offer of coexistence at the time, in the twenty-first century, Loos hoped that it might be possible for Morrill's descendants via his marriage with Eliza Ross and his Aboriginal descendants to 'look back with pride at their ancestor who tried to intervene in this 19th century holocaust to prevent more bloodshed'.[27]

The Bowen Historical Society had already produced a new edition of Morrill's story for the twenty-first century. Published in 2002, *James Morrill: His Life and Adventures* began with an account of the events of the Australia Day celebration in 1964, complete with photographs

---

24  Loos, 'Frontier Conflict in the Bowen District'; Loos, 'The History of North Queensland in Black and White'.
25  Noel Loos, 'The Spirit of Renconciliation [sic]', *Townsville Bulletin*, 31 July 2004, 27.
26  Noel Loos, in conversation with the author, 2 December 2010; Loos, 'Koiki Mabo: Mastering Two Cultures', 1–20.
27  Loos, 'The Spirit of Renconciliation [sic]', *Townsville Bulletin*, 31 July 2004, 27.

of the monument and ceremony. Morrill was re-commemorated as the 'first white resident', and the story of his rescue from obscurity by the society's founding generation was retold, largely as it had been 40 years earlier. In one sense, the new edition was unremarkable; the society's previous edition had been printed four decades earlier, which meant that there were probably no copies left for distribution—this was simply a matter of putting the story back into circulation.[28] Yet, at the turn of the new century, the story appeared in a new light, among different historiographical possibilities.[29]

As a historian who began to study Australian history in the reconciliation era, I came to this booklet sharing Loos's aspirations for Morrill's story: that it might become a story through which the descendants of Aboriginal and settler North Queenslanders might explore their connections and look into the past, possibly standing side by side. As I collected retellings of Morrill's story, I found myself listening out for fresh new versions that directly confronted the conflicts in the region documented by Loos and other historians across the previous decades. I was also working in the shadow of the 'history wars', which had been in full swing when the Bowen Historical Society produced their new edition. As Anna Clark has shown, these debates created a polarising space for the discussion of Australian history, a space in which if you were not wearing a 'black armband' then you must be sporting a 'white blindfold' instead.[30]

An earlier episode in the life of Morrill's story shows how it could spark outrage in historians and others who wished to shape public opinion at a time when history-making was becoming more and more political. Morrill's plea to the two stockmen as he perched on the fence railing formed the 'seed' of David Malouf's 1993 novel *Remembering Babylon* (though he made the disclaimer that 'otherwise this novel has no origin in fact').[31] It was received with ambivalence. Discussion centred on the ethics of fiction and its power to occasion worthwhile self-examination. Malouf's story was childlike; when his scrawny and rather idiotic character Gemmy stammered 'don't shoot—I'm a B-b-british object' it was to a child toting

---

28   Bowen Historical Society, *James Morrill: His Life and Adventures*. The text of the original story follows Gregory's third edition of 1896. The society's newsletter simply thanked the two members who gave their time for the 'preparation of the booklet' and hoped that 'we will be able to reprint several other booklets now out of print'. See *Bowen Historical Society Bulletin* 44 (November 2002): 1, 2.
29   Bradford, '"A Timeless Now": Memory and Repetition', 190, 204–06.
30   Clark, 'The History Wars', 152, 157.
31   Malouf, *Remembering Babylon*, 202.

a stick, a make-believe rifle. Gemmy told his story with the assistance of the local minister in front of children at the local school.[32] The novel's focus is on the settlers who re-adopt Gemmy, and find him so disturbing because of his sullied whiteness and his relationship with the wild country in which they have taken up land. Malouf chose not to engage explicitly with the violence of the historical frontier or with Aboriginal people and their histories. Germaine Greer condemned the novel for its 'lack of commitment to historical truth' and 'monolithic insensitivity'. Yet, others found the novel a penetrating study of settler shame, fear and the unremitting need to demarcate a clear boundary between whiteness and the unknown. Even so, as Victoria Burrows asked, was Malouf's depoliticised, nostalgic *fiction* defensible in 1993, the International Year of Indigenous Peoples?[33] The venom provoked by Malouf's juxtaposition of childish innocence with Morrill's historical story points to how highly attuned the minds of historians, including myself, and other intellectuals have become to the lack of innocence in Australian history. In one sense (though not necessarily deliberately), Malouf was holding a mirror up to the life of Morrill's 'true' story and history-makers' and readers' expectations of it in the late twentieth century, showing that it continued to be an important part of local and regional settler history, as well as a touchpoint for revisionist histories of the frontier.[34]

Some of the questions invoked by Malouf's work could be asked of the Bowen Historical Society's act of republication. In terms of what it did *not* seek to do—that is, reassess Morrill's story for the twenty-first century or include intersecting Aboriginal histories—the society's 2002 booklet might be seen as inadvertently continuing the dogged avoidance of recognition that Ross Gibson has described as characteristic in the region: 'this is how the colony was maintained: by sensing but trying not to see, by fearing and knowing but trying not to acknowledge'.[35] Yet, this

---

32  Ibid., 1–3, 8, 16–21.
33  Germaine Greer, 'Malouf's Objectionable Whitewash', *The Age*, 3 November 1993, Features, 11; Kinnane, '*Remembering Babylon*', 7–12; Stockdale, 'I Dreamed of Snow Today', 1–10; Burrows, 'The Ghostly Haunting', 124–32.
34  As Jackie Hogan observed of Baz Luhrman's *Australia*, which met with similar criticism in some respects, the novel itself is perhaps an exercise in 'wish fulfilment' at the same time as it creates opportunities to view these wishes with a sense of irony. The theatrics of a slightly absurd representation of history invite the audience to respond in a variety of ways, including with outrage. See Hogan, 'Gendered and Racialised', 64, 71, 75.
35  Gibson, *Seven Versions*, 90–94.

answer does not help to explain what the volume *does* do, and what other responsibilities the society's members might have considered central to their task.

There were, perhaps, several reasons for the Bowen Historical Society to retell Morrill's story as told by its founders. For example, one that emerges in the society's *Bulletin* is respect for those who established the organisation, and a *sense* of solidarity with previous members. The deaths of long-time members were felt keenly, for 'whilst not blood relatives, we are still all one family here at the museum'.[36] Further, there was a sense of deliberateness and care involved in retelling the story as it was told in 1964, as it had been inherited from storytellers of previous generations. A new story about Morrill would have required renegotiation of the place of Aboriginal history within the organisation, as well as an active 'forgetting' of previous histories.[37] The shaping of history by institutional continuity and loyalty seems strange to the revisionist impulses that characterise much academic history-making; however, these influences cannot be overlooked. Certainly, for the Bowen Historical Society, for which Morrill's story is an important part of the history of the society itself, it would seem to have been important.

Part of the founding members' project was the ordering of history into a timeline of inaugural events that established the comprehensibility of local history as a 'linear pattern … of development and progress'. However, it should not be assumed that this ordering of history is no longer necessary for later generations; rather, these timelines need to be maintained and expanded in a continual cycle. This is an important part of what Graeme Davison called a 'preservative' impulse, a feature of much local history making.[38] As Elizabeth Furniss has observed of Mt Isa, and Heather Goodall of the 'black soil plains' of the New South Wales – Queensland border, efforts to 'establish the long tenure' of the white community in rural and regional local contexts in the present can be understood as a response to social and economic pressures that threaten the life patterns

---

36  Addressing the 40th anniversary Annual General Meeting, the president exclaimed: 'If only we could have Vic Jones, Henry Darwen and Walter Cottrell with us tonight to see that forty years on, the Museum continues to run like clockwork in the hands of volunteers'. *Bowen Historical Society Bulletin* 45 (October 2003): 4, 7; *Bowen Historical Society Bulletin* 43 (November 2001): 3.
37  Bradford, '"A Timeless Now": Memory and Repetition', 205. As Humphrey McQueen has observed, it can be difficult to write new stories from within old organisations amid a comfortable 'tolerance' for the inherited ways in which Aboriginal history has been negotiated. McQueen, *Gallipoli to Petrov*, 107–18.
38  Furniss, 'Timeline History', 284–86; Davison, *The Use and Abuse*, 13.

and livelihoods of those communities. Part of this pressure comes from the increased visibility of Aboriginal history-making and local native title processes. In this sense, timelines of pioneer histories help to mark out a present and a future in which 'colonial authority is established, unproblematic and unchallenged'.[39]

Economic change and changing landscapes in the ever more highly capitalised rural and mining industries can also contribute to a sense of incipiency that can make the re-inscription of historical order socially necessary.[40] For much of its existence, Bowen has been the 'Cinderella of the eastern coast', waiting to be 'roused to her great importance' as a port. Whereas a local history cum promotional booklet of 1920 predicted that 'in the inside of ten years the population of this place should count up to well over 50,000', the actual population of the Bowen Shire in 2002 was a little over 12,000, and was just beginning to rise again after steady population losses each year from the mid-1990s. In 2012, the Whitsunday Regional Council anticipated that 'the Bowen and Collinsville communities are well positioned to become an economic powerhouse of the North Queensland region', a development that would ensure the region's growth and result in a radical change in the life patterns of its residents.[41] In this context, repeating founding moments, particularly those that signify Bowen's precedence in the region, may be understood as a securing of the past in the face of an uncertain future. As Furniss observed, though, even history that is 'conservative in language' can be 'creative in application', and the meaning of local historical practice can only really be understood in the 'social contexts of their creation, use and reception'.[42] With this in mind, I travelled north in December 2010.

Bill Murray, engineer, former mayor of Ayr and keen local historian, pointed out to me the different homes he and his wife had lived in along Kilrie Road, running along the southern side of Ayr, about half way between Townsville and Bowen. Some of the other houses belonged to his children, or were their past or future homes; almost every block had a

---

39   Goodall, 'Telling Country', 168; Furniss, 'Timeline History', 288.
40   Goodall, 'Telling Country', 177–79.
41   Doherty, *The Bowen Book*, 11–47. See also Whitsunday Regional Council, Development, accessed 23 March 2012, www.whitsunday.qld.gov.au/. Many of those leaving Bowen probably did so for nearby mining centres, or for other regional centres like Townsville and Rockhampton with more extensive employment prospects. 'Bowen Shire LGA profile', December 2007, prepared by AEC group for the Mackay-Isaac-Whitsunday Regional Economic Development Corporation, accessed 18 July 2018, pandora.nla.gov.au/pan/80338/20080111-0033/www.bowen.qld.gov.au/industry/Bowen%20 Profile%20-%20Industry%20Page.pdf.
42   Furniss, 'Timeline History', 292–94.

connection. We were on the way to see a marker commemorating Morrill's return to civilisation, a large, attractive stone sitting in the grounds of Airville State School. It was organised by the Burdekin Historical Society and unveiled (from beneath an Australian flag) in July 1981 by Percy Jack, great-great-grandson of Morrill via his marriage with Eliza Ross.[43] The plaque reads:

> This monument commemorates the saga of shipwrecked mariner James Morrill ... Last survivor of the brig 'Peruvian' ... Reunited with Shepherds Hatch and Wilson on Sheepstation Creek near here January 1863. After living 17 years with Aborigines.

The memorial's use of the word 'saga' to characterise Morrill's story was possibly borrowed from the title of the lecture Victor Jones had delivered in Townsville two years earlier, which members of the Jack family had attended.[44] A 'saga', in the strictest sense, is a Norwegian or Icelandic story of heroic achievement or marvellous adventure that embodies the traditional history of a family across several generations.[45] Although, in common English parlance, its meaning has changed to signify a long and complicated series of events, its more precise definition may have reflected the Burdekin Historical Society's broader intention to engage Morrill's white family in this local story, as well as the Jack family's pride in claiming the story as the beginning of their history in the region. The Jack family also funded a memorial to Morrill at the head of the 'avenue of pioneers' at Home Hill, on the south bank of the Burdekin River, as part of the Burdekin Shire Council's celebrations of National Family Day.[46]

About a year before my meeting with Bill Murray, I came across an article in Brisbane's *Courier Mail* celebrating the centenary of Federation— the dignified 'path that led to nationhood ... a journey punctuated by debate and deliberation, not the bullets and bloodshed typical of other great democracies'. The story of Morrill and his descendants was told to illustrate this narrative of peaceful progress. When Morrill and his party of 'starving and exhausted survivors' washed up in North Queensland:

---

43 *Ayr Advocate*, 24 July 1981.
44 Jones, 'The Saga of James Morrill'. Jones also spoke at the unveiling of the monument, *Ayr Advocate*, 24 July 1981.
45 'Saga', *Oxford English Dictionary*.
46 'Pioneer Avenue, Eighth Avenue, Home Hill, Queensland', and Ian Frazer, 'Home Hill Hero: Descendants Honour Shipwrecked Sailor', undated and unsourced newspaper clippings, Phillip Murray, Private Collection, Townsville.

None expected their descendants would live in the same area. They certainly would not have visualised the thousands of hectares of sugar cane farms that now exist inland of Cape Cleveland, and pictured their great-grandsons working one of those farms more than 150 years later. But that is just what has happened and Morrill's cane-farming great-grandsons could not be prouder of their ancestor's role in the history of the north.[47]

Imperialism, settlement and farming in North Queensland is a matter of family and inheritance, founded in suffering and achieved by the ancient and universal process of human increase across generations.[48] This Genesis-like narrative has something in common with Bill's story of Kilrie Road. When he made Kilrie Road his home in the 1960s, there were a number of Aboriginal camps on the other side of the creek. Some of the Aboriginal people who lived there had helped on his and his neighbours' properties. Now, in Bill's mind, Kilrie Road belongs to his family. 'It's not PC' he told me, 'but I call myself a white Murri'.[49] Bill wanted me to meet one of Morrill's descendants, a member of the Jack family, and a few days later we drove over to Brandon together; unfortunately, no one was home. Bill encouraged me to contact the family when I returned to Sydney; he wanted me to see Morrill's journal, to which his descendants had added a family chronicle. On the northern side of Plantation Creek, opposite Bill's place, near where the Aboriginal camps had been, is the Gudjuda Centre. When I told Bill I was going to visit the centre on that first afternoon, he warned me not to expect to learn a great deal from the people there. Yet, he was extremely proud of a local history book that he had helped bring into being during his time as mayor: John Kerr's *Black Snow and Liquid Gold*. Bill called me back to his home a few days later to supply me with further copies of its pages, in which Kerr described the small settlement of Aboriginal people and islanders along Plantation Creek, with huts 'scattered … amidst banana trees, pawpaws and sweet potato patches', leasing the land from adjacent farmers. Kerr noted, with a sense of justice, that Birri-gubba ancestral remains were repatriated at Plantation Creek Park in 1987, signifying the official recognition of Aboriginal history at this place.[50]

---

47   Chris Jones, 'Survivor Braved All … with a Little Help from His Friends', *The Courier Mail*, 1 August 2001, published as part of a special Centenary of Federation supplement titled 'Birth of Our Nation'.
48   Curthoys, 'Mythologies', 14–17; Curthoys, 'Expulsion, Exodus and Exile'.
49   Bill Murray, in conversation with the author, 1 December 2010.
50   The book's title refers to the ash from cane burning and the region's underground water supplies. Kerr, *Black Snow*, 187.

Eddie Smallwood, chairman of the Gudjuda Corporation, was working the day I passed through Ayr. However, he took time out to meet me in the shady park next to the Gudjuda Centre, where a large sculpture of a python presided over a Dreaming story and the repatriated remains of a number of Birri-gubba ancestors. The next few days were not going to be good for learning about Birri-gubba history and culture, Eddie told me. There was some sorry business taking place at Palm Island, and an important funeral in Bowen. Eddie encouraged me to return in the new year, when I might be able to see the bush foods garden beside the centre (flooded at that time), visit the turtle-tagging project that is part of their cultural and natural resources management program, and talk with some of the Elders. He offered to take me up Mt Elliot and show me the rock carvings there—not because they hold any specific information about Morrill's story, but because they had been part of his country. Eddie told me that Morrill fathered a number of children with a Birri-gubba woman or women; that many of their descendants, and other members of the Birri-gubba community, were forcibly relocated away from the area in the 1920s and later on; and that some of them were still living in the area. There is an old story about a young Aboriginal girl with light skin who wandered onto Inkerman Station and was taken in by the Ross family. Yellow Gin Creek, flowing into the sea near Wunjunga, is named after her, and it is thought that she might also have been Morrill's daughter.[51]

When I asked Eddie whether Morrill's story is now a story about shared history, he responded that its importance for the Birri-gubba community is in its attestation that Aboriginal people were in this area before colonisation, with their own language and customs. Eddie was advocating the identification of the traditional owners of the region with the language group, Birri-gubba, rather than the 'nations' or clan groups under this umbrella (i.e., Birri-gubba, Juru, Wulgurukaba and Gia) that are delineated by contested boundaries and cause argument and division in the present.[52] The very basic ethnography and geography and lack of personal names in Morrill's *Sketch of a Residence* are, from this perspective, something of a blessing—the story attests to the Birri-gubba presence generally, without fuelling debate about who belongs to and speaks for which country, or who is descended from whom.

---

51   Eddie Smallwood, in conversation with the author, 1 December 2010.
52   Ibid.

Morrill's story holds a similar place in the Townsville Cultural Centre, which opened in 2005, and was founded with a board of eight directors: four from the Wulgurukabba and Bindal communities (both of the Birri-gubba language group), two from Torres Strait Islander communities and the remaining two from any other Aboriginal traditional custodian group.[53] The centre presents a many-layered account of Aboriginal and Torres Strait Islander life in North Queensland in its interpretive gallery. The visitor encounters Morrill just inside the entry to the circular gallery space. An account of Morrill's rescue by a group of Aboriginal men investigating the cause of persistent shooting stars over the place where he and his companions struggled for their lives is followed by a brief summary of his adoption; the role of Morrill's published narrative in attesting to the distinctive life ways and languages of Aboriginal people in the region is also outlined.[54] In the process of this telling, Morrill's Birri-gubba knowledge had been converted into ethnography, a way of thinking in which many Aboriginal people have become highly literate. Today, as Birri-gubba communities work on native title histories, local heritage matters and public history-making, Morrill's story is a valuable reference point. Unlike the historians and anthropologists who made the first attempts to recover Aboriginal life in North Queensland in the 1970s and 1980s, and who found Morrill's story wanting, Eddie Smallwood and others do not expect Morrill to provide a 'complete' account. Instead, working backwards from contemporary traditions and links with the land, they are grateful for what Morrill did say. In a sense, after being used against Birri-gubba people for a century, Morrill's knowledge is now being repatriated.

The use of Morrill's story as an assertion of Aboriginal history is nowhere more tangible than in the mural located in the Bowen State Primary School. Bowen is a town of murals; 24 of them decorate the compact town grid, painted on the walls of public buildings between 1988 and 2001. The first eight depicted the growth of agriculture and industry in the region: white men and their machines. In 1991, as a corrective of sorts, a mural depicting pioneer women was added, sponsored, like its predecessors, by the Bowen Murals Society. The triptych on the tennis court wall at the school was not funded by the Murals Society; instead,

---

53   The website of the Cultural Centre, Townsville, staff and board of directors, accessed 18 July 2018, www.cctownsville.com.au/about-us/ (page discontinued).
54   Interpretive Gallery, the Cultural Centre, 2–68 Flinders Street East, Townsville, North Queensland, opened September 2005. I visited in December 2010.

it was funded by the Aboriginal and Torres Strait Islander Commission, possibly via the Girudala Community Co-operative, and was painted by a local Aboriginal artist, Robert Paul.[55] Paul familiarised himself with Morrill's story by reading *Sketch of a Residence*. He painted Morrill and other survivors leaving the stricken *Peruvian* on their raft; Morrill and his Aboriginal rescuers overcoming their initial mutual fear with peaceful gestures; and a central cameo based on the studio portraits of Morrill after he 'connected up back' with his own people, as Paul put it.[56]

Paul went on to paint a second mural the following year, which is known in the official guide as the 'Aboriginal and Islander History' mural. It depicts Elders passing on a Dreaming story to younger listeners 'while other members of the tribe depict a good hunting season in their paintings', as well as 'Islanders working on one of the many Chinese farms in the Bell's Gully area' in the early twentieth century.[57] For some locals, Paul's Morrill mural registers strongly in their thinking about the meaning of Morrill's story. Henry Young, a member of the Murals Committee, identified Paul's two Bowen murals, and a third mural about blackbirding and the use of South Sea Islander labour in the region, as the only ones that acknowledged the contribution of 'dark people' to Bowen's history; he also saw the Historical Society's 1964 obelisk as a belated nod to Aboriginal history. Endorsing the visibility of Aboriginal history, Young declared that Paul did a 'damn fine job'.[58]

---

55  The official murals guide, while it notes that this artwork was funded by 'ATSIC' (fewer readers will know what this acronym signifies as time passes), does not identify Paul as an Aboriginal artist, or include any references to his interpretation of the story.
56  Robert Paul, in conversation with the author, 19 November 2010.
57  The Whitsunday Regional Council, 'Bowen Murals', accessed 18 July 2018, pandora.nla.gov.au/pan/80338/20080111-0033/www.bowen.qld.gov.au/tourism/MuralNineteen.html. This publication was widely available as a hardcopy booklet.
58  Henry Young, in conversation with the author, 23 November 2010.

Figure 2: Mural representing the story of James Morrill in the grounds of Bowen State Primary School, painted by Robert Paul in 1992, and restored by the artist in 2012.
Source: Photograph supplied by Robert Paul and included with his permission.

Paul's mural subtly reminds viewers that Morrill's story is part of local Aboriginal history as well as local pioneer history. Paul based his narrative on the same version of Morrill's story that white local historians use, and he employed a similar kind of visual language to the other Bowen murals. His understanding of the story is that it shows 'two cultures of the land' coming together through Morrill's adoption by Birri-gubba people.[59]

Bill Murray warned me not to fall prey to the Bowen Historical Society's claims (or anyone else's for that matter) to know everything about Morrill. My meeting with Phillip Murray, psychologist and amateur archaeologist (and no relation of Bill's) in Townsville a few days later helped me to make sense of Bill's territorialism. Phillip and Bill are both intensely interested in the burial place of Morrill's fellow castaways, Captain and Mrs Pitkethly.[60] The Bowen Historical Society's *The Story of James Morrill* (1964) concluded with a call to mark their grave and, in 1979, members of the society were contacted by an archaeologist who had found skeletal remains, perhaps belonging to Alice Pitkethly. The remains might have been relocated to the new museum building had they not been so

---

59  Robert Paul, in conversation with the author, 19 November 2010 and 15 December 2017.
60  Morrill stated that he had asked the group caring for the stricken Captain to bury rather than cremate him. Morrill, *Sketch of a Residence*, 12–13. By the time he had heard of the Captain's death and returned, Mrs Pitkethly had also died. Eugene Fitzalan's poem provided some further clues as to the location of the grave.

fragmented.⁶¹ Bill Murray, who has dedicated considerable time and effort to locating and researching local graves outside formal cemeteries, firmly believes that the couple's grave is located at Wunjunga near Upstart Bay, marked by a cairn of small boulders.⁶² However, Phillip Murray is convinced that a site on the adjoining Abbott Bay is more likely. He has been involved with a number of university-sponsored excavations associated with the grave and has communicated with a representative of the Pitkethlys's family in Scotland. Phillip has also investigated other aspects of the geography of Morrill's story, including the location of the wreck of the *Peruvian* and the site where the raft landed. His files on Morrill's story include many carefully annotated maps and plans. In the course of his investigations, Phillip has collaborated with Birri-gubba elder Jim Gaston. The two men have been on at least one trip to Mt Curlewis together, perhaps enabling Phillip to engage with Birri-gubba country in a qualitatively different way.⁶³

Through my conversations with Phillip and others, the perceived limits of academic disciplines such as archaeology, geography and history emerged as one of the forces at play in the retelling of Morrill's story. As Denis Byrne has observed of professional heritage workers (like myself), we tend to reproduce a segregated landscape as long as we continue to work within established fields of practice. Archaeology, with its emphasis on the material life of prehistory, attests to an Aboriginal presence in the landscape—almost everywhere on the continent, and for a very long time. Conversely, the discipline struggles to recognise Aboriginal knowledge and the relevance of the 'objects' it identifies to living Aboriginal people. At the same time, heritage histories can easily erase the Aboriginal presence from 'post-contact' spaces too, by focusing on archives and fields of human endeavour that do not include Aboriginal histories, relying on archaeology to document the Aboriginal presence in a place as 'prehistory'. While this does not necessarily reflect the practitioners' own beliefs or values as individuals, the result is nevertheless a disentangled history that looks a lot like Australia's history of segregation itself.⁶⁴ The conflict between settlers and the Birri-gubba people and their neighbours in the 1850s and

---

61   Major L. W. Hill to Mrs and Mrs Cottrell, 23 February 1979; Mr and Mrs Cottrell to Major L.W. Hill, 10 March 1979, file on the Pitkethlys's burial place, Phillip Murray, Private Collection, Townsville.
62   Bill Murray, in conversation with the author, 1 and 3 December 2010; Melissa Ketchell, 'Mystery Graves Found: Couple Shipwrecked in 1846', *Sunday Mail*, 24 November 2002, 40.
63   Phillip Murray, in conversation with the author, 3 December 2010.
64   Byrne, 'The Ethos of Return', 83.

1860s is well documented in the newspapers of the time and in published diaries and reminiscences of settlers themselves, and can be confidently included in histories of the region. However, other aspects of Morrill's personal story and his legacy are less readily explored from within the documentary history tradition.

In one of his local lectures, Phillip brought his psychological interests to bear by imagining a therapeutic session with Mrs Pitkethly, exploring what her feelings may have been as she encountered the Birri-gubba and was scrutinised by them. More cautious in his engagement with Morrill, Phillip turned our conversation to a novel that, by chance, I had read a few days earlier. The thesis of Alan J. Morris's novel, *The Sole Survivor,* is that Morrill survived with the Birri-gubba people because he reached out to them, relinquished his Britishness and accepted their teachings. Unlike the other castaways, Morrill recognised that he must assimilate to survive. When Alice Pitkethly's character said to Morrill, 'you're a good man, Jimmy … but I'm afraid you're going to turn into one of them', he replied, 'yes Alice, if I'm to become a survivor I must become exactly like them'.[65] In narrating Morrill's willing and apt transformation into an Aboriginal man, as well as some of the dramas of his Aboriginal life, Morris engaged with a part of Morrill's experience that is not directly accessible through documentary sources, but must be imagined by those who are prepared to cast themselves away from the safe vessel of documented fact. Preferring not to confuse his historical understanding of Morrill's story with fiction, Phillip told me that he had decided not to read Morris's book.

One of my email correspondents, a keen local historian based in Ayr, Glenis Cislowski, furnished the following as part of her response to my query about Morrill's descendants:

> James Ross Morrill married Ellen Flynn in 1889. They had Ellen born 1890/C7184, Gertrude born 1892/C11604, Dorcas Cecilia born 1894/C10951, Jane Isabel Morrill born 1898/C71078, Lorna Clare 1904/C11388, and Edith Ann born 1906/C10931. Dorcas married Robert Jack of Brandon. They had Percy and Dave Jack. Dorcas Cecilia Jack died 12/12/1970 and is buried in the Ayr Cemetery … The Jack family still farm out past Brandon.

---

65 Morris, *The Sole Survivor*, prologue, 3. Morris thought of himself as inhabiting a chronologically segregated landscape as he wrote, dedicating his novel to 'the Brindle [sic] Tribal people who are now extinct'. Perhaps some of this freedom to imagine came from a conviction that no-one living could answer him.

> A man with Morrill as his surname came into our workshop some years ago to get my husband to do a job for him. He claimed that he was a descendent of James Morrill and a native woman. It is openly stated that Morrill had a wife and family from the local tribe.[66]

Whereas a precise account of the Jack family can be made, complete with dates of birth, birth certificate numbers, Christian and middle names, tracing Morrill's Aboriginal descendants back to him takes place through family stories. These two kinds of information can be genuinely difficult to combine into the same history. Glenis felt that I would not be able to include a family story like this in my doctoral thesis because it was not the sort of 'evidence' usually admitted to the scholarly realm. Her concern mirrored Bain Attwood's observation:

> Aboriginal pasts occur in forms and forums that refuse to conform … to the discipline of history's conventional protocols and procedures for determining whether an account of the past is factual and thus true or not.[67]

Although historians are yet to find a single, perennial solution to this dilemma, there are many models for rigorous, reliable history that bring together qualitatively different kinds of evidence.

The Bowen Historical Society followed the usual disciplinary conventions in its retelling of Morrill's story. Dilys Maltby, one of the compilers of *James Morrill: His Life and Adventures* showed me around the society's museum. She was at ease with the idea that Morrill had most likely fathered children during his time with the Birri-gubba, and might have Aboriginal descendants who still live in the region. I recounted some of the more risqué and romantic detail of *A Sole Survivor* to Dilys and asked if she had read the novel. Some of the tutelage the fictional Morrill receives is from a young woman who becomes his wife after desire blossoms during their language sessions: 'she pointed to her lips and said sweetly "moolin". It was too much for Jimmy Morrill. He kissed her quickly as he repeated the word moolin and said loudly "kiss"'.[68] Dilys, who had not read the book, laughed and said it sounded plausible, after all he was a young man who had lived as part of the community for 17 years. She recalled that, in *Sketch of a Residence,* Morrill referred to the offer of a

---

66 Glenis Cislowski, correspondence with author care of Loftus Dun, 24 January 2011.
67 Attwood, 'Aboriginal History, Minority Histories', 177.
68 Morris, *The Sole Survivor*, 66. The pair's bonding over language is a more explicit rendition of the kind of affection and eroticism Kate Grenville imagined behind the vocabulary Pattyegarang and Lt. Dawes shared. Grenville, *The Lieutenant*, 158–65. See also Carter, 'Repetitions at Night', 81–82.

wife, but not whether he accepted or not. Dilys then told me that, over the past few years, a number of enquiries had been made at the museum by Aboriginal people who thought they might be Morrill's descendants, thinking that the society might hold information that would provide proof of this. The society's researchers told them that they were sorry, but there was no such proof as far as they knew. Dilys explained that this is why the museum's displays and their booklet about Morrill do not include reference to Morrill's Aboriginal descendants, because the society deals in verifiable facts, and there is no documentary proof in this case.[69]

In promotional material, Morrill's story is cited as one of the main reasons to visit the museum;[70] yet, when I visited in 2010, Morrill occupied only a small corner—between geological specimens and a large, typographical-style display of Aboriginal weapons and tools, opposite the explorers' wall. Studio portraits of Morrill and his son, and a copy of the title deed for Morrill's lot on the corner of Brisbane and Poole streets, joined photographs of the 1964 monument and its dedication ceremony in which Morrill's granddaughters and step-granddaughters are pictured clustered around the monument. Although the society commemorates its own commemoration of Morrill—a relatively 'new' addition to Morrill's story—a way of including contemporary Birri-gubba stories touching on Morrill had not been found.

Berber Bevernage has made a study of the sense of chronology that is closely tied to the concept and process of reconciliation: the up-to-date, the destination and the desired future (as opposed to a past characterised by denial).[71] It would be easy to say that Morrill's storytellers are *running late* for reconciliation, but the reality is more complex, as the landscape of the story is truly current. As a number of Birri-gubba groups pursue native title claims, as the Bowen Historical Society continues to tell a story of white discovery and progress, and as Loos attempts to bring

---

69 Dilys Maltby, in conversation with the author, 2 December 2010. The imperative to establish European-style family trees as good evidence for 'traditional ownership' within the native title system and elsewhere has provided the motivating factor for this kind of research within many Aboriginal communities. See Goodall, 'Telling Country', 184.
70 In 2011, the museum's 'Museum and Gallery Services' listing began: 'Did you know … We hold records of the shipwrecked survivor, James Morrill, who lived for 17 years with Aborigines?' Museum and Gallery Services Queensland, Museum and Gallery Profiles, 'Bowen Historical Society and Museum', accessed 8 August 2011, www.magsq.com.au/01_cms/details.asp?ID=389 (site discontinued).
71 Bevernage, 'Writing the Past', 122–23.

the parties together, Morrill's story plays a part in regional 'matters of history—of possession and dispossession—[that] remain as important as they ever were'.[72]

A reconciliation horizon is not the only possibility for Bowen. Local self-determination initiatives work towards other futures in which stronger legal and economic positions, from which Birri-gubba people can engage in social and cultural development on their own terms, are sought, rather than a resolution of histories.[73] Gillian Cowlishaw asked of history-making and identity in Bourke: what if the reproduction of difference and segregation is not understood as 'a pathology, a gaping wound that must be healed before normal life can begin again … What if it is the disputation around the division that gives social life its meaning?'[74] Morrill's story, while it remains 'entangled' in Aboriginal and settler pasts and presents and their connections, provides a platform for the assertion of separate histories, not least through the tripartite narrative consolidated in *Sketch of a Residence* and its firm separation of ethnography from experience. Indeed, the story as it was told in *Sketch of a Residence* remains at the centre of things, unreconstructed but constantly re-contextualised. Precisely because of its brevity and sobriety, it remains capable of holding all manner of meaning.

---

72  Attwood with Doyle, *Possession*, 320.
73  Johnson, 'Reconciliation, Indigeneity', 189, 198.
74  Cowlishaw, 'On "Getting It Wrong"', 202.

# Part 2: The Many Truths of Bennelong's Tragedy

# 4

# Bennelong's Rise and Fall

Bennelong's was by no means the only Eora face that the first Sydney colonists recognised, yet he is singled out in public memory as an intermediary between the present and the past.[1] Australians, and Sydneysiders most especially, have returned over and over again to the history of the colony at Sydney Cove. In history books, children's books, songs, poems, plays and blogs, Bennelong is often awarded at least a cameo appearance, and is often responsible for conveying something of the larger story of what happened to Aboriginal people after British invasion and settlement. Historian Lyndall Ryan has described the famous Tasmanian intermediary Trucanini as 'a resilient figure in debates about the future of Australian Aboriginals today' and a 'site of struggle for ownership and possession of the colonial past'.[2] Like Trucanini, Bennelong's life offers considerable dramatic potential to the storyteller: his kidnap by Phillip, escape, convincing display of gentlemanly manners, deep involvement in Aboriginal and European politics, journey to England and back, and death in relative obscurity. Like Trucanini, Bennelong was a go-between,

---

1   For example, journalist Tony Stephens followed Peter Read in thinking of Bennelong as the first of the 'stolen generations'; however, Read did not name Bennelong. Read was thinking of Arabanoo, Colbee *and* Bennelong, Phillip's three captives, the other two of whom Stephens did not know about (confirming Brook's suspicions), or did not see as significant enough in the public view to mention. Tony Stephens, 'Bennelong, the First of the Stolen, Comes Back: Sorry Day', *The Sydney Morning Herald*, 26 May 1998 [late edition], 6, referring to Read, *A Rape of the Soul*, 17. See also Brook, 'The Forlorn Hope', 36–47.
2   Ryan, 'The Struggle for Trukanini', 154.

trader, diplomat, and builder and crosser of bridges—his life is rich in possible interpretations, and these interpretations are interwoven with ideas about Aboriginal presents, futures and pasts.

Stories about Bennelong proliferate in what folklorist Linda Dégh has called a 'fast-breaking process'; indeed, since the 1960s, there has been so much storytelling about Bennelong that it is impossible to trace lines of tradition through a clear genealogy of versions.[3] Yet, while stories of Bennelong are myriad, they are not 'promiscuous', to borrow a term from Keith Jenkins. That is, they do not make use of just any available narrative form to suit the requirements of the immediate present.[4] Instead, most popular and public storytellers adhere to a strong tradition, which itself carries many layers of meaning; Bennelong is cast in a tragedy of sorts, in which he rises to the dizzying heights of fame and friendship with the governor, before falling into despair and disrepute on return from his great journey to England. This short entry on Bennelong in a 1980 *Dictionary of Australian History* encapsulates this view:

> **Bennelong** (?–1813). Aboriginal who accompanied Governor Arthur Phillip to England in 1792. Governor John Hunter brought him back to Sydney in 1795. For a time he continued his association with the Europeans but eventually abandoned his clothes and began to drink heavily, becoming an outcast to both Europeans and Aborigines.[5]

Like the story of James Morrill's story, the story of Bennelong's story is a tale of repetition; though they wish to communicate a range of historical, political and ethical meanings, storytellers have often followed a well-worn path.

I have become fascinated with how storytellers navigate the later years of Bennelong's life. Often, I have wanted to defend him: What was the real evidence for his alcoholism? Who can prove he was no longer loved and respected by his community? I have to admit, I have feelings for Bennelong, feelings no more or less well founded than those of any of his storytellers. Walking on the same ground as Bennelong, through the storied landscape of Cadigal Eora country and Sydney, one encounters Bennelong often, at the Sydney Opera House, in the Botanic Gardens, where the first Government House was built, at Manly and on the

---

3   Dégh, *Narratives in Society*, 361–62; Hamilton, 'Memory Studies', 83.
4   Jenkins, quoted in Curthoys and Docker, *Is History Fiction?*, 6.
5   Larkin, *Dictionary of Australian History*, 27–28.

## 4. BENNELONG'S RISE AND FALL

Parramatta River. Sometimes, he seems almost familiar—an 'old friend'. Yet, his presence is also disconcerting, particularly for those, such as me, whose own understandings of the man and his times have shifted and multiplied over the years. American poet Yusef Komunyakaa frequented Sydney in the 1980s and 1990s, became familiar with the city, its history and daily race politics, and gained respect for the land rights movement and the poetry of Aboriginal activist–writers like Kath Walker, Jack Davis and Colin Johnson.[6] His poem 'Bennelong's Blues' animates an impromptu meeting with Bennelong in the present, looking back. The speaker's address is familiar yet uneasy, admiring but clear-eyed. He feels nostalgic for a happier time, when Bennelong's story seemed simpler too, and acknowledges that Bennelong was always more formidable, and more entangled, than he had realised:

> You're here again, old friend.
> You strut around like a ragtag redcoat
> bellhop, glance up for a shooting star
> & its woe, & wander in & out the cove
> you rendezvoused with Governor Phillip
> after Wil-le-me-ring speared him beside a beached
> whale. We've known each other for years.
> You're unchanged. But me, old scapegoat,
> I never knew I was so damn happy
> when we first met. Each memory
> returns like heartbreak's boomerang.
> You didn't tell me you were a scout,
> a bone pointer, a spy,
> someone to stand between new faces
> & gods. I didn't know your other four
> ceremonial names, hero in clownish clothes,
> till another dead man whispered into my ear.[7]

Over the past few decades, there has been a movement to recognise the significance of Bennelong's other four ceremonial names, and to acknowledge that Aboriginal people were not necessarily as they appeared, or as they sounded, to the British colonists.[8] Historians are attempting to step back from Bennelong and to confront him, as the speaker in Komunyakaa's poem does, as a stranger again, as a person in his own elusive story, as someone we might gain a new understanding of, now

---

6   Gotera, 'Lines of Tempered Steel'.
7   Komunyakaa, 'Bennelong's Blues', 35. Cited in full with permission of Yusef Komunyakaa.
8   See, for example, Troy, 'Language Contact', 33–50; Karskens, 'Red Coat, Blue Jacket', 1–36.

that more time has passed and Australian history has grown and changed. However, before this is possible, it is necessary to reflect on the powerful association that generations of storytellers have made between Bennelong's story and tragedy.

In her epic novel of 1941, *The Timeless Land*, Eleanor Dark sought to tell, for the first time, 'a story of the white settlement partly from the black man's point of view'. Her drafts featured a long prologue depicting Aboriginal life before the arrival of the First Fleet; the novel was immense and war was looming. Dark decided to focus the story more intensely on a 'clash of values' within white society. On publisher William Collins's suggestion, she funnelled her prologue into a much terser tableau focused throughout on Bennelong, one of her chief Aboriginal protagonists.[9] So it is Bennelong who both begins and ends her story, transformed from a sweet child trailing after his fictional father, Wunbula, in the first paragraphs, to the broken adult of Dark's epilogue. In the novel's final scene, Bennelong revisits the rock platform where Wunbula had made a carving of Cook's ship, and where father and son had looked out to sea together. He is drunk and angry. When he stumbles across the carving, he throws himself down and starts to vandalise it until he collapses, overwhelmed by alcohol and a sense of loss:

> The ground lurched, and the whole world spun. As he pitched forward across the rock a bit of broken bottle gashed his arm, and blood ran into the defaced grooves of Wunbula's drawing. Bennilong lay still, snoring heavily, while the merciful, swift twilight of his land crept up about him to cover his defeat. The End.[10]

Dark's Bennelong was drawn into the 'alien world' of the white men by a 'thread of destiny' that would 'hold him there even after death'. Taken captive by Phillip, Bennelong's initial anger subsided as he recalled his destiny and found himself wanting to be like those fascinating strangers—'proud to wear the clothes they gave him, [he] walked often in the sunshine so that he might admire his shadow, which was now the same as the shadow of a white man'.[11] Yet, Bennelong was destined to fail. Dark's Aboriginal characters were self-sufficient and creative within their own culture, but, imagined through a Social Darwinist lens, they were depicted as the 'monkey-like' 'children of the human family', hard-wired

---

9   Brooks with Clark, *Eleanor Dark*, 347–50; Wyndham, *A World Proof Life*, 180–81.
10  Dark, *The Timeless Land*, 539–44.
11  Ibid., 49, 264–65.

to an unchanging existence. All Dark's Aboriginal characters faced an intractable cultural dilemma with the arrival of the colonists. They were a 'timeless' people; change brought the sustaining certainty of their law-governed tribal life to an end.[12] In the light of this preconception, Bennelong's rush towards cultural exchange was Icarus-like.

To fill out her picture of life at Port Jackson, Dark researched Aboriginal life ways across Australia, in the process lavishing a degree of care on her Aboriginal characters that was unusual and daring at the time.[13] When published, Dark's novel was both celebrated and criticised as being almost closer to history than to fiction, providing an unprecedented view of cross-cultural relations in the colony. The trilogy, of which *The Timeless Land* is the first volume, has been in print in Australia for most of the 60 years since its publication (but without a critical introduction until 1990). In the 1950s, it was set as a school text; in 1980, it formed the basis for a television mini-series broadcast by the Australian Broadcasting Commission (ABC).[14]

Dark later wrote Bennelong's entry for the 1966 edition of the *Australian Dictionary of Biography*. Her biographical entry was dry and without pathos. She concluded simply that Bennelong had fallen between two stools in his later years, saying that after his return from England, 'references to him are scanty, though it is clear that he could no longer find contentment or full acceptance either among his countrymen or the white men'.[15] Though different in genre and mood, Dark's biographies of Bennelong both rested on a pair of powerful and interrelated narrative elements that have come to characterise much of the storywork surrounding Bennelong over the past four decades; namely, that Bennelong was *culturally* changed (or even damaged) by his contact with the colony, and that this led him

---

12   Ibid., 151, 177. Dark wrote that Bennelong's wife, Barrangaroo, sensed a danger but could not apprehend it, as 'the passing centuries, going quietly over the heads of her ancestors, had evolved in their brains no machinery for the understanding of Change', p. 406. Reynolds, *Nowhere People*, 67–72; Brooks with Clark, *Eleanor Dark*, 364–65.
13   Humphrey McQueen reminded us that the novel appeared just after New South Wales had 'celebrated its Sesqui-Centenary with an official story that turned its back on the convicts and ignored the destruction of Aboriginal society'. McQueen, 'Introduction', in Dark, *The Timeless Land*, xix, xxii.
14   Brooks with Clark, *Eleanor Dark*, 357–59; Brooks, 'Introduction', in Dark, *The Timeless Land*, vii–viii; McQueen, 'Introduction', in Dark, *The Timeless Land*, xix, xxii. The novel took Australian history to an overseas audience, being a bestseller in the United States in 1941, topping the Times Literary Supplement Christmas Fiction List in the United Kingdom, and later being translated into German and Swedish.
15   Dark, 'Bennelong (1764–1813)'.

to a lonely and (in the view of many of his biographers) disgraceful end, which heralded an ominous beginning for Aboriginal–white relations in Australia.

Manning Clark claimed that Dark's novels inspired him to write his own monumental *History of Australia*.[16] However, Clark was much less interested in Aboriginal protagonists. Although his history was driven by flawed male characters, and infused with a 'historical melancholy' that was partly absorbed from his perception of Aboriginal dispossession, he largely turned his back on the ethnographically informed insights into Aboriginal society and politics that Dark had woven into her story.[17] Bennelong did not rate a mention in Clark's history until he and Yemmerawannie joined Phillip's voyage back to England in December 1792, three years after his kidnap, on Phillip's orders, in November 1789. Bennelong, Yemmerawannie and two convicts who also departed the colony with Phillip are gathered around the great man. Their chief purpose in the narrative is to demonstrate Phillip's magnetism, his 'power to attach people to his person'.[18] Clark's Bennelong was returned to New South Wales in 1795 for the purpose of displaying 'to other aborigines the benefits of civilisation'. Yet, only two pages after his return, Bennelong instead demonstrates the awful and ironic reality that Hunter faced in his task of preparing Aboriginal people for civilisation: that 'the closer his contact with civilisation, the more the aborigine was degraded'. This was the only form of mediation that Clark gave Bennelong credit for—his early intimation of the doom awaiting the Aboriginal people, demonstrated through the course of his own life. Bennelong took to drinking too much and behaving badly; he 'disgusted his civilisers and became an exile from his own people, and rushed headlong to his dissolution as a man without the eye of pity from the former, or affection from the latter'. The next time we meet Bennelong in Clark's history, he is already in his grave.[19]

The double 'exile' that Clark and Dark imagined for Bennelong on his return from England was quite different from the way in which earlier storytellers had seen Bennelong's later years. Leon Ducharme, a French–Canadian political prisoner who was interned in the colony in the early 1840s, spent part of his term labouring at a penal settlement known as

---

16   Brooks with Clark, *Eleanor Dark*, 427.
17   McKenna, 'Clark, Charles Manning (1915–1991)'.
18   Clark, *History of Australia*, 131.
19   Ibid., 143, 145, 346.

Longbottom, overlooking Bennelong's country on the Parramatta River. In his brief and disdainful account, Ducharme wrote that Bennelong—once returned from England:

> Was no sooner ashore on his native land than he stripped himself of all his good clothes, cast them aside, and, rushing into the depths of the bush, went off to re-join his beloved tribe … he was seen again wandering about just as wild as his brothers, and following all native inclinations.[20]

Ducharme's protagonist makes a more radical break with the colony than would have been possible for Bennelong in life, but he does so amid his 'beloved tribe'. Similarly, a Bennelong of the 1940s remains in his fine London clothes until a joyful reunion with his old friend Colbee results in the 'awakening' of his old savage self. His wife in the story is greatly relieved to see him return to his pre-kidnap priorities.[21] In these and many other stories into the 1960s, Bennelong continues to be embraced either by the colonists or by his own people. Even when he appears as a 'quarrelsome' drunk beset by troubles, he is still a social being, unlike the terminally isolated figure Clark depicted, who would increasingly stand in for Bennelong over the next few decades.[22] Keith Smith, seeking to 'rehabilitate the received image of Bennelong that has for so long been copied from one history to another with no questioning of the secondary sources or interrogation of the primary historical evidence', found it important to counter this de-socialisation of Bennelong by everyone from Clark to the historically inclined former Labor Party politician, Bob Carr.[23]

W. E. H. Stanner, giving the prestigious Boyer Lectures in 1968, thought he could perceive a slow revolution underway, in which the 'Aboriginal question' was rising to the surface in Australian social and political discussions. This was a revolution that he himself had been trying to bring into being as a journalist, anthropologist and administrator since the beginning of his academic career in the 1930s. He felt that a new kind of history, one entirely different from what had gone before, was necessary—one that acknowledged the Aboriginal side to the story.[24]

---

20  Longbottom was a small peninsula in the vicinity of today's Exile Bay, Canada Bay and France Bay, named after the French–Canadian prisoners. Ducharme, *Journal of a Political Exile*, 34–35, 46.
21  McCarter, 'They Began It'.
22  For example, Sadleir, *Aborigines of Australia*, 25; *The Sydney Morning Herald*, 29 January 1898, 4; Levy, *Wallumetta*, 10–13; Chadwick, 'Governor Phillip and the Natives', 267–72; Stephensen, *The History and Description*, 321.
23  Smith, 'Bennelong among His People', 8, 21–24.
24  Stanner, 'After the Dreaming',7, 25–26; D. J. Mulvaney, 'Stanner, William Edward (Bill) (1905–1981)'.

This new history may have been an opportunity for an open-minded assessment of Bennelong's story; yet, Stanner's own view of Bennelong was jaundiced. When he asked his listeners to imagine Aboriginal men and women of 'outstanding ... character and personality', he made the following qualification: 'I am not thinking of mercurial upstarts like Bennelong'.[25] A decade later, in an article written for the first issue of the journal *Aboriginal History*, he described Bennelong as a 'volatile egotist, mainly interested in love and war; a tease, a flirt and very soon a wine-bibber; a trickster and eventually a bit of a turncoat'.[26]

Stanner also credited the readily pleased and soon 'mendicant' Bennelong with being at the head of a chain reaction that 'forced one tribe after another into some sort of dependency on Europeans'.[27] In light of contemporary economic realities, this assessment was unfair. Aboriginal people of south-eastern Australia, in particular, continued to feel the effects of a sharp downturn in employment prospects as agricultural practices were mechanised and centralised, and postwar European migrants competed for seasonal employment. The 'dependency' of the many people who lost their paid work due to these developments was new, and had nothing to do with their character.[28] It was also something of an about-turn in thinking about Bennelong. Nineteenth-century thinkers had found Bennelong's biography predictive of the lives of Aboriginal people of following generations. The conclusion they usually reached was that Bennelong had been educated in British ways, but had rejected them in favour of his own self-sufficient culture and community. A *Sydney Gazette* article of 1834 echoed David Dickinson Mann (who departed the colony in 1809) when it recalled Bennelong's case to temper public expectations about the 'education' of a group of Aboriginal prisoners on Goat Island. Bennelong, of course, while having great capacity for learning, had 'preferred the freedom of his own wild woods'.[29]

---

25   Stanner, 'After the Dreaming', 45.
26   Stanner, 'The History of Indifference', 19–20.
27   Ibid; Stanner, 'After the Dreaming', 7–11.
28   Goodall, *Invasion to Embassy*, 312–14.
29   *The Sydney Gazette*, 11 July 1835, 3; David Dickinson Mann, *The Present Picture of New South Wales* (London: John Booth, 1811), quoted in Smith, 'Bennelong among His People', 19–20. See also Bond, *A Brief Account*, 6–7. Sometimes, Bennelong's case was cited and then dismissed as a failed 'early experiment', with other examples, such as the Aboriginal Institution at Parramatta, providing precedents for success in civilising the Aboriginal people. See George Howe, 'Chronology of Local Occurrences', *New South Wales Pocket Almanac* (1818), quoted in Smith, 'Bennelong Among His People', 19; *Illustrated Sydney News*, 21 January 1871, 3.

## 4. BENNELONG'S RISE AND FALL

Stanner's Boyer Lectures and 1977 article remain touchstones for historians today as we trace the history of the transformation of Australian histories to include and recognise Aboriginal histories.[30] The association that Stanner made between Bennelong (and his fall) and the wider 'Aboriginal question' was lasting. Following the 1967 Referendum, and as the much televised Aboriginal Tent Embassy was repeatedly established and removed from the lawns of Parliament House, bringing Aboriginal people and their fight for civil rights and land rights to public attention, biographers of Bennelong increasingly invested his story with explanatory power. Stanner's assessment of Bennelong and his legacy both shaped and was shaped by contemporary anthropological thinking, as discussed below. However, even as later generations of anthropologists and others have re-thought urban Aboriginality, Stanner's portrait of Bennelong as a weak and compromised character has echoed through subsequent biographies.

In the mid-1950s, Bennelong Point was conclusively selected as the site for the Sydney Opera House. This landform was known as Jubgalee by the Eora people, and was the site of a compact brick house built for Bennelong on the order of Governor Phillip. After Bennelong's death, the point was home to Fort Macquarie, completed circa 1819, then a tram depot from 1903, which was demolished for the laying of the foundations of the Sydney Opera House in 1959.[31] When the Opera House was opened in 1973, Bennelong was accorded a level of interest perhaps unequalled since the 1790s. He appeared in the opening ceremony in the shape of Aboriginal actor Ben Blakeney, who delivered a 'stirring oration' from the topmost peak of the tallest shell, heralded by a Royal Australian Navy fanfare:

> Here my people chanted their stories of the dreamtime—of spirit heroes, and of earth's creation—and our painted bodies flowed in ceremony. On this point my people laughed and they sang while the sticks clacked in the rhythm of the corroborees. I am Bennelong—and my spirit and the spirit of my people lives; and their dance and their music and their drama and their laughter also remain.[32]

---

30  See, for example, Attwood, 'The Past as Future'.
31  Kenny, *Bennelong*, 67–73.
32  Ziegler, *Sydney Has an Opera House*, n.p.

Figure 3: Depiction of Bennelong with the Sydney Opera House, *National Aboriginal Day Magazine*, 1981, artist unidentified.
Source: Reproduced with permission from the Department of Training and Workforce Development, Western Australia.

This Bennelong, of heroic proportions, probably did a great deal to bring Bennelong forward in popular imagination, as an accessible and even friendly figure—a mediator between the present and the past. He seems rehabilitated from the crisis that tore him apart at the end of *The Timeless Land*. He haunts the Opera House, certainly. However, where Trucanini has often been imagined haunting modern Australia in a spectral, reproachful way, violated and inconsolable, as she does in David Boyd's series of paintings and sculptures first exhibited in 1959,[33] Bennelong seemed to give his blessing.

However, the Opera House did not reciprocate Bennelong's sponsorship. Blakeney's script trod a delicate line between the acknowledgement (or, perhaps, the assertion, as Blakeney spoke) of an Aboriginal presence, and the appropriation of a past Aboriginal culture for this new, distinctively Australian, cultural and architectural landmark. Indeed, an embrace of Aboriginal iconography on the national and international arts scene, as well as in tourist literature and elsewhere, was widespread in the postwar decades. Yet, it did not generally reflect opportunities for Aboriginal people to be heard, even as performers of their own cultural inheritance.[34] The Opera House's first season gave little space to Aboriginal performance. The Marionette Theatre of Australia derived its children's show, 'Tales from Noonameena', from 'Aboriginal legends'; however, the only Aboriginal performance was apparently subsumed into the all-singing, all-dancing spectacle of the 'South Pacific Festival' produced by Victor Carell and Beth Dean.[35]

The notion that the Opera House, by virtue of its location, might constitute a memorial to Bennelong has often been invoked. The first issue of *The Benelong Bugle*, a newsletter circulated among construction workers at the Opera House, declaimed rather circuitously that 'such a remarkable character … deserves a place in the annals of his native land, and it is not unfitting that one of the famous buildings of the world should occupy a site which bears his name'.[36] P. R. Stephensen, also writing as the Opera House was in the early stages of construction, suggested that 'if the Opera House is not to be considered as Bennelong's monument' (he did not elaborate on why it would or should not be), then perhaps some sort of

---

33   Ryan, 'The Struggle for Trukanini', 161–65. See also Boyd's sculpture 'Truganini—the offering', and paintings 'Dream of childhood', 'Truganini and the sealer', and 'Truganini last of the Tasmanians', in *David Boyd: Retrospective 1957–1982*.
34   Kociumbas, 'Performances: Indigenisation', 134–35.
35   Hubble, *Sydney Opera House Official Souvenir*, n.p.; Kociumbas, 'Performances: Indigenisation', 134.
36   *The Benelong Bugle* 1 (1962) (Sydney: J. Parks, Sydney Opera House Site): 17. John Kenny declaimed in 1973 that 'who, indeed, was Bennelong for in the justice of history no one can be worthier of sharing the historic and contemporary lustre of the Opera House and Sydney Cove'. Kenny, *Bennelong*, 5. The 1981 National Aboriginal Day magazine declared that the location of Bennelong's exact place of burial is of no consequence as 'Benelong [sic] has no need of a second memorial. The name, Benelong Point [sic], will remain as long as Sydney survives'. 'The Governor's Friend', *National Aboriginal Day Magazine*, 1981, 31.

memorial could be erected nearby. That this magnificent building should directly pay tribute to Bennelong was, apparently, not something that Stephenson could take seriously. Instead, its demonstration of Australia's immense wealth and global standing as a modern nation prompted him to think of a modest tribute to this most famous of the colony's Aboriginal people.[37]

The Opera House did not need Bennelong's patronage. In the *Sydney Opera House Official Souvenir* booklet, Bennelong and his contemporaries are dwarfed by the towering modernity of the building's physical properties and the ingenuity of its construction. Bennelong makes only a fleeting appearance in a role with a laughably official title: 'liaison officer between the commander of the First Fleet, Captain (later Governor) Arthur Phillip R. N., and the Aboriginal people'.[38] The Opera House's World Heritage Nomination of 2006 suggested that the building had no need of history, for it appeared to the viewer to be an 'obvious, immediate and evident' part of the landscape 'as though *only* [Utzon's] typical "shells" could occupy Bennelong Point'.[39]

Two biographies of Bennelong were published to mark the opening of the Opera House. In one, commissioned by the Royal Australian Historical Society, author John Kenny found Bennelong instructive as:

> The first of his people to be a well-documented example of their social incompatibility with their conquerors—an incompatibility which has persisted, afflicting the conquerors' conscience and mocking their compassion and ingenuity.[40]

Founding chairman of the Council for Aboriginal Affairs H. C. 'Nugget' Coombs provided the foreword to Kenny's book, and agreed that the relationship between Phillip and Bennelong was 'disturbingly pertinent to our respective positions to-day … a sombre episode [that], with minor

---

37   Stephensen, *The History and Description,* 321. As an ardent nationalist seeking to break the ties of Australian cultural life with Britain, partly by enriching it with Aboriginal symbols and ideas, Stephensen may have recruited Bennelong to lend the Opera House an even more 'Australian' quality, rather than to direct the fame of the Opera House towards Bennelong. Goodall, *Invasion to Embassy*, 282–83.
38   Hubble, *Sydney Opera House Official Souvenir,* n.p.
39   Nomination by the Government of Australia of the Sydney Opera House for Inscription on the World Heritage List 2006, prepared by the Australian Government and the New South Wales Government, p. 35, UNESCO World Heritage website, Sydney Opera House documents, accessed 18 July 2018, whc.unesco.org/en/list/166/documents/.
40   Kenny, *Bennelong,* 5.

variations, has been replayed countless times throughout Australia'. In Kenny's account, Bennelong again suffers, not so much from loss of land and resources, political, social and economic upheaval, or loss of family and allies through smallpox; instead, he is, above all, the victim of 'an ignorant and futile attempt to civilise him [that] made him a pathetic victim of confusion of his own and the founders' cultures'.[41] If Bennelong was more pathetic failure than tragic hero, then the notion that his story was predictive of Aboriginal stories across the continent lent the matter a gravity of magnitude.

A second biography was a coffee-table book by journalist Isadore Brodsky. He, too, found that 'the discussion of *Bennelong* is timely in the affairs of the Aborigines in 1973, perhaps as a contribution to their emancipation and proper recognition in Australian life'. To this end, Brodsky set out to do Bennelong's 'memory some justice' by resurrecting his subject as 'a man within his own rights'.[42] However, Brodsky was not equipped to do this, his lack of historical and cultural insight ultimately undermining his project. Like Eleanor Dark, he understood Bennelong to be a 'Stone Age' man, caught between childhood and adulthood or, more precisely, 'manhood', on an evolutionary scale. Brodsky related Bennelong's inability to meet him 'man-to-man':

> It was predictable that it would not be possible to treat *Bennelong* both as a man and a child. You can play with [a child] on the floor, and in fun and with mutual enjoyment. But a man wants to know the rules of the game, what losing entails, and the rewards of winning. *Bennelong* alternated between child and man.[43]

Marylin Lake's analysis of the 'White Australia Policy', which was finally completely dismantled in 1973, helps to make sense of Brodsky's emphasis on 'manhood'. The policy's proponents argued that, to maintain Australia as a 'civilised community', each man must be equal to the last: self-sufficient, supporting his family and taking part in the body politic on an equal footing. Aboriginal men, and others, had been excluded

---

41 H. C. Coombs, 'Foreword', in Kenny, *Bennelong*, 1; Kenny, *Bennelong*, 5.
42 Brodsky, *Bennelong Profile*, 10, 16–17. Later, Brodsky described Phillip as wanting to 'afford [Bennelong] the appearance of equality' where of course there was none, p. 57.
43 Brodsky, *Bennelong Profile*, 76. Ironically, it is partly the nature of Brodsky's attempt to address Bennelong as a 'man' that leads to this view of a half man. Brodsky explicitly confined his attention to Bennelong. He perceived Bennelong as acting alone, apart from Aboriginal networks, politics or economy. Thus his 'behaviour' appeared to be inconsistent, 'oblique and bizarre', and seemed to be driven by 'emotional' rather than rational motives, pp. 40, 49, 50, 58–59, 73.

from full citizenship because they were not man enough.[44] Also in full view for Brodsky was the 1967 Referendum, popularly understood as the admission of Aboriginal people to Australian citizenry and, thus, perhaps in Brodsky's mind, to full Australian manhood.[45] In the event, Brodsky set up his own objective, of promoting social justice in the present, to fail, for in finding Bennelong part child, he questioned whether Aboriginal men were ready to become, or even be capable of being, citizens.

A few years later, the Tasmanian Aboriginal community was finally able to secure the release of Trucanini's remains from the Tasmanian Museum, cremate them, and scatter her ashes over the D'Entrecasteaux Channel. A small posse of historians promptly made a reactive grab for Trucanini's story. The Tasmanian Museum had recognised the contemporary Tasmanian Aboriginal community; Vivienne Rae Ellis and N. J. B. Plomley published a pair of books arguing strenuously for their extinction. Ellis's book depicted Trucanini as 'actually personally responsible for [the] demise' of her people, and gave graphic descriptions of the exhumation of her body (so recently put to rest) for science. Ellis and Plomley, like Brodsky, were reasserting the relevance of powerful old narratives in response to landmark Aboriginal achievements.[46] In linking Social Darwinism with the political and social developments of the day, Brodsky's book seemed to suggest that this notion had continued relevance, notwithstanding enhanced rights for Aboriginal people. Like the Opera House itself, Brodsky was a fickle friend to Bennelong's memory; he inflated Bennelong's importance and then stuck a pin in, leaving him something of a mock-hero, and re-relegating Aboriginal history to the dim-distant past. His biography of Bennelong served to legitimise the concerns of a subset of Australians about the absolute legal and constitutional equality of Aboriginal people.

In Brodsky's account, a childlike attempt by Bennelong to become a civilised man constituted *hubris*, an overblown ambition that was punished by fate, a compelling force for a tragedy.[47] Brodsky sent Bennelong on a value-laden trajectory: a rise towards 'civilisation' and then a fall when he failed to maintain its standards. Despite, at times, attempting to step back from the attitudes he found in late eighteenth-century sources,

---

44  Lake, 'On Being a White Man', 100–05.
45  Casey, 'Referendums and Reconciliation', 146.
46  *Aboriginal Information Service Newsletter,* April–May 1976 (Hobart: Aboriginal Information Service Inc), n.p.; Plomley, *The Tasmanian Aborigines,* 29, 39; Ryan, 'The Struggle for Trukanini', 167.
47  Wallace, *The Cambridge Introduction to Tragedy*, 3.

## 4. BENNELONG'S RISE AND FALL

Brodsky saw Bennelong as a savage who was raised towards a civilised state during his captivity in Phillip's house. However, not long after his return from England, Brodsky reported that Bennelong's 'newly found standards had slipped' and he tumbled into 'progressive degradation', 'falling from grace'.[48] Brodsky wholeheartedly sympathised with Judge Advocate David Collins' indignant comments about Bennelong's conduct in 1795–98, including his exasperated summation: 'This man, instead of making himself useful, or showing the least gratitude for the numberless favours that he had received, had become a most insolent and troublesome savage'.[49] Ironically, a book written for children, published just two years after Brodsky's biography, portrayed Bennelong as a thinker grappling with momentous change. No grand trajectory of civilisation was invoked, no final judgement of Bennelong's success or failure was handed down and, as a result, it perhaps achieved Brodsky's stated aim of showing Bennelong as a 'man within his own rights'.[50]

Some of the generalisations drawn from Bennelong's story seem overblown and implausible; others seem unjust. Many are easy to critique. Yet, I am not advocating a return to a more 'innocent' age, when Bennelong could be depicted simply as an interesting character of early Sydney,[51] such as the journal of the Royal Australian Historical Society, which included the following micro-biography by John McGuanne in 1901:

> He called Phillip 'Beuga' or father, while Phillip called him 'Dorroow' or son. He went to England with Phillip, was introduced to George III, was lionised, taught to box, to smoke, and drink, and swagger. On his return to Sydney with Governor Hunter he became an intemperate hero, jealous and quarrelsome, eventually ending his days in a brawl among blacks.[52]

This Federation-era Bennelong is an action figure whose life and deeds can be marvelled at without entering into any consideration of the changes that shaped his life, or their effect on Aboriginal people more generally. This was a form of historiographical hygiene that operated on many levels in the early twentieth century. Past Aboriginality was separated from present, 'authentic' Aboriginality quarantined from the 'Aboriginal problem', and readers kept safely sealed off from their own

---

48  Brodsky, *Bennelong Profile*, 3, 26–28, 67–70, 75.
49  Collins, *An Account of the English Colony*, quoted in Brodsky, *Bennelong Profile*, 71.
50  Phipson, *Bennelong*.
51  See, for example, Heaton, *Australian Dictionary of Dates*, 6; Suttor, *Australian Milestones*, 63.
52  McGuanne, 'Bennelong Point', 9.

outrage, empathy, pity, disgust, shame and other strong feelings about the past and history.[53] Now that these matters have risen to the surface again, as Stanner hoped they would, the disjunction seems disingenuous. From the 1960s, some storytellers continued to appeal to McGuanne's carefree 'once upon a time' mode;[54] however, increasingly, as we have seen, they sought to characterise the cross-cultural exchanges in which Bennelong participated, and thereby to both derive and propound an understanding of Australian race relations. As Bennedetto Croce might have put it, the story of Bennelong has re-awoken from its slumber in the Australian chronicle, becoming history once more in an era in which Aboriginal and settler relations again seem pressingly important.[55]

As the 1988 bicentenary of the arrival of the First Fleet approached, Aboriginal people of the Sydney region, in particular, readied themselves for highly ambivalent commemoration, and reflected on the history of first contact at Sydney Cove. Many Aboriginal people and their supporters who had told stories of Aboriginal survival over the preceding 20 or so years had found 'resistance' historiography appealing, inspired by the power and drama of the Vietnamese anti-colonial struggles, and an Aboriginal activism characterised by violent confrontations with the police and the 'belligerent rhetoric' of the Black Power movement.[56] In a lecture celebrating the discovery of the site of the first Government House in 1984, archaeologist John Mulvaney said he doubted that Bennelong was 'much honoured today by his people'. He anticipated that, as Aboriginal people sought to tell their bicentennial stories, they would turn instead to Pemulwuy, a man who could be remembered as a resistance hero.[57] Sydney Aboriginal man Gavin Andrews, who traces his family line back to Tharawal ancestors, recalled that many of Sydney's Aboriginal people had indeed come to see Bennelong and Pemulwuy in this light. For Andrews, this 'politicised' way of understanding the past failed to recognise what Bennelong experienced with the arrival of the British colony, and what he survived.[58] When Sydney Botanic Gardens Aboriginal Education Officer John Lennis was establishing the *Cadi Jam Ora* garden some time before

---

53  Healey, 'Years Ago Some Lived Here', 18–34.
54  See, for example, *Benelong Bugle* 1 (1962): 16–17; Barnard, *A History of Australia*, 651.
55  Bennedetto Croce, 'History and Chronicle' (1921, as reprinted 1959), quoted in Curthoys and Docker, *Is History Fiction?*, 92–93.
56  Reece, 'Inventing Aborigines', 16–17.
57  Mulvaney, *A Good Foundation*, 14.
58  Gavin Andrews, in conversation with the author, 2 September 2011. Geoffrey Moorhouse was also left with this impression after asking some Aboriginal people at The Block, Redfern, about Bennelong in the late 1990s. Moorhouse, *Sydney*, 50.

2002, he was surprised to hear Andrews describe Bennelong as a hero, as other people had told Lennis that Bennelong had 'sold out' to the British. It is Andrews's assessment of Bennelong as a man who 'wanted to know the white man's world so he could explain it to his people' that stands as Bennelong's epithet in the gardens, alongside a short biography that embraces the ambivalence Lennis found when he asked people about Bennelong.[59]

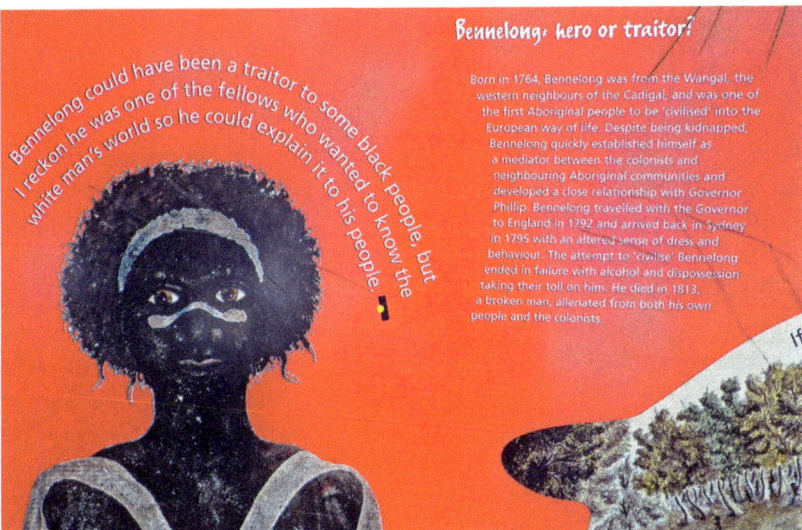

Figure 4: Bennelong featured in the *Cadi Jam Ora* garden panels, Royal Botanic Garden, Sydney.
Source: Photograph of the panels taken by author.

A number of other Aboriginal thinkers and writers, grappling with how to represent the establishment of the Sydney colony and understand its ongoing effects, were, like Andrews, unwilling to dismiss Bennelong. Eric Willmot, in his novel *Pemulwuy: The Rainbow Warrior*, first published in 1987, certainly depicted Bennelong as a 'loser', but all his characters were losers (except, perhaps, the charismatic Pemulwuy himself). Bennelong was simply the most spectacular loser, with Governor Hunter a close second. However, he was not the pathetic victim of one culture crashing against another, like wave against cliff, as Kenny and others would have us believe. Rather, in Willmot's novel, he played hard at politics and he

---

59  Gavin Andrews, in conversation with the author, 2 September 2011; Hinkson, 'Exploring Aboriginal Sites in Sydney', 65.

fell hard.⁶⁰ He was a 'good' loser, the kind of loser one can respect, giving his all for his cause, which was to gain and keep the initiative in dealings with the British.⁶¹ He felt frustrated and 'used' by both the British and the Eora at times, and he knew when he had been trumped, but he continued regardless.⁶² Willmot's Pemulwuy and Bennelong shared the same camp fires and struggled with the same dilemma—how much to resist and how much to adapt to ensure the survival of their people.⁶³

Charles Perkins, contributing to the bicentennial *Encyclopaedia of the Nation*, contrasted the political 'approaches' of Bennelong and Pemulwuy as a way of introducing a discussion of Aboriginal 'political objectives'. Not surprisingly, as a leader deeply involved in the politics of negotiation (Perkins was secretary of the federal Department of Aboriginal Affairs at the time), Perkins found Bennelong's diplomatic style of leadership more instructive. He found Bennelong leading 'a school of thought among the Eora people … that the British arrival was an important event from which both peoples had much to gain', and admired his 'statesmanship' and 'vision'. He characterised Pemulwuy's brand of violent resistance, along with submission, as a strategy of last resort. That the British had favoured Bennelong, and that he had gained considerable experience in the British way of life, was no cause for Aboriginal people to repudiate him in Perkins's view.⁶⁴ Perkins himself was one of those 'difficult young men with overseas experience' who influential policymakers like Stanner and Coombs, dedicated as they were in the 1960s to improving the lot of Aboriginal people in non-urban northern Australia, found it difficult to comprehend or categorise. Like Bennelong, Perkins was also no stranger to the charge that he had 'sold out'. In the 1980s, Noonuccal activist and poet Kath Walker exclaimed, 'public servant, oh yuck! … [they] buy you body and soul', citing Perkins as an example par excellence. Particularly in the late 1980s, following the thick tangle of backroom negotiations surrounding the Brisbane Commonwealth Games, and as Perkins faced charges of mismanagement of the Aboriginal Development Commission,⁶⁵ retrospective repudiation of Bennelong may have carried a sting for him, and for other Aboriginal people like him working 'from the inside'.

---

60   Willmot, *Pemulwuy,* 30, 54, 173, 219–20, 268–70.
61   Curthoys characterised a 'good' loser as being like the ANZACs. Curthoys, 'Mythologies', 23–25.
62   Willmot, *Pemulwuy,* 173–74, 192.
63   Ibid., 180–90; Willmot, 'Beyond Contact', 4–5.
64   Perkins, 'Political Objectives', 235.
65   Read, *Charles Perkins*, 149, 261–63, 330–37; Kath Walker, quoted in Mitchell, *The Matriarchs,* 207.

Alongside the interpretations offered by Perkins and Willmot, others continued to build on a view of Bennelong as a lost soul. Much loved non-Indigenous country singer and songwriter Ted Egan versified:

> I couldn't help thinking that Benelong
> Never again sang the eagle song
> For he seemed just like a man whose spirit left him.
>
> Doomed was he forever more
> He lost his way as he lost his law
> And the white sea eagle sings its song alone.[66]

At the beginning of the new millennium, histories popular and official, long and short, across traditional and new media, carried Egan's understanding forward. In a recent children's book, the sections narrating Bennelong's return from England are titled: 'A lonely man', 'Rejecting tribal law', and 'Drunkenness and death'.[67] In the Sydney Opera House's World Heritage Nomination in 2006, Bennelong was relegated to an extremely brief entry in an appendix, which concluded with the line: 'Bennelong dies in 1813, alienated from both Aboriginal and European cultures'.[68] Similarly, the Marrickville Council website described him as 'increasingly depressed, drunk, aggressive and vengeful' in the period leading up to his death.[69] In early 2009, Bennelong's entry in Wikipedia concluded that 'Bennelong quickly became alienated from his own people after [his] return' from England and claimed that he was 'marginalised and died in obscurity'.[70] Thomas Keneally, in the epilogue to his *Commonwealth of Thieves*, wrote that Bennelong 'found himself fully accepted neither by the new administration in Sydney Cove nor by his own people' and cited Bennelong's increasing fondness for alcohol.[71]

---

66  Egan, *The Aboriginals Songbook*, 36–37.
67  Sheppard, *The Life of Bennelong*, 26–27.
68  Nomination by the Government of Australia of the Sydney Opera House for Inscription on the World Heritage List 2006, prepared by the Australian Government and the New South Wales Government, Appendix 10D, p. 112, UNESCO World Heritage website, Sydney Opera House documents, accessed 18 July 2018, whc.unesco.org/en/list/166/documents/.
69  Marrickville Council, Cadigal Wangal, 'Bennelong', accessed 27 March 2012, www.cadigal wangal.org.au/MenulessPages/native_landuse_popup_bennelong.aspx?Id=74 (site discontinued).
70  'Bennelong', Wikipedia, updated 26 January 2009, accessed 20 February 2009, en.wikipedia. org/wiki/Bennelong. On 18–19 June 2010, I revised this entry, providing an account of Bennelong's latter years based on Keith Smith's research and removing unreferenced allusions to a 'tragic' end. I have monitored the entry since then, interested to observe whether Bennelong's tragedy might be reasserted by other editors. To 27 September 2011, although many minor changes have been made, this has not been the case.
71  Keneally, *Commonwealth of Thieves*, 446.

Increasingly, storytellers follow on from the stories of Bennelong's generation with an affirmation of a strong and ongoing Aboriginal presence in Sydney. Lucy Hughes Turnbull, in her 1999 'biography' of Sydney, found that 'there are descendants of the Dharruk and Dharrawhal living here today. Many of Sydney's Kooris can trace their ancestors back to the early colonial days'.[72] Hughes Turnbull did not believe Bennelong's legacy was entirely bleak; however, she found the story of his last years saturated with loss and failure. On his return from England, she noted that he 'moved uneasily between European and Aboriginal cultures, and neither considered him to be part of their group'. Further, he lost the affections of his wife and 'despite (or because of) his new-found "sophistication", he could not persuade any other women of the extent of his charms and so was lonely for the rest of his life'.[73]

In *Dancing with Strangers*, a widely read history book that was both celebrated and criticised for its re-readings of first-hand accounts, Inga Clendinnen made a close re-examination of the social, political and cultural exchange that occurred in the first years of the colony. In returning to colonial relationships, her project was to recover the fragile optimism of first contact, and to see whether there was any possibility beyond cross-cultural failure. She found in Bennelong a complex and intelligent mediator who nevertheless failed to bridge the cultural divide that defined the relationship between his people and the colonists. When Clendinnen's Bennelong returned from England, he was a virtual 'Englishman' who had 'decided to commit himself to the British account of things'; yet, he found his influence with the colonists far less potent, he experienced terrible luck with women and obliterated his disappointment with rum. Clendinnen concluded:

> Baneelon, with his anger and his anguish, simply drops from British notice. He did not die until 1813 … Over the last years of his life Baneelon abandoned the British in his heart, as they had long abandoned him in the world. At fifty he fumed his way to an outcast's grave. He should have died earlier, in the days of hope.[74]

---

72  Hughes Turnbull, *Sydney: Biography*, 54. See also Moorhouse's history, in which Bennelong similarly loses his self-respect and independence, and Moorhouse is then incensed by the injustice of Aboriginal deaths in police custody, partly through his conversations with Aboriginal people at The Block, Redfern. Moorhouse, *Sydney*, 47–51.
73  Hughes Turnbull, *Sydney: Biography*, 35–54.
74  Clendinnen, *Dancing with Strangers*, 265–67, 272.

## 4. BENNELONG'S RISE AND FALL

Clendinnen acknowledged that the last years of Bennelong's life are little known, but she was content to imply that they were characterised by smouldering anger and exile from both Aboriginal and European society. Her final sentence in the excerpt above was almost hyperbolic, and not so different from Eleanor Dark's dramatic curtain fall 65 years earlier.

Keith Smith concluded his 2001 biography as Bennelong sailed for England. His justification was that he saw Bennelong's latter years as discontinuous with the diplomat's life to that point:

> In this second part of his life, Bennelong was a changed man. He abandoned the white settlement, took to drink and was frequently wounded in payback battles ... That is another story.[75]

Smith did not want to write a tragedy and felt that curtailing his narrative was the only way to avoid it. However, he has since completed more extensive research on Bennelong's place in Eora kinship systems, and has reassessed the evidence for the latter part of Bennelong's life. In work published in 2006 and 2009, Smith refuted the claim that Bennelong lost respect in the eyes of his own people and the Europeans, referring to sources such as a letter from Henry Waterhouse to Phillip in 1795 mentioning that Bennelong had 'got his old wife' again, and the memoirs of Joseph Holt, who wrote of Bennelong as the leader of a large group of Aboriginal people in the Rydalmere area in about 1802. According to Smith, after his return from England, Bennelong reintegrated himself into Eora networks and patterns of life, which had changed with the presence of the colony.[76] Somewhat persuaded, Thomas Keneally offered a circumspect view of Bennelong in *Australians: Origins to Eureka*, asking readers to consider the truth of Bennelong's posthumous role as 'archetype of his people's tragedy'.[77] *The Sun Herald*, reporting on investigations surrounding the location of Bennelong's grave at Kissing Point on the Parramatta River in March 2011, created a redemption of sorts by narrating Bennelong's post-voyage 'exile', followed by a relocation to the northern bank of the river, where he became leader of a local clan.[78]

---

75  Smith, *Bennelong: The Coming*, viii.
76  Smith, *Wallumedegal: An Aboriginal History of Ryde*, 25–26. See also, Smith, 'Bennelong: Ambassador of the Eora Part II', 79–81; Smith, 'Bennelong among His People', 7–30.
77  Keneally, *Australians: Origins to Eureka*, 219.
78  Eamonn Duff, 'Found: Long-Lost Grave of Bennelong', *The Sun Herald*, 20 March 2011, 9.

Understanding Bennelong's place in Eora networks (rather than viewing him as a man acting on his own, only loosely moored to Eora ways of being and ready to drift towards the British) seems key to this more positive evaluation. As Isabel McBryde began to demonstrate from 1989, Bennelong's was a complex and ambiguous ambassadorship that must be understood in the context of contemporary Eora life and politics. McBryde placed Bennelong's relationship with Phillip among other cross-cultural relationships, and posited political motives for many of the puzzling exchanges in which Bennelong was involved. She examined his role as a key trader in the status-enhancing exchange of the curiosities of each culture, engaging in strenuous diplomatic work and, at times, holding the diplomatic advantage. As Smith was to do, she found that Bennelong's status remained high into the nineteenth century. Although his semiofficial role as mediator had waned, he continued to command attention from 'persons of the first respectability', and continued to play an important role in trade, social and ceremonial life, and in maintaining relationships between his Aboriginal community and the settlements at Sydney and Parramatta.[79] With a more integrated understanding of Bennelong, we might imagine his motives and self-conceptions quite differently. For example, Gerry Bostock has speculated that Bennelong, as an Eora man, may have remained captive in the settlement longer than he needed to in 1789 so that he could acquit the special responsibilities associated with that place because someone had 'to sing back the spirits of [the Gudjigal people] who died outside their country', even if he was not yet fully trained for the task.[80]

Smith's findings, which he has shared with local public audiences, and Keneally's changed assessment, perhaps indicate that fertile ground for a more sanguine view of Bennelong's final years now exists among middle-class Australian readers and history buffs. The play *I am Eora*, directed by Wesley Enoch, premiered at the Sydney Festival in 2012. Drawing on historiography that contrasts Bennelong and Pemulwuy, and reflecting on Bennelong's changing relevance to Aboriginal people, the play charts a rejection and re-acceptance of Bennelong, the 'interpreter', by Sydney's

---

79  McBryde recognised 'tragic aspects' in the lives of Bennelong and Bungaree, but did not find this the sum of their lives. McBryde, *Guests of the Governor*, 15, 21, 27–29, 51; McBryde, 'Barter ... Immediately Commenced', 255–60. Attenbrow also depicted Bennelong as an active participant in Eora life and the life of the colony, as one of those Eora people whose frequent and often frank communication with the British allowed her to reconstruct the life ways of Aboriginal Sydney. Attenbrow, *Sydney's Aboriginal Past*.
80  Bostock, 'Colebe', 613–18.

Aboriginal people. Bennelong appears near the beginning of the play as a character thoroughly at odds with his community and its project of cultural revival. However, later (commencing with a rendition of 'tooralai – ooralai – attity / Bound for Botany Bay'), Bennelong speaks as a wise old man who can remember the colony, the time before the colony, and the important stories of his country. He is interpreter, commentator and witness. Slowly, one by one, the other actors sit down to listen to him. When he dies at the conclusion of the play, the warrior Pemulwuy (or his returned spirit) is the reverent bearer of his body.[81]

Grace Karskens recently asserted that 'stories of Bennelong as the "first drunken Aborigine", shunned by women of both races, a man hopelessly and helplessly "caught in a void between two cultures" are myths'.[82] So we must ask, why has tragedy been such an appealing mode for biographers of Bennelong across half a century? My answer to this question is that Bennelong's tragedy seems to storytellers to be true: true to history, true to commonsense, true to human nature. Tragedy has given a comprehensible shape to Bennelong's story, and seems to make sense of the way in which the colonists' opinions of Bennelong changed over the years, the ambiguous clues to his own behaviour found in the primary sources, and the fragmentary records for his later years. Bennelong's cultural crisis and fall into despair and alienation also seems to reflect contemporary reality, and to explain how the present came to be. The tragic narrative maintains a mutually affirming relationship with a nest of notions about Aboriginal history and cross-cultural relations that have held continued claims to plausibility despite radical changes in the making of Australian history. So, while it can be shown that Bennelong's own life is not necessarily best represented by a tragic story, storytellers have found a powerful nexus of overlapping social, moral and narrative truths in his tragedy, that may shift over coming years, or may see Bennelong's tragedy continue to be retold into the future.

---

81  Bennelong is cast as 'interpreter' in the play, Pemulwuy as 'warrior' and Barrangaroo as 'nurturer'. Bennelong first takes the stage in an old suit, railing against a ceremony about to take place and the right of a young business-suited man to strip to his ceremonial painting. Enoch and Heiss, *I am Eora*.
82  Karskens, *The Colony*, 422–24.

# 5
# History, Tragedy and Truth in Bennelong's Story

Storytellers' insights into Bennelong's character and his relationships are made possible by the first-hand accounts of the First Fleet's commissioned diarists and letter writers. Together, the journal writers offer a lively and detailed coverage of Bennelong's relationship with the colony across the period 1789–92: his kidnap and residence at Government House, his behaviour when Phillip was speared at Manly, his aptitude in learning English language and manners, and what they learned from him about the life ways of the Eora people. In Hunter's published journal, Bennelong is an almost constant presence between September 1790, when he conversed with Phillip before Phillip was speared at Manly, and September 1791, when Bennelong attempted to arrange the birth of his child in the governor's residence.[1] The excitement of the diarists as they observed the Eora world, often through Bennelong, is palpable. For Tench in late 1790, 'our greatest source of entertainment now lay in cultivating the acquaintance of our new friends, the natives'.[2]

Twenty-three years later, *The Sydney Gazette* summed up his life:

> Of this veteran champion of the native tribe little favourable can be said … The principal officers of the government had for many years endeavoured, by the kindest of usage, to wean him from his original habits and draw him into a relish for civilised life; but every effort was in vain exerted

---

1 Hunter, *An Historical Journal*, 305–60.
2 Tench, *A Narrative of the Expedition*, 160.

and for the last few years he has been but little noticed. His propensity to drunkenness was inordinate; and when in that state he was insolent, menacing and overbearing. In fact, he was a thorough savage, not to be warped from the form and character that nature gave him by all the efforts that mankind could use.[3]

The diarists' close and often sympathetic reportage creates an illusion of completeness for the years that are easy to imagine as Bennelong's prime. By contrast, the sparseness of information for the last two decades of his life, along with *The Sydney Gazette*'s dire assessment, give the impression that he fell into an abyss after his return from England. In combination, these sources suggest a certain shape for Bennelong's story: a rise and fall. Many of Bennelong's storytellers have assimilated this pattern, rather than reflect upon it.

As Hayden White observed, it is easy for both historians and their readers to remain unaware of the narrative structure of a history, believing that its shape is simply the shape of the past itself. In White's analysis, all narrative histories within the Western tradition operate within literary modes, presenting and explaining the past to their readers using the storylines of tragedy, romance, satire and comedy. White perceived these storylines as indispensable (and also inescapable) for the historian in the task of forging a coherent story from the chaotic and incomplete evidence left behind by the past. He argued that any history thus has two interwoven levels of truth: 'correspondence' to the past and 'coherence'.[4] It is worth scrutinising Bennelong's stories from this point of view, to see whether we can distinguish between these two levels.

Accounts from Bennelong's own lifetime only show a rise and fall for Bennelong if they are interpreted uncritically. As Isabel McBryde pointed out, European attitudes towards Eora people changed as the settlement became more secure. By the time Bennelong returned from England, the two groups were no longer 'new friends'. In fact, in the late 1790s and early years of the new century, Aboriginal people of the Cumberland Plain and Hawkesbury River were in open conflict with the colonists.[5] We should be wary of adopting (as Brodsky did without question four decades ago) the frustration Collins expressed in 1798, protesting that Bennelong could have enjoyed a legitimate and comfortable place

---

3   *The Sydney Gazette*, 9 January 1813, 2.
4   White, *Tropics of Discourse*, 122–23, 128–29.
5   McBryde, *Guests of the Governor*, 27.

living with the governor into the nineteenth century, but threw this chance away.⁶ Yet, the bitterness lingers. Keith Willey made a revealing half circle of historical thinking in his 1979 book *When the Sky Fell Down*. He discussed 'the end of the Noble Savage', by which he meant the demise of Rousseau's ideal in the hearts and minds of the Sydney colonists. He found that Bennelong's 'rapid degeneration' contributed to this demise, but he did not come full circle to ask whether this ideological shift may, or may also, have shaped how the authors of our sources perceived or reported on Bennelong's behaviour.⁷ Inga Clendinnen similarly forgot to take out her Enlightenment gentleman's eyeglass when she saw Bennelong tragically 'reduced' as he gained a reputation as an 'irreconcilable savage'.⁸ In doing so, she confused an assessment of Bennelong's own life prospects (which were no doubt constricted and compromised in some ways) with the rapidly declining capacity of the British to imagine and relate to Eora people in any way other than to judge them as more or less successfully civilised.

The written sources produced inside the colony, no matter how sensitive or enlightened we might find some of the diarists, were centred in European thought articulated from the small fragments of empire at Sydney Cove or Parramatta. When the writers felt that Bennelong was drawing closer to them and their way of thinking, he appeared to be safe in the bosom of civilisation. When he appeared less often, and undressed, the colonists felt he was drifting away from what Tench described as 'the comforts of a civilised system', back to 'a precarious subsistence among wilds and precipices'.⁹ As Maria Monypenny demonstrated in the Tasmanian context, the ongoing use of this pseudo-geographic 'coming in' and 'going out' is part of the maintenance of a Eurocentric perspective.¹⁰ In the case of Bennelong's story, it forms the foundation for a perceived 'fall', or at least a sudden transition from fame to obscurity. For example, Manning Clark referred to Bennelong's increasingly frequent 'absences from the Governor's house' on his return from England. These absences signified 'presences' somewhere else, but they were not presences that Clark was interested in investigating. By contrast, interpreting some of the

---

6   'Instead of living peaceably and pleasantly at the governor's house, as he certainly might always have done, Ben-nil-long preferred the rude and dangerous society of his own countrymen.' Collins, *An Account of the English Colony*, 134.
7   Willey, *When the Sky Fell Down*, 128.
8   Clendinnen appearing in Nowra and Perkins, 'Episode 1: They Have Come to Stay'.
9   Tench, *A Narrative of the Expedition*, 108.
10  Monypenny, 'Going Out and Coming In', 73.

same sources differently, and with insights drawn from archaeology and anthropology, McBryde discerned a pattern in Bennelong's movements in and out of the settlement, which she described as 'independence'.[11]

Of course, many stories of Bennelong have no direct relationship with primary sources and first-hand accounts. They rely on other 'second order' storytellers for both information and its interpretation. Yet, whether a storyteller has returned to Tench and Collins themselves, 'the birth of a new version' of Bennelong's story does not occur in a vacuum. As Hayden White and Martin Jay argued, existing versions of stories, and points of consensus within a writing and reading community, exert considerable influence on the way stories are told; even before a storyteller begins a new version, some explanations seem logical and others outlandish.[12] Bennelong's story told as a tragedy, or a fall or failure, has a logical feel to it. For white Australian storytellers and audiences, it is specious, credible, fits into what we know of the world, and seems to help make sense of Australian history.

Tragedy arrived in New South Wales as part of the cultural baggage of the First Fleet; Watkin Tench reached for a line from Joseph Addison's well-known early eighteenth-century tragedy *Cato* to help express the gravity of the moment as the ships approached Botany Bay.[13] History has long sailed in the company of tragedy, and the two have met and mingled both in Bennelong's own story and in the larger cultural traditions that have helped to shape how we tell it. Among Europe's cultural elite, tragedy was considered to be at the apex of literary achievement during the nineteenth and early twentieth centuries. Animated discussions ensued about tragedy's relationship with history, and these trickled down to influence Australian historians. Manning Clark followed the epoch-making Leopold von Ranke in deriving the framework for his history from the genre of tragedy.[14] Bennelong's storytellers have called

---

11  Clark, *History of Australia*, 143; McBryde, 'Barter … Immediately Commenced', 238–77.
12  White, *Tropics of Discourse*, 128.
13  Tench, *A Narrative of the Expedition*, 37.
14  Hirst, *Sense and Nonsense*, 57–58; Curthoys and Docker, *Is History Fiction?*, 71–73, 86–87, 180. As Curthoys and Docker noted, whether or not Thucydides' *History of the Peloponnesian War* could be considered a tragedy, and where this placed history in relation to literature, was a matter of energetic debate in Europe in the early twentieth century. Clark employed a dramatic opposition of 'barbarism within (Aboriginal culture) and civilisation without' as the setting for his history.

on tragedy by reaching for themes, narrative devices, features of character and ideas about how tragedy feels that are recognisable as part of our contemporary culture.[15]

Stories of Aboriginal decline and death have formed a constant background for the retelling of Bennelong's story across the twentieth century. They are part of a grand narrative that gained momentum from the seventeenth century and consolidated into a 'discourse of the triumph of Saxondom over the whole globe' by the end of the nineteenth—the narrative of the inexorable extinction of primitive races.[16] In the late nineteenth century, such stories were often expressed in a regretful voice, evincing ambivalence about the success of the pioneers in the certainty that it was 'too late', or impossible, to make amends.[17] Histories of the early twentieth century expressed less regret, but no less certainty. A 1910 history of Australia proclaimed: 'it is possible to calculate with almost certainty a date on which "the last post" will be sounded over the Australian, as it has been over the Tasmanian aboriginal race'.[18] Although it was becoming patently clear in the postwar period that Aboriginal populations were maintaining themselves or, in fact, increasing, as Charles Duguid sought to bring to Australians' attention, the narratives of fatal impact continued.[19] In 1962, Manning Clark declaimed:

> When those aboriginal women uttered their horrid howl on first seeing the white man at Botany Bay in April 1770, that howl contained in it a prophecy of doom … For the culture, the way of life of the aborigine was doomed.[20]

As Grace Karskens observed, 'in settler history we seem to be searching constantly for beginnings … but in Aboriginal history of the colonial period so often the search is for endings'. This does not need to be so. In her recent history of Sydney, Karskens looked to a much longer Aboriginal story that is not one of failure or 'fatal impact', but of Aboriginal people responding to change. She asked: if the taken-for-granted failure of Bennelong is not true, is it perhaps necessary to rethink 'what happened

---

15   Particularly the ancient Greek mythic tragedies, which are constantly reinvented, and Shakespeare's works, which have featured on school curricula for generations and are performed by the John Bell Shakespeare Company to more than 80,000 Australian students each year. Christopher Bantick, 'Why Shakespeare Still has a Role in the Curriculum', *The Age*, 27 April 2014.
16   Brantlinger, *Dark Vanishings*, 1–10.
17   Foster, Nettelbeck and Hosking, *Fatal Collisions*, 26–28.
18   Spence and Fox, *Australia*, 142.
19   See Duguid, *No Dying Race*; Kerin, *Doctor Do Good?*
20   Clark, *History of Australia*, 110.

to Aboriginal people in early Sydney', or even across the continent, as a whole?[21] As the survival of Aboriginal people and cultures in south-eastern Australia has been gradually acknowledged over the past few decades, a number of histories have been written in which an Aboriginal post-invasion 'romance' is charted, deeply infused with pain and loss, but depicting cycles of renewal, survival and transformation, as well as defeat, dispossession and death. Heather Goodall's *Invasion to Embassy*, a history of Aboriginal people's fight for land over more than 200 years, could be interpreted this way.

However, when Bennelong's story re-awoke from mere chronicle to be re-examined as history in the mid-twentieth century, it was reborn into a reciprocally affirmative relationship with powerful narratives of fateful Aboriginal decline, death and extinction. Bennelong's tragedy gives this large-scale, impersonal movement of history a human face. Conversely, as a specific instance apparently supported by historical evidence, it contributes to the truth quotient of the larger tragedy. To white Tasmanians, Trucanini's death in 1876 and the display of her remains in the Tasmanian Museum from 1904 seemed to provide both proof of the extinction of Aboriginal Tasmanians and comforting evidence of a good reason for their extinction (i.e., their presumed place on the bottom rung of the human evolutionary ladder).[22] In a similar way, Bennelong's tragedy is often understood as the opening chapter of a more general Aboriginal tragedy, and has seemed to provide evidence that the decline and death of the Aboriginal race was unavoidable once Aboriginal people had come into contact with European culture.

Tragedy does not simply denote a fall; it is also a riff on inevitability. A characteristic dramatic strategy of the genre is to set up a pair of irreconcilable opposites, which, just by coming into contact with each other, lead to an inexorable unfolding of events.[23] Bennelong's tragedy is emphatically a cultural tragedy, played out on the beaches where Manning Clark's 'barbarism' meets 'civilisation'. In narratives of Saxon triumph, the momentum of the British Empire, and its history of progress, set those two cultural continents on a collision course. It is the necessity of this collision that Clark's Aboriginal women recognised in their instinctive, howling 'prophecy of doom'.[24] For nineteenth-century European thinkers,

---

21 Karskens, *The Colony*, 422–24.
22 Ryan, 'The Struggle for Trukanini', 159–61.
23 White, *Tropics of Discourse*, 128.
24 Clark, *History of Australia*, 3–4, 110.

'collision' itself became a favoured metaphor for explaining movements of people around the globe, and it has continued to appeal to storytellers attempting to characterise the colonisation of Australia.[25] N. J. B. Plomley imagined a 'culture clash' occurring with the colonisation of Tasmania, in which the 'weaker' Indigenous culture inevitably came off worse. Keith Smith followed suit in his 1992 biography of Bennelong's younger contemporary Bungaree, stating that 'when the two races met, a clash of cultures was inevitable'.[26] Bruce Elder, who gave a brief rendition of Bennelong's story as part of a larger Aboriginal tragedy published for the bicentenary, set up an Eden-like Aboriginal society in opposition to the invading British:

> The fatal moment when Phillip stepped ashore was the moment when the conflict began. There was no spear thrown; no musket fired. But the course of events was set upon its inexorable path. The two cultures were so different … There was no possibility of compromise. One side respected the land; one side exploited the land. One side was basically peaceful and benign; the other was essentially sadistic and autocratic. One sought harmony; the other was driven by aggression and competitiveness.[27]

Eden was about to collide with civilisation and its power to corrupt. This powerful and indifferent force, of two cultures colliding like tectonic plates, is indeed one that could easily crush anyone standing near the edge. As it was economically put on the 'Creative Spirits' website, 'Bennelong got caught between the two worlds and he died as a lonely alcoholic with a broken spirit in 1813'.[28]

Eleanor Dark located the destructive force of colonisation within the souls of her Aboriginal characters. They are a timeless people confronting change that comes upon them like a spiritual poison, creating a 'division in their own hearts'. One of her Elders, Tirrawuul, dies because he cannot 'endure even the first faint forewarning shadow of change' to a life governed by a 'faith which never had been challenged'. She marked Bennelong, the mediator, as a man in particular danger. His fellow captive, Colbee, resolved not to engage with the captors beyond a watchful compliance and managed to remain aloof. Colbee thus remained 'whole' while Bennelong

---

25  Brantlinger, *Dark Vanishings*, 173–219.
26  Plomley, 'Book Review', 50–52; Smith, *King Bungaree*, 20.
27  Elder, *Blood on the Wattle*, 11.
28  Jens-Uwe Korff, 'Bennelong Point', Creative Spirits, accessed 16 March 2009, www.creativespirits. info/oznsw/sydney/sitescbd/operahouse.html (site discontinued). The updated site both reiterates this notion, and challenges it as 'myth', citing Keith Vincent Smith's work. See www.creativespirits.info/ australia/new-south-wales/sydney/bennelong-point-opera-house, accessed 8 July 2018.

was torn by an internal 'strife', as part of him was drawn towards the white men and the possibility of becoming like them.[29] Richard Sadleir, writing in the 1880s, had cause to examine Bennelong's inner life for a different reason. He was convinced that only religion could bring Aboriginal people into 'British' life, and felt the British were culpable for arriving in New South Wales with so little religious supervision. Bennelong's story illustrated the inevitable results of this secular approach; he perished 'a drunken savage, after all the advantages he had had of visiting England, and living at the Governor's house … We have here the failure of mere civilisation which produces only outward effects. Religion alone can reach the heart'. The problem was that Bennelong's inner self had not been transformed in the right way through his contact with the British. Sadleir declared that the 'reckless and degraded class of men' that first colonised New South Wales were not destined to 'elevate or raise' the natives, but rather to 'depress and vitiate, and ultimately to destroy them'.[30] He stopped short of finding Bennelong's own heart corrupted (perhaps to keep open the possibility of redeeming Aboriginal people on the whole via conversion). However, in using the verb 'vitiate'—to corrupt, to spoil, to make impure—he gestured towards the diagnosis that would become most prominent in stories of Bennelong's fall over the past four decades: a division or sickness in his own soul. Bennelong's tragedy emerged as storytellers began to engage with the sticky soft tissue of cross-cultural contact and attempt to make sense of Bennelong's inner life once more in the mid-twentieth century.

Fascination with self-destructive cultural transgressions has deeply penetrated the Western literary and popular imagination. The archetype is, perhaps, Joseph Conrad's character Kurtz in his 1899 novella *Heart of Darkness*. Kurtz's rule over his African workers transcends duty and comes to dominate his own identity; he is reshaped in their cultural image. Kurtz loses his senses and his colleagues are at once fascinated and appalled.[31] A not dissimilar imaginary drives Peter Goldsworthy's 2003 novel *Three Dog Night*, in which grown-up Adelaide private school boy, Felix, goes to the 'Centre' as a doctor and returns initiated as a Warlpiri man. As one review put it: 'Felix has long moved between mainstream and black society—gone to drink, chain-smoking and now, as we learn, terminal

---

29   Dark, *The Timeless Land*, 177, 179–80, 264–65. See also Clendinnen, *Dancing With Strangers*, 268.
30   Sadleir, *Aborigines of Australia*, 22–25. Sadleir recognised that the settlement of the Sydney region had deprived Aboriginal people of their food resources.
31   Conrad, *The Heart of Darkness*.

cancer'.³² His cultural crossing and illness are not explicitly causally related; yet, the two travel hand in hand in the book, and the unpredictable 'dark' side of Felix is never dissociated from his involvement in Warlpiri culture. Similarly, poet and historian Barry Hill penned an essay entitled 'Crossing Cultures' in 2003 in which linguist T. G. H. Strehlow was cast as an 'exemplary case of successful crossing', as he experienced an intense and long-term immersion in Aboriginal culture. At the same time, Strehlow:

> In agony over his internal contradictions, as *the* one who possessed the truth about Aranda culture, dropped dead in a seizure of recriminations … From beginning to end you could say he was doom-laden.³³

In mid-twentieth century anthropological thinking, the notion that Aboriginal culture could not survive the processes of transculturation that had taken place across south-eastern Australia was pervasive. Whereas the imagined 'going native' of European individuals led to madness or death, Aboriginal 'cultural crossing' seemed to lead to the extinction of a people. Stanner, as we have seen, understood Bennelong to be at the head of a chain reaction of dependency on Europeans that he felt had proceeded with settlement, or even ahead of it.³⁴ For Stanner, Clark, Mulvaney and others, Bennelong's story showed what would happen to Aboriginal people when exposed to 'civilisation', recycling, with different inflections, the nineteenth-century theory of degeneration. Though this theory was well and truly defunct in scientific terms by the mid-twentieth century, it had an ongoing life into the postwar world through eugenics, and it resonated with archaeological and anthropological scholarship, particularly through the 1970s. The theory is based in a neo-Lamarckian notion that acquired characteristics, 'both favourable and unfavourable, could alter human heredity and be transmitted down the family line'. It was up to a species to make itself 'fit', and a race could actually fall downwards on the evolutionary ladder through unhealthy living.³⁵

---

32  Goldsworthy, *Three Dog Night*; Robin Osbourne, 'Book Review–Three Dog Night and Curious Incident of the Dog in the Night Time', Northern Rivers General Practice Network, accessed 28 January 2008, www.nrdgp.org.au/columns/bookreviews/bookreview3491.html+Three+Dog+Night&hl=en&ct=clnk&cd=3&gl=au (site discontinued). The book has received considerable interest in medical circles due to Goldworthy's previous medical career and the book's subject.
33  Hill, 'Crossing Cultures', 117.
34  Stanner, 'The History of Indifference', 19–20.
35  Stern, *Eugenic Nation*, 14–15. According to Marcia Langton, traces of eugenicist ideas remain in both popular thought and public policy through the concept of the 'drunken Aborigine', bolstered by a 'once respectable' theory that Aboriginal people have a genetic trait making them peculiarly susceptible to alcohol, and a converse pride in the superior capacity of white men to hold their drink. Langton, 'Rum, Seduction and Death', 198–99.

As an anthropologist and policymaker, Stanner championed a view of contemporary Aboriginal communities as dynamic entities, engaged in a process of negotiation with Western technologies, laws and economies within their own metaphysical frameworks. Yet, as Clendinnen noted, he also had a strong emotional and aesthetic attachment to an 'unstained vision of the physical hardihood, intellectual sophistication, and spiritual exuberance of the "Traditional Aborigine"'. He repudiated the flexibility and ingenuity of the astute political operator, who, like Bennelong, he felt was 'an arch-manipulator, with wit and charm but no principles'. Although Stanner may often have used the notion of 'dependency' in a merely technical way, his association of the process with the 'turncoat' and 'trickster' Bennelong suggests a kind of moral alarm.[36] In his telling, Bennelong was responsible for leading Aboriginal people into a servile, imitative state, which was deliberately dissociated from Stanner's metaphysically independent Aboriginal communities. Bennelong's tragic fall was to be an opening chapter in a story of 'race suicide' or, in its new incarnation, the inexorable social process of cultural suicide.[37] While the ironies of Stanner's views were soon pointed out, it has taken several decades of dedicated work to dismantle the valorisation of an 'authentic' and remote Aboriginality, idealised in anthropological circles so as to be remote from anywhere the anthropologist might be. The view of Aboriginal people as rigidly 'tradition-bound' and, thus, highly vulnerable to change, has very gradually given way to a recognition that the strength of Aboriginal cultures may be in their very flexibility.[38]

Even now, Bennelong's adaptability seems to offend a deep-seated notion of cultural purity within the Western storyteller. His ambiguous flirtation with gentlemen's dress, ingestion of European fare, and willing pastiche of manners and languages, seems to infringe cultural 'cleanliness' and, thus, to invite danger not only to himself, but also to Aboriginal people in general. Following Mary Douglas's theorisation of cultural purity and pollution, Bennelong's ingestion of alcohol sees him absorbed into the British cultural and political body, and signals the contamination of the

---

36  As Alexandra Stern noted, degeneration was a concept 'imbued with both scientific and moral meaning'. Stern, *Eugenic Nation*, 13. Clendinnen, 'The Power to Frustrate', 419, 429–30; Stanner, 'Durmugam, a Nangiomeri' (1959), quoted in Clendinnen, 'The Power to Frustrate', 424.
37  Alarm about 'race suicide' swept across Theodore Roosevelt's America on the back of the notion of degeneration. Stern, *Eugenic Nation*, 13. Interestingly, Clendinnen described Bennelong's 'performance' of the irreconcilable savage as 'suicidal'. Clendinnen, *Dancing with Strangers*, 277.
38  In 1980, Diane Barwick noted the persisting preference for fighters over negotiators in revisionist accounts of Aboriginal history. See Veracini, 'A Prehistory of Australia's History Wars', 43–47, 451–52; Macdonald, 'Does "Culture" Have "History"?', 185.

Aboriginal body via Bennelong's mouth.[39] Echoing Dark, Clendinnen argued that Colbee had negotiated relations with the British with more dignity and less risk than Bennelong. She attributed Colbee's success, in part, to his maintenance of his 'wholeness', claiming that 'Colbee kept a sure footing in both camps, perhaps because he was never tempted to make any accommodation to British values, but remained always a tribal man'.[40] Clendinnen's comparison may be a valid historical one; however, it is interesting that she associated integrity with aloofness, and strength with perceived authenticity, just as Stanner had done, according to her, in his unguarded moments.

Bennelong has been, and continues to be, imagined as a kind of cultural 'half-caste', someone embodying the worst of both races and, as Henry Reynolds argued, 'commonly assumed to be morally and physically defective, unpredictable, unstable and degenerate'.[41] Plomley's 1970s account of the social place of the 'hybrid' mirrors Bennelong's imagined exile, belonging 'to neither race (shunned by both), and lacking a racial background they have no history'.[42] Bernard Smith, in his Boyer Lectures of 1980, characterised Bennelong as a man who had tried to function on both sides of a cultural divide—a 'game' that has 'always been an emotionally difficult one to play, its benefits precarious. Most became alcoholics'. Smith accorded Bennelong a legacy, passed down through a line of 'fool kings' and 'clowns' to, among others, Albert Namatjira:

> Life between the two cultures has always been fraught with these terrible tensions. Take the case of Namatjira … His tragic end is well known. In sharing liquor to which he was legally entitled with others of his tribe who were not, he was caught between the laws and customs of two societies. His trial and death shortly afterwards are now a part of the history of both cultures.[43]

Like Bennelong's, Namatjira's was a life contaminated by alcohol and overstretched to breaking point by the embrace of two worlds. Smith argued that, unlike heroic resistance leaders such as Pemulwuy and

---

39  Mary Douglas has explored the dyad of purity and pollution, a ubiquitous human preoccupation with physical and social 'cleanliness', which takes quite different forms for different peoples, but universally implies a danger in departing from purity, and associates pollution with weakness. The body of the individual can form a microcosm for the body politic. Douglas, *Purity and Danger*, 4–5, 142.
40  Clendinnen, *Dancing with Strangers*, 268.
41  Reynolds, *Nowhere People*, 3–5.
42  N. J. B. Plomley, quoted in Anderson, 'Black Bit, White Bit', 46.
43  Smith, 'The Spectre of Truganini', 37–39.

Yagan, these 'Quislings' or 'Jacky Jackies' have 'always been regarded by Aborigines with suspicion'. Not long after Namatjira's death in 1959 (and perhaps even during his lifetime), an identification with Bennelong was made.[44] The strains placed on each man as a colonised person become super-historical via such comparisons; in Smith's account, Bennelong and Namatjira succumb to an internal division and weakness that has 'always been' (as he insists through repetition). Finding this motif of internal Indigenous division a constant refrain within the discipline of anthropology, Ian Anderson replied that 'personhood is had through coherent experience … The separation of black bit, white bit is a denial of humanity'.[45]

As Mary Douglas suggested, the belief that pollution weakens is closely followed by a suspicion that only those who are weak or careless would fail to resist pollution.[46] J. J. Healy, writing for a popular audience in 1977, employed an excess of reflexive language to illustrate his conviction that Aboriginal people could be held responsible for their own tumbling descent, finding 'continuity between Bennelong and those Aborigines who would speed the dissolution of their own societies by a self-generated fascination with the artefacts of European society'.[47] Over the past 20 or so years, the use of Bennelong's story to imply that Aboriginal people's 'problems' are self-inflicted has become less explicit. However, the ongoing narration of Bennelong's story as a cultural and an alcoholic tragedy carries a persistent implication that transculturation is analogous to a shameful cultural addiction. The Barani Indigenous History pages of the City of Sydney Council website acknowledge Bennelong's importance at the same time as they disown his adoption of 'European dress and ways': 'While Bennelong suffered from the worst aspects of enculturation, he also represents those who tried to change the behaviour of Europeans on Aboriginal lands'.[48] It is as if a cleansing of his memory is required. The anthropologist's, and now the historian's, ongoing desire to escape

---

44   Ibid., 37. In 1962, Bill Beatty suggested that 'there are certain aspects in Bennelong's story that seem to find sympathetic echo in the case of … the late Albert Namatjira, torn between his tribal laws in Central Australia and the existing laws of the white man'. Beatty, *Early Australia,* 171.
45   Anderson, 'Black Bit, White Bit', 51.
46   Douglas, *Purity and Danger*, 4–5, 142.
47   Healy, 'A Most Tragic Theme', 32. Cowlishaw has shown that when the concept of race was no longer ostensibly in currency in the 1960s and 1970s, and the 'blood' of a person could no longer provide a valid indicator of their allegiance, cultural practices and even accoutrements readily became essentialised to provide the same kind of categorising information. Cowlishaw, quoted in Byrne, 'Deep Nation', 91.
48   Heiss, 'Barani: Sydney's Aboriginal History'.

the 'rotted frontier' and to find 'the unspotted savage' is, of course, much more than incidentally related to assimilation, which, in the immediate postwar decades, declared tribal life akin to an addiction that must be given up for a good, clean, modern life.[49]

Alcohol is a key ingredient in the story of Bennelong's failure. His twentieth-century biographers have reached for the bottle without hesitation, finding either that Bennelong drank 'to ease the pain of loneliness and confusion', or that it was alcohol itself that precipitated his alienation (a foreboding musical squall broke out as Bennelong took his first draught in a recent play).[50] Yet, alcohol is by no means a historiographically neutral substance. The first-hand accounts depict Bennelong engaging in both 'good' and 'bad' drinking, with Tench's admiring comment that he could hold his grog like any gentleman contrasting with the vulgar 'propensity to drunkenness' cited by the report of his death in *The Sydney Gazette*.[51] It is true that these two comments occur at opposite ends of Bennelong's association with the British. However, they are also thoroughly bound up with ideas surrounding social class and alcohol at a time when, as Stephen Garton argued, the British began to wrest local Aboriginal peoples' wealth from them and attempt to fit them into their allotted place in colonial society and economy—right at the bottom.[52] At first, Bennelong drank in the governor's dining room, the officers using wine to initiate him into 'civilised' company; by such means, the officers may have hoped to bring Bennelong into a kind of gentlemen's agreement about his role in the spread of civilisation. For his part, Bennelong seems to have been alive to the ritual significance of the consumption of wine as part of the sharing of elite male goodwill, as he demonstrated when he accepted Governor Phillip's offer of wine at the whale feast at Manly and proceeded to toast 'the King'. When Bennelong ceased to drink exclusively with the officers, their interpretation of his drinking became more closely aligned with their attitude towards the lower classes, which they disparaged for taking 'unruly' pleasure in bloodsports and drinking to excess in public.[53]

---

49  Clendinnen, 'The Power to Frustrate', 415; Haebich, 'Imagining Assimilation', 66–67.
50  Sheppard, *The Life of Bennelong*, 27; Tweg, 'Dream On', 50. Brodsky's Bennelong is also explicitly doomed from his first taste of alcohol. Brodsky, *Bennelong Profile*, 27.
51  Tench, *A Narrative of the Expedition*, 117–18; *The Sydney Gazette*, 9 January 1813, 2.
52  Garton, *Out of Luck*, 9–12, 15, 19–20, 36. See also Reynolds, 'Aborigines and European Social Hierarchy', 124–33. Reynolds presented a convincing case that nineteenth-century thinkers sought to integrate Aborigines into colonial society as landless labourers.
53  McIntyre, 'Bannelong Sat Down to Dinner', 39.6–39.10; Karskens, *The Colony*, 128.

The symbolic valency of alcohol does not diminish as we approach the present. Postwar renditions of Bennelong's story coincided with an era of strong temperance activity, reflecting theories of predisposition and approaches to alcohol abuse from medical and scientific perspectives that gained momentum from the 1890s.[54] The social understandings surrounding alcohol abuse in contemporary Australian society are so rich and various that there is room in Bennelong's story for everything from pity, as in Melinda Hinkson's 'lonely alcoholic with a broken spirit', to smutty humour, as in Keith Willey's comment that 'the nature of [Bennelong's] association with the brewer, James Squire—apart from a notable liking for his product—is not known'.[55] In the 1980s, John Mulvaney found that Bennelong's drinking reflected a lack of steadiness of character and an inability to discriminate between good and bad parts of British culture. He contrasted the way in which Arabanoo, while he savoured bread and tea, 'resisted alcoholic drinks with "disgust and abhorrence", according to the approving Tench, but his successor, Bennelong, succumbed to grog'. Mulvaney, too, approved of Arabanoo ('his conduct was something [that] modern Aboriginal people can honour'), whereas Bennelong's willingness to partake of alcohol was evidence of a lack of similar moral fibre.[56] In making this comparison, Mulvaney projected eighteenth-century ideas of class-differentiated morality onto Aboriginal men trying alcohol for the first time; in doing so, he found a readily comprehending audience in the present.

As Marcia Langton has demonstrated, alcohol has long played a part in popular and official representations of Aboriginal communities. Langton perceived Bennelong as the first 'drunken Aborigine', transformed by the alcohol that was pressed on him by the colonists, and then depicted as a 'degenerate native' lacking the restraint and dignity necessary for civilisation. She argued that, across the centuries since Bennelong's

---

54  Garton, *Medicine and Madness*, 56–57; Garton, *Out of Luck*, 104. An article about the residential rehabilitation program tailored to Aboriginal needs at Bennelong's Haven uses the language of 'habit' and 'addiction' in telling Bennelong's story. See Miller, 'A Haven for Alcoholics', 602–05.
55  Hinkson, 'Exploring Aboriginal Sites in Sydney', 65; Willey, *When the Sky Fell Down*, 146.
56  Mulvaney, *A Good Foundation*, 13. Clendinnen wrote: 'In those first encounters on the beach most Australians had shunned the wine or rum pressed on them—except for Baneelon. Restless for glory in this as in so much else, he was soon quaffing wine with all the flourishes with which the white gentlemen surrounded it'. The implication is that Bennelong's drinking was power hungry and immoderate. Clendinnen, *Dancing with Strangers*, 275. *The Sydney Gazette* of the first decade of the nineteenth century contains much correspondence on the unfortunate way in which Aboriginal people had picked up the bad language of rough London from the convicts, and how difficult it was to steer them towards good manners. See Garton, *Medicine and Madness*, 56–57.

lifetime, the image of the 'drunken Aborigine' has sustained its own momentum.[57] I agree that the association of Bennelong's fall and disgrace with alcohol has helped to sustain this story of tragedy across the latter part of the twentieth century and into the twenty-first. This story has survived because it seems to be true. We 'know' that alcohol can be addictive and that alcohol abuse can result in the breakdown of a person's relationships as they become aggressive or morose, unreliable and incompetent; thus, Bennelong's tragedy is plausible. Ideas about alcohol have undoubtedly changed over the past 200 years; however, in application to Bennelong, they translate readily. Alcohol abuse has maintained a conceptual association with the disadvantaged and Aboriginal people have remained marginalised. Research and legal processes continue to find alcohol a factor in violence occurring in Aboriginal communities at the same time as political grandstanding takes advantage of public opinion on the matter; for example, Tony Abbott proposed a 'crackdown on alcohol abuse in Aboriginal communities' in February 2010 as he sought election as leader of the opposition.[58] Thus, Bennelong's alcohol-fuelled tragedy is malleable, its truth continually and continuously reflected in the existing social order.[59]

The First Fleet diarists were keenly attentive to the responses of Aboriginal people to English food and drink, and clothing and grooming practices; Tench reported with great interest meetings at which Eora men, including Bennelong, submitted to a shave by means of a cutthroat razor.[60] As a longed-for ambassador for the British, Bennelong's receptiveness to the appurtenances of gentlemanly culture, and his aptitude for assimilating British language and etiquette, certainly excited the First Fleet diarists. Yet, Tench observed that Bennelong, coming and going from the settlement in late 1790, sometimes wore the clothes he had been given and sometimes carried them in a bag around his neck.[61] It appears that Bennelong dressed when it suited him. This left the colonists with an equivocal understanding of his place in the settlement.[62] Later storytellers

---

57   Langton, 'Rum, Seduction and Death', 195–206.
58   *The Sydney Morning Herald*, 25 February 2010, 1. See also, 'Alcohol "Primary Cause" of Aboriginal Violence', *The Sydney Morning Herald*, 9 April 2010, 7; 'Call for More Alcohol Rules to Cut Aboriginal Violence', *The Sydney Morning Herald*, 25 February 2009, 3.
59   Spillman, 'When Do Collective Memories Last?', 451.
60   Tench, *A Narrative of the Expedition*, 134–38, 142–43.
61   Ibid., 108.
62   McBryde noted Hunter's musings about whether Bennelong had perhaps simply lost the clothes that he had been given. McBryde, 'Barter … Immediately Commenced', 253.

have been much less willing to be equivocal. Few of Bennelong's modern biographers have been able to imagine him moving between the colony and Aboriginal life in a sustainable way. Uneasy when Bennelong appears to be 'in limbo between two societies', they have felt the need to push him one way or the other.[63] A 1970 children's book found that Bennelong's period of captivity transformed him. He happily adopted English dress, food and the 'easy' life, and 'liked standing in the sunlight and looking at his shadow. His shadow was no longer that of Bennelong of the Cadigals. It was the shadow of a white man'.[64] Conversely, 'Swimming Monkey', a contributor to the internet forum Everything2, used Bennelong's state of undress in his later years to evoke his despondency and disgrace:

> As the years went by his drinking became progressively heavier and he ceased to trouble himself with dressing in the gentlemanly finery he had been so fond of earlier, instead becoming contented with slinking about in dishevelled [sic] rags.[65]

According to Simon Schama, to honour the 'obligations of tragedy … we must proceed until all is known; a verdict declared; a sacrifice made ready; an atonement decreed'.[66] Once dressed, the tragic Bennelong cannot again be undressed without being naked. As Karskens observed, Europeans have been disconcerted by Aboriginal people in hybrid dress, equating part-European dress with indignity, immodesty and poverty, rather than cultural borrowing, innovation, friendship, trade and rivalry.[67]

Having once tasted alcohol, Bennelong was no longer innocent of the continuum between drunkenness and sobriety, and, upon reaching the peak of his career, storytellers have been impatient to get rid of him. Clendinnen was not alone in feeling that Bennelong 'should have died earlier'. Manning Clark disposed of him 'headlong', as we have seen, and Brodsky charted a 'downward rush [that] could not be halted'.[68] A twenty–first century biographer made an arithmetic mistake, writing 'only eight years after [Bennelong's return from England], he died an

---

63   Jill Sykes, 'Bennelong Makes a Point', *The Sydney Morning Herald*, 8 October 1988, Arts, 81.
64   Endeavour Reading Programme, *Bennelong*, 44. Dark said something only slightly different, but with quite a different meaning—that, when dressed, Bennelong's shadow was the 'same as the shadow of a white man'. Dark, *The Timeless Land*, 264–65.
65   Swimming Monkey, 'Bennelong', Everything2, 19 December 2007, accessed 17 March 2009, www.everything2.com/index.pl?node_id=1922328.
66   Schama, *Dead Certainties*, 262.
67   Karskens, 'Red Coat, Blue Jacket', 8–16, 29–31.
68   Brodsky, *Bennelong Profile*, 78.

alcoholic', robbing him of a decade of life between 1795 and 1813. This error of subtraction is part of a systematic 'misremembering' of Bennelong's latter years. As Karskens observed, storytellers have wilfully overlooked that 'Bennelong got his life back together' after facing an initial series of reversals on his return from England.[69] One of the ongoing attractions of the tragic mode is surely that it makes the evidence cohere into a compelling story, in which there is only one reversal of fortune for Bennelong, leading directly to his death. Significantly, an Aboriginal retelling of Bennelong's story provides a rare exception; a play produced by Koories in Theatre in 1995 put forward a positive metaphor for Bennelong's 'in-between' status—the platypus, an animal with a 'multifaceted nature' that must find a niche for itself in a new world.[70]

The *Bringing Them Home* report found that many stolen generations survivors have experienced feelings of not belonging in either 'world'. One contributor testified:

> Most of us girls were thinking white in the head but were feeling black inside. We weren't black or white. We were a very lonely, lost and sad displaced group of people. We were taught to think and act like a white person, but we didn't know how to think and act like an Aboriginal. We didn't know anything about our culture.
>
> We were completely brainwashed to think only like a white person. When they went to mix in white society, they found they were not accepted [because] they were Aboriginal. When they went and mixed with Aborigines, some found they couldn't identify with them either, because they had too much white ways in them. So that they were neither black nor white. They were simply a lost generation of children. I know. I was one of them.[71]

It is clear that the idea of navigating 'two worlds' has relevance to Aboriginal people facing the continuing implications of colonisation. It is possible that some of Bennelong's recent biographers have projected these experiences back onto Bennelong (and integrated them into his tragedy) after having witnessed these feelings of alienation through survivors' testimonies. They may have been encouraged by connections drawn in public history-making, such as the 1998 exhibition about the

---

69   Flood, *The Original Australians*, 42. On 'misremembering' see Portelli, 'The Massacre', 29–41; Karskens, *The Colony*, 422.
70   Koories in Theatre, 'Moobbajia: Speak an Unknown Language'.
71   Human Rights and Equal Opportunity Commission (HREOC), *Bringing Them Home*, 152.

stolen generations held at Government House titled 'In the Interest of Bennelong'.[72] The 'National Inquiry into the Separation of Aboriginal and Torres Strait Islander Children from Their Families' found that these self-understandings were nurtured by systems of removal, punishment, education and labour that were 'administered in such a way as would directly cause feelings of alienation'. Interestingly, these experiences are described as 'tragic' only a handful of times in the report, mostly in the submissions of health professionals and legal or government organisations, rather than by Aboriginal people talking about their own experiences.[73] While tragedy is an important part of Western/European culture in Australia (many aspects of which are part of the cultural vocabulary of Aboriginal people today), tragedy did not figure strongly in how Aboriginal people articulated their loss, pain, shame and displacement in the *Bringing Them Home* report. The genre's links with fate and inevitability were, perhaps, not helpful in articulating these experiences.

Instead of leading to a tragic end, Bennelong's negotiation of the cultural tensions of a colonised life can provide a reassuring example for Aboriginal people maintaining connections and cultural integrity.[74] A contributor to the *First Australians* guestbook on the Special Broadcasting Service (SBS) website who introduced herself as a Wardandi Bibbulmun woman drew a very different relationship between Bennelong's actions and his Aboriginality than Stanner and Smith:

---

72 Stephens, 'Bennelong, the First of the Stolen', 6.

73 HREOC, *Bringing Them Home*, 204. The words 'tragic', 'tragedy' and 'tragically' occur only 11 times in the 500 page report. The authors of the report described cases in which reunion was impossible as 'tragic'. HREOC, *Bringing Them Home*, 235. Health professionals and legal or government organisations described the effects of removal on stolen generations survivors and their families, or the overall system and its intentions, as 'tragic', in the sense of being deeply sad and having caused profound and sustained loss and damage. HREOC, *Bringing Them Home*, 180, 197, 286, 363, 425, 435. One stolen generations survivor cited her loving foster father explaining the 'tragedy' that her natural father must have suffered in losing his daughter, and another talked of the holistic healing necessary for recovery of body and spirit from 'all of our past pains, traumas and tragedies'. HREOC, *Bringing Them Home*, 170, 399.

74 Bangarra Dance Theatre's production 'Bennelong', which premiered at the Sydney Opera House in June 2017, looked to Bennelong as a man who had struggled with two worlds. 'Bennelong is in all of us, as we navigate the ancient and modern elements of our lives', said the company's artistic director, Stephen Page, in the production's program; yet, the production powerfully and unambiguously depicted Bennelong's exile right at the point at which his struggle with those contradictions peaked on his return from England. A precipitous end came to the resilient, intelligent and creative character we had come to know through the dancing of Beau Dean Riley Smith, as he was suddenly enclosed in a small, reflective cell (the panels placed by the other dancers), drunk and irrecoverable. See Clarissa Sebag-Montefiore, 'Bangarra's Bennelong Review—Aboriginal Warrior's Conflict Portrayed in Dramatic Suspense', *The Guardian*, Australian edition, 1 July 2017; Fullagar, 'The Story of Bennelong is Potent and Evocative—but it is Being Contested', *The Guardian*, Australian edition, 8 July 2017.

> Bennelong was an inspiration, a man who spoke the wadjela ways, but whose heart belonged to his people. We have all learnt to walk the wadjela walk, but remain embedded in our culture.[75]

This storyteller did not see Bennelong's story as determinative or predictive of the life patterns of Aboriginal people. Rather, she saw him as an ancestor who might provide an example of strength for people facing similar challenges in the present. Likewise, Kamilaroi Ngunnawal woman Pamela Young, working on a recent oral history book, looked to Bennelong to connect her writing practice with the 'ancient oral wellspring [that] is the source of wellbeing' for Aboriginal orators. Bennelong, having written the first letter by an Aboriginal person, had connected these 'two worlds', embodying the strength of Aboriginal tradition in a form recognisable to colonists, saying, in effect, 'I can play your game mate, I can write'.[76] Young did not require Bennelong to form a permanent and singular crossing between two cultural monoliths, or to stop them from colliding. Instead, she found that he began a tradition that she could draw on in her own work. Bennelong's significance as a tragic figure within a larger Aboriginal tragedy, which has seemed so pertinent to non-Indigenous Australians, is, perhaps, not as relevant to Aboriginal people.

Tragedy is a literary and dramatic form with a long history of practice and philosophy, in which some of the most complex and troubling characters of Western cultural tradition have been created. Although a few of Bennelong's biographies have approached full-scale dramatic treatments, Dark's and Brodsky's among them, most of the 'biographies' considered here are pocket-sized sketches. An eclectic local production, tracing Aboriginal history from the Dreaming to the present, encapsulated Bennelong's life thus:

> He was befriended and taken to England by Captain Arthur Phillip; treated as a curiosity; learned English quickly; attempted to reconcile the English and the Eora in the early days; became a victim of alcoholism; tragic life story—wafting from the white world to the black. He was from the Cadigal Clan.[77]

---

75 'Trish Hill-Wall', 21 October 2008, SBS First Australians, Your Comments, accessed 20 March 2009, www.sbs.com.au/firstaustralians/.
76 Carrington and Young, *Aboriginal Heritage and Wellbeing*, 35.
77 Ellis, *Aboriginal Australians*, 113.

This summation of Bennelong's life is cursory, by no means masterfully written, and probably has no direct relationship with the primary sources. Yet, it manages to convey a powerful impression. The adjective 'tragic' functions as a flag; it signals agreement with other accounts of Bennelong's pitiable failure, recruits the reader's prior knowledge of this failure and gives the tragic wheel another spin. Even if the reader has no prior knowledge of Bennelong, the compact evocations of his alcoholism and unsuccessful attempt to reconcile 'two worlds' provides ample explanation of an inevitable and partly self-destructive course towards alienation and despair. The equally economical fall of Bennelong in Andrew and Nancy Learmonths's *Encyclopaedia of Australia* suggests that this understanding was already well established by the late 1960s:

> One of two Aborigines captured, befriended and trained by Phillip who took them to London … Bennelong returned with Hunter, living at the Governor's house, almost as an exhibit, but he returned to the bush where he was rejected by his own people. Drink and degradation made him the first of many tragic failures to reconcile Aboriginal with European culture.[78]

Eschewing the imperialist rhetoric of Brodsky, the literary drama of Dark and the academic-speak of Clendinnen, the down-to-earthiness of these micro-biographies helps to give Bennelong's tragedy a patina of realness that contributes to an intertextual consensus that Bennelong lived a tragic life. Perhaps, most importantly, the adjective 'tragic' gives a signal to the reader about how they should feel.

In 1985, Eric Willmot warned the 'dragons' of history (i.e., white historians who wanted to keep the past to themselves) that a generation of Aboriginal scholars was about to emerge and make Australian history its own. Like Mulvaney, Willmot felt that the story of Pemulwuy would be the one that these Aboriginal historians would most want to tell (as he himself did shortly afterwards). Although Willmot viewed Bennelong's story as tainted, he did not see this as Bennelong's failure; instead, the taint came from the long period his story had spent in the keeping of the dragons.[79] The fabric of Bennelong's tragedy is a closely woven web of veracities: historical, allegorical, literary and moral. The threads are not easy to disentangle; however, in the light of a body of evidence for the varied fortunes and strong relationships of Bennelong's last 18 years, it is

---

78  Learmonth and Learmonth, *Encyclopaedia of Australia*, 54.
79  Willmot, 'The Dragon Principle', 44–48.

clear that we must reflect further on his story and on its uses. Tragedy is not life, nor is it history. Tragedy is a dramatic or literary construction with its own logic and genealogy. If Bennelong's life is 'tragic', then it is his storytellers who have made it so.

# 6

# Ambassador between the Present and the Past

Bernard Smith, in his 1980 Boyer Lectures, called on writers to engage with the tragedy in Australian history because tragedy embodies a moral commitment and has the power to act as the midwife of 'atonement'. He felt that Australians had avoided tragedy because 'the tragic muse was an old Aboriginal woman, surviving precariously as a fringe dweller in some unknown country town'—and white Australians wanted to forget her. He argued that engagement with the tragedy of Aboriginal history would spur the 'concerned conscience' to agitate for the improvement of legal, health and education outcomes for Aboriginal people. Yet, tragedy's potential to play a constructive role in the 'education of democratic citizens' has long been in dispute; philosophers from Plato to Nietzsche have variously found that tragedy has the potential to morally corrupt or to undermine genuine moral responsibility. Smith himself acknowledged the danger that a tragic history 'could readily fall into sentimentality, making oppressive institutions tolerable, even enjoyable, in the very process of exposing them'.[1]

---

1   Smith remarked that 'at times it would seem as if all the culture of old Europe were being brought to bear upon our writers and artists in order to blot from their memories the crimes perpetrated on Australia's first inhabitants'. It did not occur to him to examine the implications of mobilising this cultural armoury in the service of *remembering*. Smith, 'The Spectre of Truganini', 16, 22–34. Kaufmann, *Tragedy and Philosophy*, quoted in Muldoon, 'Thinking Responsibility Differently', 246.

Paul Muldoon, in an essay examining the limits of justice as a paradigm for reconciliation, noted that 'when historians refer to the fate of the Aborigines as a "tragedy" … the only element that generally remains of the original Greek signification is that of a necessary or unavoidable catastrophe'. For tragedy to have the transformative power that the ancient Greeks endowed it with, it must be uncomfortable, it must decentre or disturb the audience, prompt each audience member to look into their own all-too-human soul and know that they could share the fate of the protagonist. To transform, tragedy must make the assumed foundations of social endeavour quiver beneath the feet of the audience, showing how civilisation itself, far from being a safe refuge, has terror and confusion on its underside. If a 'tragedy' is simply inevitable, its audience achieves easy absolution via the kind of sentimental masochism that Bernard Smith worried about; as Muldoon put it, when tragedy is reduced to 'misfortune', it becomes 'a category of event to which the concept of responsibility has little or no application'.[2] W. K. Hancock, charting Australia's great romance with wool in 1930, rendered Muldoon's point with exactitude. Hancock explained Aboriginal history in terms of Social Darwinism, stating that 'the advance of British civilisation made inevitable "the natural progress of the aboriginal race towards extinction"'. Though he did not interrogate this 'natural' explanation, Hancock was able to offer an acute account of the level of responsibility it might engender:

> Australian democracy is genuinely benevolent, but is preoccupied with its own affairs. From time to time it remembers the primitive people whom it has dispossessed, and sheds over their predestined passing an economical tear.[3]

A tragic outcome for Bennelong has a bearing on the level of responsibility that storytellers and their audiences might feel for Aboriginal history across the subsequent two centuries. As Mark McKenna stated of local historians in south-eastern New South Wales who have added Aboriginal history back in over the last few decades:

> Acknowledging that the settlers had poisoned or shot Aboriginal people … allowed historians to remove them from their historical narrative. Once the unpleasantness was out of the way, history could continue as a non-Aboriginal story.[4]

---

2   Muldoon, 'Thinking Responsibility Differently', 245–48.
3   Hancock, *Australia*, 32–33.
4   McKenna, *Looking for Blackfellas' Point*, 94.

It has become increasingly relevant in academic and public spheres to suspend the doom of 'the fatal moment when Phillip stepped ashore' and to re-examine contact history, focusing on the texture of what actually happened, the variety of relations that were entered into, the kinds of cooperation that made European settlement possible, and the agency and strategies of Indigenous peoples in accommodating, as well as combating, the colonists.[5] Inga Clendinnen returned to colonial relationships in *Dancing with Strangers* in this spirit, hoping to recover the many-coloured and fragile optimism of the 'springtime' of first contact. However, she found resounding failure in the persons of Phillip and Bennelong. For Clendinnen, these men were the leaders of two peoples on whose shoulders the weight of history rested. She found that Phillip and Bennelong had the best chance of setting up enduring good relations between European colonists and Indigenous Australians; instead, they established a course through uncertainty, conflict and mutual disrespect across the continent. Thus, 'each failed, to their own and their people's injury, and to ours'.[6] One implication of Clendinnen's interpretation is that Phillip and Bennelong, right back there at the 'beginning', should bear more responsibility than those who came after them for the pain and violence in Australian history.

According to Tim Rowse, history-making almost inevitably involves the making of 'counterfactual' claims for, in maintaining a conviction that the course of history is not inevitable, we imagine other courses that history might have taken. Rowse has challenged Australian historians to be reflective about the nature of these claims that are closely bound up with the ways in which we imagine our own complicity in the dispossession of Aboriginal peoples.[7] Underlying Clendinnen's analysis of Bennelong and Phillip's failure is a powerful counterfactual claim that, had goodwill been maintained, the British colonisation of Aboriginal lands might have been mutually beneficial. The nature of the failure she perceived, and the character of her counterfactual claim, made it possible for her to call for a reconciliation based on a renewal of the mutual curiosity and concern that she found in early British–Aboriginal relations in the Sydney area.[8]

---

5   Elder, *Blood on the Wattle*, 11; Byrne, 'Archaeology in Reverse', 240–41.
6   Clendinnen returned to the history of the Sydney colony in pursuit of 'social justice between Australia's original immigrants, and those of us who came later'. Clendinnen, *Dancing with Strangers*, 5, 286.
7   Rowse, 'Historians and the Humanitarian', 254–56.
8   Clendinnen, *Dancing with Strangers*, 287.

Rowse identified a similar strain of 'humanitarian' argument running through the 'history wars'—namely, that 'the "rule of law" could have limited the extent to which the usurping Britons used physical force to secure their dominion'. He argued that Clendinnen's implicit claim 'can never lose its pertinence for Australians who wish to ameliorate the impact of a colonisation that they cannot reverse'.[9] Historians have responded to Clendinnen's counterfactual scenario from various directions. Gordon Briscoe, appearing back to back with Clendinnen on the *First Australians* television series, stated that he had found no evidence that the British were attempting to establish a future based on mutual understanding; rather, it was clear from the outset that change was to be imposed.[10] For John Hirst, the notion that more goodwill in the beginning may have resulted in a better outcome for Aboriginal Australians was a 'liberal fantasy'; he argued that the 'concerned conscience' becomes absorbed in the colonial phase of Australia's history at the expense of acknowledging the relentless bureaucratic 'second attack' on Australia's Indigenous peoples in the early twentieth century.[11]

Clendinnen's imagined audience, drawn into a sympathetic circle of readers by her frequent use of the first person plural, was characterised by Alan Atkinson as 'Australians … probably of British descent, but not British ourselves, well informed, well travelled and with a distinctive moral attitude'.[12] Members of Bennelong and Surrounds Residents for Reconciliation, an active group based in the federal electorate of Bennelong (inner north-western Sydney) might be included within this circle. This group, which backed Maxine McKew's challenge of then Liberal Prime Minister John Howard in the Bennelong electorate in 2007, gained inspiration from Clendinnen's ideas about Bennelong. Having recently read *Dancing with Strangers*, in her maiden speech to Parliament, McKew said:

> It is a complex story, the story of early European settlement … [It should be known] that there were … moments when trust and goodwill ruled hearts on both sides of the divide. The universal disaster did not have to happen and it does not have to happen now. For Bennelong there was no happy ending. When he returned to his own land after three years in England, he was scorned by the Europeans and by his own people.

---

9   Rowse, 'Historians and the Humanitarian', 254.
10  Nowra and Perkins, 'Episode 1: They Have Come to Stay'.
11  Hirst, *Sense and Nonsense*, 82, 88–90.
12  Atkinson, 'The Charmed Circle', 9–10.

He was the first of tens of thousands of Aboriginals who have attempted or been forced to straddle both worlds, only to end up lost between both. A question for us all as we start out on the road to reconciliation is to ask: what was Bennelong trying to do in forging a friendship with the British? At the very least, we can say he was making a connection, attempting to build a bridge. And that is what we need to do.[13]

Neither McKew nor the Residents for Reconciliation denied responsibility for the present. McKew took up Clendinnen's call for a reconciliation inspired by past goodwill. For their part, the Residents for Reconciliation dedicated significant time, energy and resources to actions ranging from participation in the 'Stop the Northern Territory Intervention' campaign to the promotion of local Aboriginal artists; they also planned to dedicate a memorial to Bennelong.[14] In addition, the organisation supported and publicised Keith Smith's work on Bennelong, helping him to 'rehabilitate' Bennelong from the myth of his 'pathetic demise'.[15] Of course, no reader is captive to a single interpretation of Bennelong's story. Members of this group may have drawn inspiration from both Smith's and Clendinnen's works, as well as rethinking the relationship between the two under the tutelage of Keneally's *Australians: Origins to Eureka*.

McKew's version of history contains a mixture of recognition and insistence on destruction that are inseparable. How should her impulse to destroy Bennelong in narrative, even as historical goodwill and mutual understanding are remembered, be understood? Does this kind of insistence on destruction point to a thread of hostility intermingled with the very goodwill involved in remembering Bennelong?[16] As we have seen already, Bennelong has been remembered by many storytellers over the past 40 years as a friend to the colony, with the obliteration of his health, family life, self-respect and future prospects following close behind. Explaining this, Andrew Lattas suggested that storytellers and their audiences might feel cleansed by Bennelong's comprehensive failure, his 'Christ-like suffering' restoring 'settler Australians to a lost moral order'.[17]

---

13   McKew, First Speech to Parliament, 14 February 2008.
14   Judy MacGregor Smith, Bennelong and Surrounds Residents for Reconciliation, personal communication with author, 13 November 2008.
15   Smith, 'Bennelong among his People', 8, 24. The Bennelong and Surrounds Residents for Reconciliation hosted a talk by Smith about Bennelong and the Indigenous history of Ryde in conjunction with a visit to Bennelong's grave at Kissing Point in October 2008.
16   Rutherford, *The Gauche Intruder*, 10–13.
17   Andrew Lattas 'Aborigines and Contemporary Australian Nationalism: Primordiality and the Cultural Politics of Otherness', quoted in Broome, 'Historians, Aborigines and Australia', 71.

Sherman Alexie, of the Spokane/Coeur d'Alene people of Washington, provides an ironic recipe for nation-defining popular fiction across the Pacific that has distinct affinities with Bennelong's tragedy. The readers of Alexie's 'Great American Indian Novel', imagined to be beneficiaries of settler-colonialism, will be offered both absolution and ascendancy by the plot's spectacle of 'Indians [with] tragic features: tragic noses, eyes and arms', and the travails of the hero, who will be a 'half-breed, half white and half Indian'. The narrative will transform the truth of American history, making real the settler fantasy of being one with the land, without predecessor; in this novel 'all of the white people will be Indians and all of the Indians will be ghosts'.[18]

Andrew McCann linked the ubiquitous rendition of the vanished or vanishing Aboriginal race with white Australians' desire to identify with the land. He argued that it is the writing of an Aboriginal tragedy (anticipating an Aboriginal extinction that has not yet arrived but inevitably will) that has allowed settlers to engage in a 'romance' with Australia, in which it is the settlers who struggle, who sacrifice, who shape and are shaped by this harsh landscape.[19] Bennelong's tragedy, like the overarching tragedy of Aboriginal extinction, may be a 'melancholy footnote' to white history, but it is a footnote on which this history depends. As Frances Peters-Little observed, it is Aboriginal *history* that has been made to disappear by these narratives:

> Bennelong's children survived, as did a lot of Aboriginal people's children … But they were told they were no longer Aboriginal because they didn't live in a certain way … That's been the process of genocide. It's being told you're not what you are. They're around, they're everywhere.[20]

Bennelong's contribution to the romance of 'progress' is not always related to his suffering. His friendship with Governor Phillip and its 'metaphorical clasping of hands, the black and the white' has, at times, carried a hovering implication that this mateship, or paternal-filial bond, absolves the white hand for its dispossession of the black, or even constitutes an agreement

---

18   Alexie, 'How to Write the Great American Indian Novel', in *The Summer of Black Widows*.
19   McCann, 'Unknown Australia', 37–50; McCann, 'The Literature of Extinction', 48–54. Brantlinger coined the term 'proleptic elegy' to show how this 'wished-for lack' has become a central part of nationalist celebration for 'settler' societies to the present. Brantlinger, *Dark Vanishings*, 3, 189–90.
20   Frances Peters Little, personal communication, quoted in Smith and Plater, *Raging Partners*, 79.

of some kind.[21] A 1969 children's book created a clasping of hands in which a handover was very strongly implied. In the story, Bennelong is depicted as hating Phillip and the British for intruding and staying in his country; however, he comes to understand that these strangers now own 'the land'. Bennelong broadcasts this to his people and works through the resentment that he feels as a result of this new reality. The book reaches an almost homoerotic pitch when Bennelong makes an (ahistorical) visit to Phillip's bedside as he convalesces after being speared at Manly:

> Phillip was in bed, but he received him, and for a few moments the two men were quite still—each regarding the other. Then both smiled—and Bennelong shot out his hand … Their paths had crossed before; this time they met—and it was in friendship.[22]

Relinquishing his dream of seeing the next generation of boys become strong hunters, Bennelong sailed to England with the virile Phillip, never to return.[23] This narrative of assent and forgiveness implied a mutual understanding between Bennelong and Phillip that the Aboriginal epoch had passed, symbolised by a peaceful handover to British Australians that even Bennelong acknowledged as progress.

Like the rhetorical recruitment of the Opera House as a memorial for Bennelong, a number of popular and official stories have created a similar sense of 'rightness' by finding that Bennelong, with his enthusiastic appreciation for British culture, is aptly commemorated by the continued growth of the nation. A 2005 children's book included a section dedicated to 'Bennelong today', in which an unproblematic continuity was drawn between Bennelong, the Opera House and a raft of commercial and political ventures that have taken his name. 'On Sydney Harbour today', we are told, 'residents and tourists can enjoy luxury cruises in the motor

---

21  Brodsky, *Bennelong Profile*, 37. In the 1980s television series based on Dark's *The Timeless Land*, we are confronted with Phillip's face looking lovingly towards Bennelong like a new father. *The Timeless Land: The Early Days of British Settlement in Australia*, disc 1. The notion that the two men exchanged names as 'a sign of their deep affection for each other' continues to circulate unaccompanied by comment on the nature of kin ties and their formal and political meanings for the Eora. See Hinkson, *Aboriginal Sydney*, 7.
22  Wilton, *The Unknown Land*, 19.
23  Ibid., 20. Similarly, Eleanor Dark and the children's book that follows her story created a fictional father for Bennelong who had seen Cook's ship, and who always wished that his son would travel in such a 'magic boat': 'It is the wish of my father, the wish of Wunbula, that I stay here with the white men. For one day Wunbula's wish will come true. Wunbula's son will travel in the magic boats, the magic boats of Wunbula's corroboree'. Endeavour Reading Programme, *Bennelong*, 44–45.

yacht MV *Bennelong* on the waters once fished by Bennelong and the Wanghal people'. Thus, 'Bennelong lives on' (apparently) through these various ways in which his name is 'honoured'.[24]

The implications of this grafting of the goods of the present onto Bennelong's story are brought into sharp relief by John Birmingham in his conclusion to *Leviathan: The Unauthorised Biography of Sydney*, in which he imagines the ghost of Arthur Phillip returning to Sydney in the present: '[I'd] shout him the most expensive lunch. I'd tell him that, all things considered, he'd done well … The city he helped raise is one of the finest in the world'. However, Birmingham flinches as the ghost asks him what has happened to the descendants of Aboriginal people he knew. Birmingham realises that if Phillip's apparition were to appear, so might Bennelong's, and that this Bennelong might not be satisfied by the naming of an electorate after him, or any other gesture of 'tribute' to his memory. Birmingham encounters Bennelong with some trepidation; he cannot think of anything to say except an inadequate 'sorry' and stops short of trying to imagine what Bennelong's ghost might say in reply.[25] Here, as in Yusef Komunyakaa's poem, it is as if a happy innocence in Australian history, once sponsored by Bennelong, is being relinquished.[26]

Henry Reynolds encountered many people who felt 'let down, cheated, sold short' by their school education. His book *Why Weren't We Told?* provided an account of his own gradual recognition of frontier conflict, repressive legislation and racist ideology in Australian pasts and presents. Reynolds's research shook his belief that 'Australia was a society that valued equality above all other virtues and was committed to a fair go for all' and forced him to relinquish the notion that Australia had been peaceably settled.[27] Likewise, a contributor to the *First Australians* online comments page recoiled from the saccharine version of Bennelong's friendship with Phillip he had been taught as a child: 'We were never taught of these atrocities at school … I do remember learning the charming story of the friendship between Philip [sic] and Bennelong—not so "charming" now'.[28]

---

24  Sheppard, *The Life of Bennelong*, 29.
25  John Birmingham wanted to write a happy, carefree history of the city he loved, but that was not what happened; to his own surprise, he produced a 'black armband biography'. Birmingham, *Leviathan*, 509–10.
26  Komunyakaa, 'Bennelong's Blues'.
27  Reynolds, *Why Weren't We Told?*, 2–9, 135–38.
28  'Ross Mac from Moorooka', 22 October 2008, SBS First Australians, Your Comments, accessed 20 March 2008, www.sbs.com.au/firstaustralians/.

It is perhaps this rejection of a 'charming' colonial history that leads to an interpretation like McKew's and Bernard Smith's, in which Bennelong's obliteration must be recognised by the 'concerned conscience'.

Muldoon found that, for tragedy to transform the citizen and engage his sense of responsibility, a level of awareness is required; audience members must enter into a contract of sorts and must recognise their own participation in a theatrical or literary process in which they will be reorientated towards the reality of their own lives.[29] The complex relationship of Bennelong's story with truth makes this self-awareness difficult to gain. As I have argued above, Bennelong's example has become not simply an ordinary truth, tied to evidence, but an allegorical truth of the kind better captured in drama than by historical investigation.[30] The problem is compounded as Bennelong's life is often narrated in the language of the theatre, partly due to the location of the Opera House on Bennelong Point, and also the temptation to understand the early Sydney colony as a kind of 'stage' of history. In 1977, J. J. Healy undertook to flesh Bennelong out as a fully fledged 'actor' on history's stage, in which he had often been depicted contemptuously as a 'marionette' dressed up in English clothes. In this work, Bennelong returned from London intoxicated by British culture, like an actor drunk on bright lights and applause, and unable to separate 'role' from reality. Healy's Bennelong was a prophetic player *acting out* a story that interpreted the future.[31] Clendinnen too, at times, characterised the colony as a kind of tableau and referred to 'players' on the colonial stage; one of her reviewers validated this approach by complementing Clendinnen on her staging of 'a classic drama of human will'.[32] Under such circumstances, when the distinction between theatre and life is muddied, Hayden White's call to a circumspect and reflective use of dramatic tropes in history is, perhaps, even harder to hear than usual.

---

29 Muldoon, 'Thinking Responsibility Differently', 245, 248.
30 Felicity Collins examined the question of what kind of truth can arise from fiction, allegory and film, and whether it can be admitted as 'historical truth'. She concluded that some aspects of the past, perhaps particularly traumatic ones, are examined to advantage via dramatic modes, and that these can create a constructive dialogue with more traditional historical forms of investigation. Collins, 'Historical Fiction', 55–71.
31 Healy, 'A Most Tragic Theme', 30–32.
32 'Enter Banleelon' is one of Clendinnen's chapter titles; when she discusses 'roles' available to Aboriginal people, it is with a nod to the theatrical. Clendinnen, '*Dancing with Strangers*', 277. Fox, '*Dancing with Strangers*', 456–58.

In 2001, the Melbourne Theatre Company and Indigenous performance group Jagera Jarjum staged a production of Shakespeare's *The Tempest*, reinterpreted as an exploration of reconciliation. Shakespeare's character Caliban was remodelled on Bennelong, played by Indigenous writer, director and actor Glenn Shea. The conclusion of the play is ambiguous for Bennelong, he leaves the stage unreconciled, deaf to the cries of the Ancestors.[33] One reviewer made a revealing assessment of this ambitious project:

> Bennelong may have seemed like a good idea initially as Caliban's model but it effectively straitjacketed the actor Glenn Shea, preventing him from giving life to the character the play text itself offers and sending him offstage to an uncertain freedom, especially with Bennelong's tragic, alcohol addicted end in mind.[34]

While Shea's performance may or may not have been constrained by his understanding of the historical Bennelong, this reviewer's understanding of the play was certainly constrained by hers. Before she saw the play she knew, presumably from retellings of his story, that Bennelong died an alienated alcoholic. Thus, even as an experienced theatregoer perceiving him on a fresh stage, she struggled to accept a different dramatic outcome for Bennelong. Unaware of the 'theatre' already inherent in the familiar story of Bennelong, the reviewer could not be touched by the cathartic power of Bennelong's appearance in *The Tempest*. In Muldoon's terms, she had become a spectator rather than a citizen.[35]

Aristotle felt that the tragic hero needed to be 'highly renowned and prosperous' so that his or her story would be of some consequence, but also be enough 'like ourselves'—the flawed human audience—to make us sympathetic to his or her plight, partly through fear that the same kind of disaster could strike us.[36] In a culture in which non-Indigenous Australians compete with each other to be at the centre of narratives of victimhood

---

33  Tweg, 'Dream On', 51.
34  Ibid.
35  Muldoon, 'Thinking Responsibility Differently', 245, 248. A similar rejection of new dramatic possibilities for Bennelong is apparent in the media response to Enoch's *I Am Eora*. One article cited actor Jack Charles's affinity with his character, Bennelong, and Charles's recovery from addiction and incarceration at the same time as reasserting Bennelong's ongoing alienation (whereas the play itself seems to suggest otherwise): 'Charles said that as a man who had lived through addiction, jail time and racist abuse, he had a deep understanding of Bennelong. However, while Bennelong died a lost soul, Charles said he had "jumped off" his addictions to become an elder and "law man" within his Melbourne community'. Lissa Christopher, 'Black Perspective Sheds Light on Early Sydney', *The Sydney Morning Herald*, 9 January 2012, 4.
36  Aristotle, *Poetics*, quoted in Sayre, *The Indian Chief as Tragic Hero*, 3.

and struggle, Aristotle's famous and wealthy hero might elicit anything but sympathy.[37] Indeed, Bennelong has been criticised for arrogance and ambition; however, more often he is pushed off the bottom of Aristotle's scale, as a protagonist that we might pity or even despise. If he seems essentially weak, primitive or corruptible, as he does if the audience accepts the racial or cultural determinism we have seen in so many histories, then Bennelong is, by definition, not 'like ourselves'. 'Classical amateurs' in the colony toyed with the notion of sympathising with Aboriginal people by semi-facetiously identifying Bennelong and his peers with the most ancient of Greek heroes.[38] 'Atticus', writing to *The Sydney Gazette* in 1817, compared Bennelong with Theseus who lived in a time before history, went naked and engaged in violence against women and children. Nevertheless, he made Bennelong's hyper-primitive difference clear by reminding the reader more than once of his difference in colour.[39] Isadore Brodsky, apparently missing the sense of absurdity infusing Atticus's comparison, felt it necessary to redeem Theseus from this debasing association, declaring that (while each was superior to his countrymen as 'Atticus' had claimed), 'where Theseus scaled the great heights, Bennelong only plumbed the depths'.[40] Contempt for Bennelong has pervaded his story. Peter Read remembered learning, via history materials at primary school in the 1950s, that Bennelong was a 'white man's dog'.[41]

Australian sympathies may have an egalitarian tenor, but moral fibre, constancy, self-reliance and an anti-servile disposition are, perhaps, no less important for their engagement than the 'greatness' Aristotle required.[42] Bennelong's self-respect and respect-worthiness are often reflected on in stories about his younger contemporary, Bungaree. With his king plate and cast off fancy dress, as a mimic and performer, and as a drunk, Bungaree was Bernard Smith's archetypal 'fool king'. In Smith's account, he outdid Bennelong both in genius and in self-abasement; yet, at the same time, reflected both these 'achievements' back onto Bennelong.[43] F. D. McCarthy's short 1966 biography of Bungaree was dripping with

---
37  Curthoys, 'Expulsion, Exodus and Exile', 2–3, 6–8.
38  *The Sydney Gazette*, 13 January 1805, 2; 14 July 1805, 2; 29 March 1817, 1–2.
39  *The Sydney Gazette*, 29 March 1817, 1–2.
40  That this comparison was made in jest is signalled at the beginning of the article when 'Atticus' makes fun of Napoleon for identifying himself with both Caesar and Alexander. *The Sydney Gazette*, 29 March 1817, 1–2; Brodsky, *Bennelong Profile*, 79.
41  Peter Read, personal communication with the author, 19 October 2011.
42  Curthoys, 'Expulsion, Exodus and Exile', 6–8.
43  Smith, 'The Spectre of Truganini', 37. See also Clendinnen, *Dancing with Strangers*, 273; Moorhouse, *Sydney*, 47–51.

contempt as it described him as the leader of a 'pathetic remnant' of Aboriginal life that constituted the 'township Aboriginals', a position he held not by virtue of 'tribal authority', but through his adaptability, talent for 'facile exhibitionism' and the 'completely fictitious' title of king.[44] Bungaree is a parody of Aristotle's royal yet accessible tragic hero, losing sympathy both because of his self-aggrandising posturing and because that posturing has no basis. Phillip O'Neill's exploration of the mixture of humour and seriousness in Bungaree's performances and the presence of power in his impersonations, throws into sharp relief the will of McCarthy and others to despise him, and to disqualify him—in spite of (or because of) his fame—from being a hero whose story might shake the foundations of the colony.[45]

A hero may indeed be a victim of forces beyond their control; however, if they are to engage an audience on an ethical level, they must ultimately take responsibility for the choices they make.[46] A puppet opera conceived and performed for the 1988 bicentenary provided a rare opportunity for Bennelong to do just this. Two singers stood side stage next to the orchestra, while life-sized puppets with jointed arms and legs and mobile eyes played Bennelong and a range of supporting characters, including Phillip, King George and Gooroobarabooloo, Bennelong's second wife. The Bennelong puppet, pictured in *The Sydney Morning Herald*, appeared erect and dignified, as well as somewhat knowing and conspiratorial. Brodsky's epithet, 'the most observed of all observers', was evocative of its facial expression.[47] A reviewer felt that one of the production's main successes was that:

> Bennelong was as much responsible for his fate as [Governor Phillip] … Whether this was truly so or not, it helps to put Bennelong out of range of the kind of sentimental condescension that would insist on picturing him simply as a victim. This Bennelong knows how to exploit his own charm, understands how to use his white sponsors for his own purposes and, at the end, refuses the unction of pity.[48]

---

44  McCarthy, 'Bungaree (?–1830)'.
45  O'Neill, 'Putting the English in Drag', 69–86.
46  Muldoon, 'Thinking Responsibility Differently', 249–50.
47  Sykes, 'Bennelong Makes a Point', 81. However, the article also referred to a 'clash between cultures' and described Bennelong as 'the Aboriginal introduced to white man's ways by Governor Phillip' who, left 'in limbo between two societies', became 'acceptable to neither, and died a drunkard'. Brodsky, *Bennelong Profile*, 10.
48  Roger Covell, 'No Room for Pity in Black Puppet History', *The Sydney Morning Herald*, 12 October 1988, Arts, 22.

The reviewer felt it was partly the production's 'humorous exaggeration of very serious matters' that allowed it clarity and incisiveness. It was a tragicomedy akin, in some ways, to Willmot's *Pemulwuy*, in which the occasional indignity was not damning, and the divide between success and failure itself was interrogated.[49]

When understood as a lurching, querulous drunkard at the time of his death, Bennelong fails to regain the respect of the audience. It often seems to be assumed that readers of Bennelong's stories have no connection with a sodden Bennelong of 'diminished responsibility'. However, there was one place in which Bennelong's drinking was intimately associated with personal responsibility. Benelong's Haven, a residential treatment centre on the north coast of New South Wales, was a 'place where Aboriginal people with alcohol and drug problems can come together to undertake treatment'. Staff and residents believed, like many of our storytellers, that Bennelong 'epitomised the fate of other Aboriginals who have succumbed to alcohol since the British landed in 1788'.[50] Here, his story functioned as an 'archetypal alcoholic's story'—a starting point for participants' own recovery and regeneration. A 1982 profile of the program featured a small portrait of Bennelong, wreathed with the motto 'Love, Dedication, Loyalty' drawn by former resident, Pop Patterson, and subsequently used as a letterhead for the organisation.[51] At Benelong's Haven, Bennelong was part of a community of fellow sufferers taking responsibility for their problems and working towards a better life. If he was shamed here, it was through a socially reintegrative process that leads to mutual acceptance, and in which Bennelong and his storytellers shared shame and moved forward together.

In brief biographical narratives, Bennelong's alcoholism often functions as both a cause of early death and an epithet, as in a *Sydney Morning Herald* article that recounted Tench's description of Bennelong as 'stoutly made' with a 'defiant' countenance, 'yet he died an alcoholic in 1813 aged 48'. The effect is very different when the order of these two elements is reversed, as in the *Encyclopaedia of Aboriginal Australia*, which employs very similar wording, but mentions his alcoholism first and then allows

---

49   Covell, 'No Room for Pity', 22.
50   Benelong's Haven was established in 1973 by Valerie Bryant-Carroll in Marrickville. Until November 2017, when it closed, it was located at the former Kinchela Boys Home on the north coast of New South Wales. Chenhall, *Benelong's Haven*, 1–2; Miller, 'A Haven for Alcoholics', 602–05.
51   Miller, 'A Haven for Alcoholics', 602–05. The piece also recounts that one of the residents sang a song about Bennelong as part of his contribution.

Tench the last word on this 'bold, intrepid' man.[52] Here, as at Benelong's Haven, Bennelong becomes a 'survivor', a man whose stature is shaped, but not reduced, by his acknowledged addiction and the pain and loss he experienced. When Bennelong is a survivor of colonisation, rather than its victim, there is far greater potential for the exposure of his pain and loss to raise a corresponding sense of shame in his storytellers and their audiences. As Rosamund Dalziell observed, shame can lead to sympathetic emotions and social action, whereas guilt, with its direct link to blame, gives a reader the choice between accepting a burden and rejecting it (on the grounds that they were not directly involved in the act at hand).[53] In counting Bennelong a survivor, and acknowledging the many people who are descendants of his generation, non-Indigenous storytellers may also be more likely to acknowledge that Aboriginal and Torres Strait Islander people will be among their audiences, and will have responses to the stories that they tell, and to any apologies they offer or call to action they make.[54]

In invoking tragedy and employing its well-known features to tell Bennelong's story, storytellers have variously combined misfortune with Aboriginal culpability; put forward notions of cultural temptation or incompatibility to explain Aboriginal dispossession to an exclusion of material and political factors; and cast Bennelong as a historiographical go-between who hands over Australia to the British, or simply provides an answer to our questions about what went wrong back there at the beginning. When all this is viewed from the high moral ground of tragedy, non-Indigenous storytellers risk making Bennelong's tragedy merely enjoyable, a speech given in their own defence, and not a call for justice in the present.[55] As Aboriginal and Torres Strait Islander Social Justice Commissioner Tom Calma observed in 2008:

---

52  Stephens, 'Bennelong, the First of the Stolen', 6; Horton, *The Encyclopaedia of Aboriginal Australia*, 118.
53  Dalziell, *Shameful Autobiographies*, 1–11. A survivor, as the members of the stolen generations are at times depicted. For example, Stolen Generations Alliance, 'Welcome to the Stolen Generations Alliance', accessed 8 July 2018, www.nsga.org.au/about-the-stolen-generations/current-state/; The Stolen Generations Testimonies Foundation, accessed 8 July 2018, www.stolengenerationstestimonies.com/.
54  There is a tendency in the Australian context to overlook Indigenous peoples' responses to attempts at apology for past and present wrongs. See Dortins 'Apology and Absolution'.
55  Casey, 'Referendums and Reconciliation', 137–48. John Frow discussed the meaning of 'apology' in the context of the stolen generations. He argued that acknowledging the suffering of others may involve the taking on of the responsibility of transforming present relationships, or it may simply strengthen the listener: '"forgive me", it says, "I was wrong": the apologist gains honour, and nothing changes'. Frow, 'A Politics of Stolen Time', 362–63.

> The Australian community had become so accustomed to stories of Indigenous disadvantage that they had become immune to it, and came to expect it … the community and government have come to believe that this situation is intractable … and for some people, the fault of Indigenous peoples themselves … So while I firmly believe that these stories of disadvantage and dysfunction should be told, I also believe that they should not be told just for the sake of it.[56]

Retelling Bennelong's story in the present as an allegory for Indigenous failure is gratuitous. However well intentioned, it can end up simply indulging what Calma described as the 'industrial deafness' of other Australians. The repetition of Bennelong's failure becomes a 'repeated act of colonisation' too. When the events associated with British colonisation are reiterated in the present in the guise of misfortune, tragedy becomes farce, as in Marx's famous dictum—a story of someone else's trauma told with indifference.[57]

The 'concerned conscience' has been a major force in Australian history-making and politics since Bernard Smith evoked it in 1980. It can be seen in the movement for reconciliation and in the replacement of John Howard with a new prime minister who would make an apology to the stolen generations within a few months of his election. Since the 1970s, the retelling of Bennelong's story as a tragedy has reflected a disaster that continues to unfold for the concerned conscience in the present—a realisation of the continued culpability of non-Aboriginal Australians in the destruction of Aboriginal lives, life ways, culture and society. Yet, as Bennelong's tragedy was once used by the ardent monarchist Brodsky to reassure white Australians that Aboriginal people did not merit equality, it has also held its reassurances for the concerned conscience, along with an uncomfortable continuity with old narratives of Aboriginal death, decline and corruption. Gratuitous lamentations about the long-dead Bennelong's fall into disgrace, and the irreversible rupture in cross-cultural relations that this is held to signify, provide a large target for conservative accusations of 'conspicuous compassion' on the side of the political left, a cheap expenditure of tears and talk that obviates 'sensible action'.[58]

---

56  Calma, 'Essentials for Social Justice: Reform'.
57  Weaver, *Other Words*, 142; Tumarkina, 'First as a Tragedy', 24–26. Marx, quoted in Curthoys and Docker, *Is History Fiction?*, 124.
58  Mason, 'The Tragedy of Conspicuous Compassion', 6. In the early twenty-first century, this 'sensible action' has functioned to valorise conservative policy, and actions such as the Northern Territory Intervention, at the same time as rejecting the importance of campaigns like the one for a statement acknowledging Indigenous Australians in a new preamble to the Constitution, with the notion that this would be merely 'symbolic'.

Renewed conservative claims on Australian history at the turn of the twenty-first century saw Bennelong adopted by the Bennelong Society, a conservative think tank on Aboriginal policy founded in 2001, as a poster child for assimilation. The society's Bennelong, having readily perceived the 'benefits' of the British lifestyle, was deemed to have succeeded in British terms, which is what the society would have liked Aboriginal people to do in the present and future. Bennelong was depicted as a 'master of adaptation and improvisation' who, in collaboration with Phillip, 'devised' the 'peaceful coming-in of the Eora' to Sydney in 1790.[59] The society found it necessary to dissociate itself from Bennelong's latter years. Special care was taken on its website to explain that Bennelong's drinking problem began during his time in England; while he was engaged in diplomatic work, his drinking was under control—it was 'good' social drinking.[60]

Eve Vincent attended the society's 2006 conference and gave an account of her experience in *Arena Magazine*. She did not find the conference a comfortable place to be. Most difficult was the barely submerged implication that the Aboriginal realm, when distinctive or 'segregated' from 'Australian civilisation', was 'depraved, disordered, sick, illiterate, brutal and addicted'. Delegates derided and shouted down 'romantic' notions of self-determination and the sustainability of remote communities, and aligned themselves with an ideology-free pragmatism. For Vincent, the most disturbing aspect was 'the relative terms—civilised, savage' that the society wanted 'to invest anew with power and meaning'.[61] As I hope I have shown, the telling and retelling of Bennelong's story as a cultural tragedy over the past 70 years has helped to maintain the relevance of these value-laden poles of civilised and savage. The society's Bennelong represented a self-conscious response to the downbeat, dead end of Bennelong's tragedy. It was in the interests of the society and its supporters to hold a monopoly on 'sensible', constructive action—the solution to the 'Aboriginal problem'—which those who have promoted

---

59  Gary Johns, 'The Failure of Aboriginal Separatism', presented to Workshop 2000: 'Aboriginal Policy: Failure, Reappraisal and Reform', The Bennelong Society, accessed 17 February 2009, www.bennelong.com.au/conferences/pdf/Johns2000.pdf (site discontinued); Dirk van Dissel, 'Woollawarre Bennelong, the Bush Politician (1789–1792)', The Bennelong Society, accessed 17 February 2009, www.bennelong.com.au/articles/bennelongbio.php (site discontinued). The society was disbanded in 2011. Some of its 'Bennelong Papers' have been transferred to the Quadrant website, see www.quadrant.org.au/blogs/bennelong-papers.
60  Dirk van Dissel, 'Woollawarre Bennelong'.
61  Vincent, 'Who is Bennelong?', 47–48.

self-determination have only further compounded.⁶² The society's no-nonsense, go-ahead Bennelong endorsed Aboriginal participation in the mainstream capitalist economy, leaving soft questions about culture and history, loss, shame and responsibility behind.

The telling of Bennelong's tragedy in the years following the history wars might be read as a reassertion of the relevance of mutual grieving, apology, atonement and the need for reconciliation on a number of levels—not only the 'practical' level offered by the Bennelong Society. The *First Australians* series showed several historians talking about Bennelong's life. Peter Read's Bennelong 'goes out' of Sydney Cove in his later years in a situation of relative equality. Having seen all that Europeans have to offer, he ultimately rejects the new settlement, choosing his own life, not unlike the traveller Gulliver who sallies forth into the world, encounters difference, difficulty and adventure, but returns to his own society and manages to reintegrate himself—changed by his new experiences, but not broken by them.⁶³ Inga Clendinnen had the last word on Bennelong: 'to see that light-footed man, that man of so much political skill and resilience so reduced is, I think, tragic'.⁶⁴ In the book that accompanied the series, Marcia Langton affirmed Clendinnen's interpretation, giving Bennelong a central place in the 'dance' with the colonists. When Bennelong returned from England he was:

> Left to survive in the profoundly changed circumstances of his country. He had changed, too, not least because of his alliance with Phillip. At the end of his days, his mood of increasing bitterness and alcoholic decline reduced him from his warrior's countenance to a weak, defeated man.⁶⁵

---

62   See, for example, Comrie-Thompson, with Johns and Mundine, 'Nugget Coombs Revisited'.
63   We leave Gulliver settled to contented reflection in his 'little garden at Redriff', reconciling himself gradually to life in close quarters with humans once more. Swift, *Gulliver's Travels*, part IV, chapter 12.
64   Nowra and Perkins, 'Episode 1: They Have Come to Stay'. At least one viewer, whose thoughts were made more public than most via a review of the series in *The Age*, found Clendinnen's account the most satisfying, describing Bennelong as 'the remarkable 18th century Aborigine, an audacious wag who was kidnapped by Governor Arthur Phillip and became his interpreter and mediator. Bennelong learnt to speak English, lodged with the governor, and even sailed to England in 1792 where he charmed London society. But Bennelong died in ignominy, a man caught between cultures'. Gabriella Coslovich, 'Uncovering History in Black and Whitewash', *The Age*, 25 October 2008, Insight, 9.
65   Nowra and Perkins, 'Episode 1: They Have Come to Stay'.

In *First Australians*, Bennelong's story appeared among many stories of hope, friendship, massacre, cruel institutions, death, pain, survival and celebration across the continent and across more than two centuries. In choosing once more to follow the well-worn pathway of Bennelong's political and personal obliteration, did Langton and Clendinnen mean to come together around Bennelong's story to grieve for generations of talented Aboriginal men cut off by war, incarceration, accident and suicide? In implying, as so many had done before them, that Bennelong was at least partly a victim of his own success, what was it that they meant to say to the young men and women of today?

# Part 3: Friendship Beyond the Grave

# 7
# A Family Heirloom

The opening episode of the *First Australians* television series concluded with a story of friendship, jointly told by Wiradjuri Elder Dinawan Dyirribang, formerly Bill Allen, and David Suttor, owner of Brucedale, a cattle farming property near Bathurst. Suttor introduced his great-great grandfather, William—a 17-year-old, ambitious to succeed in the new world he saw opening up to him as more extensive settlement was permitted beyond the Great Dividing Range in the early 1820s. Dinawan Dyirribang introduced his ancestor, Windradyne—a fiery young warrior, family orientated and strong in his culture, who met the newcomers with dignity. Wiradjuri people guided William and his father, George, to land with good water, and Brucedale was established. William was left to manage the property with instructions from his father to respect the Wiradjuri. He took these instructions to heart, learning some of the Wiradjuri language. When violence ignited under the pressure of rapidly increasing settler and stock numbers in Wiradjuri country, the ties between the Suttor family and Windradyne and his people held.

A flashpoint came when a farmer offered Wiradjuri people some of his potatoes, but then, when some of the same people returned the following day to help themselves, he rounded up an armed posse to help him 'defend' his crop. Several of Windradyne's family members were killed. Soon afterwards, Windradyne and a group of warriors surrounded William Suttor's hut at night. William came to the door and spoke with Windradyne in the Wiradjuri language. After extended discussion, the warriors departed. Thirteen other settlers were speared and burned to death in their huts over the following month, and the stock of many farmers scattered, but Brucedale was spared. The settlers retaliated, killing Wiradjuri men, women and children. Governor Brisbane declared martial law in the Bathurst district on 14 August 1824, and the Wiradjuri faced a military contingent, as well as continued action by landowners and their servants.

Eventually, perhaps recognising the toll the conflict was having on his people, Windradyne and 130 other warriors walked to Parramatta to attend the governor's annual Aboriginal conference and negotiated peace with Governor Brisbane. Windradyne returned to live on his own land, which included Brucedale, and was buried there in the Wiradjuri way. The story closed with Dinawan Dyirribang calling for recognition of the harm and pain caused on both sides of the conflict, and David Suttor thanking the Wiradjuri people for their mercy on that fateful night in 1824; without their goodwill, Suttor said, 'we might not be here today'.[1]

As the voices of Dinawan Dyirribang and David Suttor entwine, their story of friendship takes on a redeeming quality, transcending the larger narrative of war of which it is a small part. The viewer is left with a sense of hope; perhaps difference can be overcome through a common humanity? The cross-cultural friendship of the 1820s is mirrored in the contemporary bond between the two storytellers, brought together by a shared history.

This retelling of the story of Windradyne and William Suttor on *First Australians* was an episode in a long tradition. Each generation of the Suttor family at Brucedale had commemorated their friendship with Windradyne and his people. Successive generations dedicated monuments in literature, concrete and law, adapting the story as the foundations of Australian history shifted beneath it, and as the meaning of friendship itself evolved.

Wiradjuri people, remembering their connections to Windradyne as an important ancestor and cultural and historical figure, have renewed the friendship with the Suttor family, and the two groups of descendants have been telling the story together for more than two decades. My account seeks to understand how this story of friendship has been shaped by its own retelling. It seeks to draw out the possible contemporary meanings of the Suttor family's commemorative acts through the nineteenth and

---

1   Nowra and Perkins, 'Episode 1: They Have Come to Stay'.

## 7. A FAMILY HEIRLOOM

early twentieth centuries, and to consider the significance of the coming together of the Suttor family's story traditions with those of the Wiradjuri descendants of Windradyne.

Windradyne's grave is at the centre of the story and the friendship. He is believed to be buried on a rise above Winburndale Rivulet, a little over a kilometre from the Brucedale homestead, in a burial ground that holds the remains of at least three other Wiradjuri people. The graves are surrounded by a rich commemorative landscape that continues to evolve, reflecting the developing relationship between the Suttor family, local Wiradjuri people and the state's national parks service, which administers a Voluntary Conservation Agreement signed in 2000 to protect the cultural values of Windradyne's grave. Between the traditional Wiradjuri graves and the commemorative additions of the early twenty-first century sits a memorial dedicated to Windradyne in 1954. It seems oddly out of place, yet it attests to the continuing friendship and is embraced as part of this *lieu de memoire*. It is here that I start.

Her Royal Highness Queen Elizabeth II visited Bathurst on 12 February 1954. The official souvenir booklet prepared by Bathurst City Council described the establishment of Bathurst as a peaceful affair. It referred to the Macquarie Memorial Cairn (erected 1930), which marked the site of that governor's founding of Bathurst, as a 'sacred spot' around which 'Bathurstians' gathered annually to tell the story of their city's beginnings. The only official Wiradjuri presence took the form of a painting of Yuranigh (guide to Surveyor Mitchell) on the decorated roadway that led the Queen's vehicle up to the 'Welcome Gates'.[2] In the Queen's wake came Anzac Day. On 25 April 1954, returned servicemen marched with the Bathurst District Band and wreaths were laid at the War Memorial Carillion. The mayor made a solemn speech, an Anzac Day sermon was given in the cathedral, and two war memorials were unveiled at St Stephens Presbyterian Church.[3] On the same day (or perhaps the following one), members of the Bathurst Historical Society drove to Brucedale to gather around a sturdy concrete plinth beside the grave mound where

---

2    Bathurst City Council, *Official Souvenir Programme*.
3    'Solemn Scenes at Local Anzac Day Celebrations', *The Western Times*, 26 April 1954, 1–2.

Windradyne was believed to be buried. Following an address recounting the life of Windradyne, Mrs Roy Suttor drew aside the Australian flag to reveal a bronze plaque.[4] The inscription read:

> THE RESTING PLACE OF WINDRADENE, ALIAS SATURDAY
> THE LAST CHIEF OF THE ABORIGINALS.
> FIRST A TERROR, BUT LATER A FRIEND TO THE SETTLERS
> DIED OF WOUNDS RECEIVED IN A TRIBAL ENCOUNTER 1835.
> 'A TRUE PATRIOT'
>
> This Plaque was unveiled by Mrs Roy Suttor of Brucedale
> 25th April, 1954.
> Bathurst District Historical Society

Figure 5: Memorial dedicated to Windradyne by Mr and Mrs Roy Suttor and the Bathurst Historical Society in 1954, with two burial mounds visible behind.
Source: Photograph taken by author.

---

4   Papers of P. J. Gresser, Australian Institute of Aboriginal and Torres Strait Islander Studies (hereafter AIATSIS), MS21/3/a, 117–18. Contrary to the memorial's inscription, Percy Gresser stated that the ceremony took place on the 26 April, *The Western Times*, 31 August 1962, 7.

Precisely what moved Roy Suttor, grandson of William Suttor, and his wife, to celebrate Windradyne's memory at this time is unknown. They may have felt a responsibility to mark the pair of fragile and slowly sinking earth graves before they ceased to have a physical presence in the landscape. The commemoration may have been inspired by the 'pilgrimage' led by the neighbouring Orange Historical Society in 1950 to Yuranigh's grave, to mark the centenary of his death.[5] Another possibility is that Roy Suttor was prompted by conversations with Percy Gresser. Gresser was a shearer who had collected Aboriginal artefacts across New South Wales and Queensland on his days off from the age of 16; he retired to Bathurst in 1953 to write an Aboriginal history of the district and attended the ceremony at Brucedale. Whatever its immediate inspiration, the commemoration, particularly in its allusions to war, stands out. According to Ken Inglis, memorials to Aboriginal people of any kind were sparse in the mid-twentieth century, and memorials to Europeans killed by Aboriginal people in frontier conflicts tended to avoid any reference to war, instead 'categorising the killing as murder'.[6] The deaths of Aboriginal men and women in the Australian military services remained largely unacknowledged until the 1980s, and it was only at this time that historians and Aboriginal campaigners began to make an explicit connection between the fallen in overseas wars and Aboriginal people who fell in defence of their country against invasion by the British. In 1981, Henry Reynolds asked:

> Do we … make room for the Aboriginal dead on our memorials, cenotaphs, boards of honour and even in the pantheon of national heroes? If they did not die fighting for Australia as such they fell defending their homelands, their sacred sites, their way of life.[7]

---

5   The party laid a boomerang-shaped wreath on Yuranigh's grave, marked by four commemorative carved trees, and a stone engraved to Mitchell's specifications in 1852 (replaced with a replica c. 1900). Percy Gresser wrote about the two commemorations back-to-back. Percy Gresser, 'The Aborigines of the Bathurst District', *The Western Times*, 31 August 1962, 7. The owner of the property on which the grave was located erected a fence around it, and later donated the land to Cabonne Shire Council. NSW National Parks and Wildlife Service, 'Yuranigh's Aboriginal Grave Historical Site: Plan of Management', July 1999, p. 7, Department of Environment, Climate Change and Water, accessed 27 May 2010, www.environment.nsw.gov.au/resources/parks/pomfinalyuranighs.pdf. The impulse may also have come through the Suttor family. Jock Suttor, who grew up on the family property at Wyagdon, spent much of his adult life travelling and living in Asia. On one of his visits home in the early 1920s, he had attempted to locate the grave of Georgie Suttor, an Aboriginal man who had taken the family name, so that he could erect a memorial. Teale, 'Suttor, John Bligh (1859–1925)'; Papers of P. J. Gresser, AIATSIS, MS21/2, 29–30.
6   Read, *A Hundred Years War*, 11; Inglis and Phillips, 'War Memorials in Australia and New Zealand', 181.
7   Reynolds (1981), quoted in Inglis, *Sacred Places*, 423–24.

Ten years later, as Chilla Bulbeck asserted, there were still 'no memorials' that responded 'to Reynolds' suggestion'.[8] The meaning of the inscription at Brucedale, dedicated amid the commemorative mood of Anzac Day in 1954, is further explored below. However, first it is important to look back at the story of friendship that Roy Suttor inherited by examining the 'monuments' left to the friendship by previous generations.

In 1826 and 1829, two letters appeared in colonial newspapers under the pseudonym 'Colo', but were addressed 'Brucedale, near Bathurst' and 'B-----e near Bathurst', respectively, which would have made their origin with the Suttor family quite clear.[9] At that time, George Suttor and his wife Sarah Maria were residents at Brucedale, probably accompanied by most of their 10 children.[10] The letters possess the authority and diplomacy of a mature writer, which might suggest George Suttor's involvement; however, his son, William, who was in his twenties when the first letter was written, is also a candidate.[11] Both letters are rich sources for understanding the nature of the friendship between local Wiradjuri people and the Suttor family. The first offered to share some 'sketches of the manners and customs ... of the Aborigines ... inhabiting the country round Bathurst' with 'fellow admirers of ... the works of God'. 'Colo' painted a harmonious scene at Brucedale that included Windradyne (referred to as 'Saturday' throughout) and his people sitting around small fires singing and laughing; 'Colo' sharing his crop of turnips with them; and them visiting the house to borrow pots and pans or, at times, a comb. In return, the Wiradjuri kept an eye on runaway cattle, a welcome service on any property.[12] 'Colo' provided a pattern for coexistence, attributing to his Aboriginal friends the idea that:

---

8    Bulbeck, 'Aborigines, Memorials and the History of the Frontier', 173–74.

9    *The Australian*, 14 October 1826, 3–4; *The Sydney Gazette*, 21 April 1829, 3. The same letter was printed in *The Sydney Monitor*, 18 April 1829, 2, and *The Australian*, 15 April 1829, 3.

10   Almost a decade after the establishment of Brucedale, George and Sarah Maria moved back to their original grant, Chelsea Farm, at Baulkham Hills, and from 1833 spent much of their time in a town house in Sydney, commuting back and forth to Chelsea Farm and Brucedale. George Suttor, *Memoirs of George Suttor*, 59.

11   William managed Brucedale soon after its establishment and formally took it over in 1834. Though he seems not to have been a writer by nature—he is renowned within the Suttor family for having written nothing at all—he participated vigorously in the public life of the colony. Percy Gresser canvassed the possibility that 'Colo' was George Suttor Jnr, William's eldest brother (b. 1799). John Suttor, in conversation with the author, 20 January 2009; Parsons, 'Suttor, George (1774–1859)'; Norton and Norton, *Dear William*, x; Papers of P. J. Gresser, AIATSIS, MS21c, loose leaf.

12   *The Australian*, 14 October 1826, 3–4. The letter is dated 25 August 1826.

> All wild animals are theirs—the tame or cultivated ones are ours. Whatever springs spontaneously from the earth, or without labour, is theirs also. Things produced by art and labour are the white fellows [sic], as they call us.[13]

The explosive conflicts in the Bathurst area had passed, but they would still have been fresh in the memories of all those who survived them. Groups of Wiradjuri people had gradually made peace with local authorities in the latter months of 1824, and the outlawed Windradyne had appeared at the native feast at Parramatta at the end of the year accompanied by a large group of Wiradjuri people, wearing a straw hat with the word 'peace' stuck in the band.[14] However, there were precedents for these sorts of gestures—they did not necessarily indicate that war was over. In 1805, Aboriginal people thronged to Parramatta from the fringes of the Cumberland Plain to reconcile with Governor King after he lifted an injunction aimed at keeping Aboriginal people out of settled and farmed districts. Yet, the people of the lower Hawkesbury and Broken Bay fought on.[15] 'Colo' sought to improve readers' impressions of Aboriginal people, in particular, those of the Bathurst district. Echoing the catalogue of virtues of the 'noble savage' that Rousseau and his followers had cited since the mid-eighteenth century, his tableau of domestic harmony and his praise of local Aboriginal people seem to have been aimed at encouraging readers to establish friendly and trusting relations on a sustainable basis.[16]

As more and more Wiradjuri country became other people's 'property', the Wiradjuri, like other Aboriginal peoples, became dependent on friendly relations with pastoralists to ensure ongoing access to their country. Gundungarra man Werriberrie or William Russell, reflecting on his life around Picton and Burragorang, mapped out a constellation of properties where he camped and worked as a young man in the mid-nineteenth century. The relationships had been established by his mother's and

---

13  Ibid.
14  In October 1824, for example, it was reported that about 60 Aboriginal people had come in to the settled district and re-established their previous 'peaceable footing', *The Sydney Gazette*, 28 October 1824, 2. Windradyne's appearance at the native feast is reported in *The Sydney Gazette*, 30 December 1824, 2.
15  This was the third 'coming in' of the Hawkesbury people after 15 years of sporadic conflict intermeshed with friendship, domestic intimacy encompassing men, women and children, and cultural exchange (including mutual education in different forms of justice and retribution, and complex patterns of loyalty), Karskens, *The Colony*, 460–90.
16  Clifford, *Political Genealogy after Foucault*, 1–4.

uncles' generation, and Russell himself continued to maintain them.[17] It is likely that Brucedale was becoming part of a network of safe places where local Wiradjuri people could continue to camp, work and meet. Reynolds observed that the 'coming in' of Aboriginal groups provided a conceptual challenge to many settlers who, during times of uncertainty and conflict, had found themselves infused by a hatred born of fear and now had opportunities to exert power over vulnerable Aboriginal people in their midst.[18] 'Colo' presented a model of benevolence for pastoralists; having accepted the friendship offered by Aboriginal people who had 'come in', he took a position of patron over them, as well as the role of host to their broader networks. He made a point of documenting the welcome he extended to large gatherings of Aboriginal people, boasting that he had accommodated at least 150 visitors from neighbouring areas on one occasion.[19]

Lively debate had occurred in public meetings and in colonial papers across the early 1820s. A number of correspondents advocated the use of 'terror' as a means of teaching the Wiradjuri groups around Bathurst how to submit to colonisation, while others sought to remind them that both races were members of the human family, and that they should reflect on the manner in which they had appropriated Aboriginal land before becoming bellicose about the spearing of a few (or even 100) sheep.[20] Many of those counselling restraint and compassion did so from an evangelical standpoint, advocating missionary work as a means to making the natives peaceful.[21] The God 'Colo' invoked drew from a secular, humanitarian model. Advocating for the Wiradjuri in the aftermath of war, he called on higher values in the reader, the British Empire and the governor alike: 'Let us hope that while Briton [sic] is making such amazing progress in Knowledge and in science, she will still enlarge her humanity'.[22]

---

17  Russell (Werriberrie), *My Recollections*. Russell was in his mid-80s when he collaborated on this brief memoir with friend and neighbour, A. L. Bennett.
18  Reynolds, *Frontier*, 63–72.
19  *The Australian*, 14 October 1826, 4.
20  See, for example, letters from 'Philanthropus' and 'Honestus', *The Sydney Gazette*, 5 August 1824, 4 and 12 August 1824, 4. As Salisbury and Gresser noted, the identities of most of these correspondents are unknown and one or more of them could also have been members of the Suttor family. Salisbury and Gresser, *Windradyne of the Wiradjuri*, 52.
21  Roberts and Carey, '"Beong! Beong! (More! More!)"', n.p. See letters to *The Sydney Gazette* from 'Philanthropus', 5 August 1824, and 'Amicitia', 19 and 26 August 1824, and to *The Australian* from 'Adaelos', 30 December 1824.
22  *The Australian*, 14 October 1826, 4. He also invoked the growing threat to good order in the district posed by bushrangers, and contrasted these wrongdoers with the 'innocent' Aborigines who were united with the settlers against them.

On one level, 'Colo' welcomed the reader into a circle of friendship with Windradyne and his people. Yet, he also set himself apart, saying: 'I have always been friendly to them, and have directed my people to avoid giving them offence. We have never suffered the smallest injury from them'. He laid the blame for the recent loss of life on both sides on 'the imprudent and *cruel* conduct of some of *our* people'—that is, those settlers who had armed their convict servants against the Wiradjuri and had themselves failed to exercise proper restraint.[23] The record of escalating violence from 1823, and the period of martial law in the latter months of 1824, leave the historian with a hazy understanding of the nature and severity of the conflicts. It seems that about 13 Europeans were killed; however, the scale of loss of life on the Wiradjuri side is much less readily estimated. The complexity of official approaches towards such conflict at the time is partly to blame for this obscurity. As Ann Curthoys explained:

> The Colonial Office never wavered in its refusal to acknowledge that a war of conquest was occurring, or in its insistence that the rule of law could and should prevail and that Indigenous life could be protected.[24]

It was important to assuage the concerns of 'the humanitarians in London' and, as Mark McKenna observed, to leave a 'record of the government's determination to defend Aboriginal rights'. However, the government was 'satisfied for the squatters to run ahead of government in their rush for wealth', and it was well understood that Aboriginal people and their rights would suffer in the process.[25] Governor Brisbane reported that the period of martial law had seen virtually no bloodshed. Some historians and storytellers have charged him with a 'cover-up'. In fact, there is

---

23  Ibid. (emphasis added).
24  Barker, *A History of Bathurst*, vol. 1, 67–72. European lives lost were carefully documented in evidence given to Major Morisset following his arrival in Bathurst in May 1824. NSW State Archives (hereafter NSWSA): Colonial Secretary; NRS 897, main series of letters received, 1788–1825, 4/1799, 31–48. Curthoys, 'Indigenous Subjects', 89. War with Aboriginal people was held to be impossible because they were to be considered 'subjects of the Queen'; it was this status that was supposed to provide them with protection. McKenna, *Looking for Blackfellas' Point*, 53.
25  McKenna examined a series of exchanges between Governor Bourke and Lord Glenelg in response to Batman's Port Phillip treaty and the colonisation of the New South Wales south coast. Governor Brisbane's proclamation of martial law was a similar record. McKenna, *Looking for Blackfellas' Point*, 52–54.

little firm evidence to support either version of events.²⁶ 'Colo' himself was not straightforwardly conciliatory, stating in principle that 'natives' might be justly 'chastised under the authority of a military officer, or some respectable, authorised, accountable person' in situations in which defensive measures were necessary. He emphasised that Wiradjuri women and children had been killed in the recent conflicts (something that the governor's proclamation of martial law explicitly sought to avoid), as if laying a charge of cowardice against the type of settler who had been involved in vigilante action. 'Colo' did not criticise Major Morisset or Governor Brisbane for their actions.²⁷

The Reverend William Walker, a Methodist minister who had been appointed as missionary to the 'black natives of New South Wales', also lamented that Aboriginal men, women and children had been 'butchered' by settlers in the west; yet, in July 1824, he had signed a landholders' petition for military intervention to 'overawe the natives' and bring them to 'a state of due Subjection and Inoffensiveness'.²⁸ George and William Suttor likewise saw their interests in productive land to the west of the ranges as legitimate, and may have felt that punitive action of some sort

---

26  Brisbane reported to Earl Bathurst that 'only seven Europeans have lost their lives ... and the number of [natives] ... can only be gathered from conjecture, but in all probability they do not much exceed double the number of Europeans'. He was 'gratified' to report that 'not one outrage was committed' during the period of martial law. Thomas Brisbane to Earl Bathurst, 31 December 1824, in Watson, *Historical Records of Australia*, series 1, vol. 11, 430–32. Mary Coe described the action under martial law as a 'campaign of genocide', and dubbed Brisbane's claim to have 'restored tranquillity without Bloodshed' the 'official cover-up'. Coe, *Windradyne—A Wiradjuri Koorie* (1989), 43. See also Elder, *Blood on the Wattle*, 49–51. Peter Read found that although some of the stories about massacres seem to have been exaggerated, it is plausible 'that between one quarter and one third of the Bathurst region Wiradjuri were killed' in these conflicts. Read, *A Hundred Years War*, 10. John Connor, in a military history of Australian frontier conflict, found that the Wiradjuri outclassed Morriset's military operations; his main expedition had difficulty even finding them. The tables were only to turn with the use of mounted cavalry—first deployed against Aboriginal people of the Hunter region in 1825. Only when settlers or soldiers came upon Aboriginal people by chance, could guns be used to kill in large numbers, as Chamberlane, William Cox's overseer did near Mudgee in late 1824. Connor, *The Australian Frontier Wars*, 52–62.
27  *The Australian*, 14 October 1826, 3.
28  Claughton, 'Walker, William (1800–1855)'; NSWSA: Colonial Secretary, NRS 897, main series of letters received, 1788–1825, 4/1799, Bathurst settlers to Brisbane, 16 July 1824, 73–76. The petition was signed by nine other landholders, including William Cox and Samuel Marsden. Several of the same men had made an appeal for government assistance, dated 3 June 1824, citing the murder of seven men by Aboriginal groups (pp. 51–54).

## 7. A FAMILY HEIRLOOM

against the Wiradjuri had been necessary.[29] As Penny Russell observed of Robert Dawson's account of his work establishing the Australian Agricultural Company operations at Port Stephens in the mid-1820s, 'Colo's' letter depicted 'his encroachments upon Aboriginal land as a story of advances in contact and friendship'. Like Dawson, 'Colo' seems to have sincerely desired to understand his presence as peaceable. While recognising some of the adverse effects of encroaching 'civilisation' upon Aboriginal people, both men 'regretted only [their] inability to prevent this—never [their] instrumentality'.[30]

In exploring the relationships between Victorian philanthropist Mrs Charles Bon and Victorian Aboriginal men William Barak, Thomas Bamfield and others, Liz Reed distinguished between Bon's advocacy on behalf of Aboriginal people and her personal friendships with them, and represented these two forms of goodwill as intimately related. Reed found that Bon's public role as a 'friend to the Aborigines' was sustained and motivated by her relationships 'with individual Aborigines in which [she] appeared to demonstrate an emotional connection and from which she derived personal comfort'.[31] 'Colo's' friendship with Windradyne and his people might be understood in a similar way. While he may have been a humanitarian on principle—George Suttor certainly counted himself a committed pacifist—'Colo's' act of advocacy appears to have sprung from genuine affection towards the Wiradjuri people whose country overlapped with Brucedale.[32] What 'Colo's' 1826 letter does not do (and I count myself slightly foolish for having hoped it might) is represent any profound friendship between the writer and any Wiradjuri individual. It evinces no meeting of minds, no deep conversation, no shared repasts—which is not to say that no such meeting of minds existed. To the contrary, if such intimacies did exist between George

---

29  When George Suttor found that the grant he had occupied on the Macquarie River was to be allocated to another settler, he wrote to Brisbane indignantly, 'granting my station to another will destroy all my hopes of prosperity there'. NSWSA: Colonial Secretary, NRS 897, main series of letters received, 1788–1825, 4/1832, letter 374, George Suttor to Brisbane, 14 June 1822, 1–2. Ann Curthoys saw a repeating pattern across the continent as settlers claimed new land and then attempted to defend their interests there, appealing for government support and sanction of punitive expeditions. Curthoys, 'Indigenous Subjects', 86–90.
30  Russell, *Savage or Civilised*, 58, 75–77. Dawson's memoir, *The Present State of Australia*, was published in 1830, after he returned to England.
31  Reed, 'Mrs Bon's Verandah', 39.1–39.2.
32  Suttor, *Memoirs of George Suttor*, 17. As a botanist, he probably also shared the respect for (and dependency on) Aboriginal expertise and assistance that his colleague and friend George Caley was forced to assert when Governor King ordered Aboriginal people out of the settled districts in 1801, Karskens, *The Colony*, 479.

THE LIVES OF STORIES

and William Suttor and Wiradjuri people, 'Colo' may well have chosen not to write about them in this rather proselytising letter.[33] While some colonists disagreed with philanthropic feeling towards Aboriginal people, its expression was much less likely to provoke the vehement opposition that intimate associations with Aboriginal people or targeted advocacy could inspire.[34] Risking the invocation of a threat to colonial order by elaborating on cross-cultural collaboration and communion would have been counterproductive to the letter's aim of normalising general interracial harmony on more or less British terms.

Virtually nothing is known about the way in which Windradyne and his family understood this friendship. If Wiradjuri people did direct George and William Suttor to the site of Brucedale, then, in doing so, they placed them on Wiradjuri country.[35] Maria Monypenny, writing of Tasmania, observed that the assimilating impulse and capabilities of Aboriginal groups are often overlooked:

> It would be a mistake … to assume that, because Aborigines were prepared to accommodate Europeans, they saw themselves becoming part of the European world. It is possible that, initially, they saw Europeans as becoming part of their world, and that it was on that basis that they were willing to co-operate with the newcomers.[36]

At least initially, the Wiradjuri may have been friendly towards the Suttor family not only, or chiefly, because they were benevolent, but also because they (the Suttors) had been satisfactorily incorporated into the local Wiradjuri world. 'Colo's' education in the structure and language

---

33 I have not discovered any more private source in which relations with Aboriginal people at Brucedale are discussed. George Suttor's brief memoirs do not discuss relations with Aboriginal people on Brucedale. I have so far found only one family letter from Brucedale in the early years. George wrote to Sarah Maria near the end of 1823 describing the new garden at Brucedale, which he and his second son, Charles (b. 1804), were tending, while William, along with his younger brother John (b. 1809), were expected to return soon from a five or six week journey into the hinterland. George evinced some concern about their welfare, but gave no details of their purpose or likely interactions with Aboriginal people. Suttor Family Papers 1774–1929, ML Manuscripts Collection, MSS 2417, item 3, 119.

34 Reed notes that Mrs Bon's cross-cultural collaborations and effective cohabitation with Aboriginal people at times led to her situation 'on the outermost boundary of acceptable European behaviour', which she was also at times accused of crossing, 'betraying her race, [and] behaving in ways unbecoming for a woman of her class'. Reed, 'Mrs Bon's Verandah', 39.3, 39.8. See also Reynolds, *Frontier*, 83–88.

35 According to Coe, the place may have been at a safe distance from sacred sites and their favourite camping and hunting grounds. Coe, *Windradyne—A Wiradjuri Koorie* (1989), 24.

36 Monypenny, 'Going Out and Coming In', 73.

of neighbouring groups appears to have been ongoing. At the time of writing, he had been introduced to people belonging to eight distinct local groups and instructed on their place in local networks.[37]

'Colo's' second letter, printed in *The Sydney Gazette* and *The Sydney Monitor* in 1829, was a report of Windradyne's death, offering a 'biography' of this famous Aboriginal man to the reading public. Following a tradition of obituary writing developed by John Nichols, editor of London's *The Gentleman's Magazine*, it provided a warm and respectful appraisal of Windradyne's character and person. 'Colo' assessed his subject as a man 'who never suffered an injury with impunity, [for] in his estimation revenge was virtue'. Yet, Windradyne also 'possessed the healing art' and was caring and compassionate in his ministrations to the sick. Whereas, in his earlier letter, 'Colo' had been content to refer to the man as 'Saturday', this time he was very clear that 'his original or aboriginal name was Windrodine'.[38]

'Colo' made it clear that the deceased had made a valuable contribution to colonial society by avoiding conflict for the latter part of his life. He wished the reader to understand that this signified conscious and deliberate restraint, rather than apathy or ignorance, speculating that Windradyne's 'high and independent spirit felt uneasy at times seeing his country possessed by the white fellows'. In a manner characteristic of his chosen genre, 'Colo' presented a clear account of the cause of death and used anecdote to illustrate the character of the deceased. Importantly, he also utilised the obituary itself as a vehicle for more general political comment, reproaching Europeans for their cruelty to this 'inoffensive race'. His description of Windradyne's 'head, his countenance, indeed his whole person, [as] a fine specimen of the savage warrior of New Holland', may be read as constituting an assertion of difference. While description of a subject's physical qualities was not unknown in *The Gentleman's Magazine*, a perusal of obituaries from 1829 suggests that, in cases in which the deceased was considered a gentleman or gentlewoman (for 'persons of interest' also graced Nichols' columns), the emphasis was on the

---

37  *The Australian*, 14 October 1826, 3.
38  *The Sydney Gazette*, 21 April 1829, 3. The letter is dated 24 March 1829. Starck, *Life after Death*, 5, 20–22, 32. In 1826, Nichols' own obituary appeared in the magazine. If George Suttor did not read the *Gentleman's Magazine* in his youth, or in the colony, then we might imagine him whiling away his hours in the court waiting room in 1810–12 (as a witness for Bligh in the court martial of Colonel George Johnston) reading the magazine's obituary columns. Parsons, 'Suttor, George (1774–1859)'.

deceased's discerning taste or intellect, with more oblique references to the physical, such as the form of the subject's handwriting or nature of his or her 'constitution'.[39]

'Colo's' mode of commemoration was not common in *The Sydney Gazette* of the time. The death notices composed by the editor were terse. Where they blossomed into compact tributes, it was usually because the deceased was 'respected by all who knew him'; little approximating an appraisal of character was offered. This pattern was enlivened by the occasional import from England, or a more extensive homegrown effort, such as the obituary of Mr Isaac Nichols, postmaster, printed in 1819.[40] Although the deaths of few Aboriginal people were noted in the Sydney press, a handful of well-known identities claimed far more column space than most eminent Europeans. Some of these were presented simply as a matter of curiosity. For example, the 1817 report of the death of 'Mirout' (or Mahroot) focused on the 'fracas' in which this man 'of docile friendly disposition' lost his life. The infamous 'Musquito' had died a decade earlier and *The Sydney Gazette* had featured a report on the elaborate funerary ceremony conducted by his friends and relatives, rather than an account of the man himself. In contrast, the Aboriginal men known as Andrew Sneap Hammond Douglas White and Thomas Walker Coke both received lengthy obituary-style tributes that assessed them in terms of their adoption of, and into, 'civilisation'. White's 1821 obituary concluded that 'all proved unavailing—ancestral habits being too indelibly engendered ever to be eradicated', while Coke's, of 1823, celebrated that, 'up to the period of his death, he gave satisfactory evidence of his acceptance with his Maker'.[41] By contrast, George or William Suttor, writing as 'Colo', provided Windradyne with a dignified tribute to his place in his own

---

39   *The Sydney Gazette*, 21 April 1829, 3; Starck, *Life after Death*, 46; *The Annual Biography and Obituary for the Year 1829*, 444, 446. The use of physical description in the obituary of a celebrated wood engraver drew attention to a difference of class: 'Mr. Bewick's personal appearance was rustic; he was tall, and powerfully formed. His manners too, were somewhat rustic; but he was shrewd, and never wished to ape the gentleman'. *The Annual Biography and Obituary for the Year 1829*, 414.
40   See, for example, the very brief death notices of Augustus Alt, *The Sydney Gazette*, 14 January 1815, 2; Captain Charles Waldron, *The Sydney Gazette*, 6 February 1834, 4; and a young man who fell from a horse, *The Sydney Gazette*, 11 February 1834, 4. By contrast, Nichol's recreational and gardening and boat building activities, as well as his efficiency as postmaster are described, *The Sydney Gazette*, 13 November 1819, 3. For an imported obituary (source not acknowledged), see that of Mrs Hannah Moore, who died in Bristol, providing an account of the literary and charitable achievements of this 'benefactress of her species', *The Sydney Gazette*, 1 February 1834, 3.
41   *The Sydney Gazette*, 23 August 1817, 3; 19 December 1806, 2; 8 September 1821, 3; 6 February 1823, 3.

society as well as his fame, or infamy, in European circles. This was the deed of a friend, not necessarily an intimate or confiding friend, but certainly a staunch and admiring one.

'Colo' probably imagined his friendship with Windradyne through the rich and flexible vocabulary of amicable relations that traversed philanthropy and sociability, available to him through the theory, literature and English practice of friendship of the late eighteenth and early nineteenth century. Although he understood that the status of 'chief' was not recognised among the Wiradjuri, in the world depicted in his letters he addressed himself to the most famous of Wiradjuri men, Windradyne, at times as a partner in a rational, pragmatic alliance between men that combined sympathy and loyalty with 'mutual interest' (such as that often forged between partners in commerce) and, at other times, in a less intimate, but no less trusting, political alliance in which he and Windradyne stood as representatives of their respective peoples. 'Colo' did not indulge in any late eighteenth-century sentimentalism in describing his own relationship with Windradyne; however, his description of the fervently loyal relationships between Wiradjuri men—to the death—might have been intended to counter the idea that savages were incapable of friendship due to a lack of moral refinement and, thus, to indicate that real friendship was possible between, and with, Aboriginal men. Conversely, 'Colo' directed his philanthropic love of humanity at the Wiradjuri in general as fellow human beings (though lower on the scale of humanity) who might be 'uplifted' by his attentions.[42]

An intensely patronising strain was evident in 'Colo's' 1826 letter to *The Australian* in which he referred to the Wiradjuri as 'rude children of nature' and advanced the opinion that:

> The laws of nature are their laws. They have not, that I can find, any other code … If knowledge be progressive in the human mind, in theirs it has hardly yet advanced one step, nor have their ideas began to shoot.[43]

Would a mutually respectful relationship with a Wiradjuri person have been possible for the writer of this letter? Reading it in the early twenty-first century, immersed in an understanding of friendships as emotionally

---

42  *The Sydney Gazette*, 21 April 1829, 3; *The Australian*, 14 October 1826, 4; Garrioch, 'From Christian Friendship to Secular Sentimentality', 185–87, 194–208; Brodie and Caine, 'Class, Sex and Friendship', 263.
43  *The Australian*, 14 October 1826, 3–4.

intimate, one-on-one relationships between equals, it is difficult to gain a footing in 'Colo's' thinking or to evaluate how different his public articulation of friendship might have been from his day-to-day interactions with Windradyne and other Wiradjuri people. 'Colo's' statement about a lack of code or law throws doubt on the depth of the writer's cultural exchange with the Wiradjuri people, as it evinces ignorance even of a kinship system into which he may himself have been adopted.

According to Russell, Dawson negotiated the complex social universe created by the interaction of Aboriginal people with Europeans of upper and lower social classes by setting himself securely atop it as 'master, arbiter and educator'. While Dawson experienced a loss of control over this universe at times, he was able to rationalise this, partly through writing about his experiences.[44] As he wrote, 'Colo' seems to have been making a transition between gentlemanly first-contact relationships with leaders such as Windradyne and 'Sunday', whom he likened to Apollo and Hercules, and the kind of intimacy he perceived as being feasible in the future. He pointed towards the 'improved ... manners' of the Aboriginal people he knew, and noted their 'docility' and potential to be 'useful and faithful servants'.[45]

The question of whether it was George or William Suttor who wrote these two letters is not insignificant for their interpretation. George was not the same generation as Windradyne; he was aged in his mid-50s in 1829, while 'Colo' estimated that Windradyne was about 30 years old when he died. If 'Colo' was George Suttor, it is notable that he singled out Windradyne as a leader and did not mention any of the Aboriginal Elders who would have been his own peers.[46] Conversely, William would have been slightly younger than Windradyne, making 'Colo's' adopted position of 'patron' even more striking. It was William and Windradyne who

---

44 Russell, *Savage or Civilised?*, 56–68.
45 *The Australian*, 14 October 1826, 3–4.
46 Dennis Foley, examining the nature of Windradyne's leadership, found that after witnessing the 'destruction and extermination of his Elder system' and fighting for his people's survival, Windradyne was heralded as a 'chief' by the Europeans. He then 'lived out his days as a token of what he had once been' as 'a warrior without Elders'. In these letters, and in much of the historiography that has followed them, Windradyne does appear as 'a warrior without Elders'. To what extent this was a failure of recognition or representation on 'Colo's' part, or a symptom of his selective socialising with Windradyne's clan, is not possible to say. Foley, 'Leadership', 180–85.

formed the friendship feted in recent retellings of the story.[47] This may have something to do with the contemporary appetite for fraternal rather than paternal-filial love, discussed further below, and is certainly related to William's part in the dramatic story preserved for posterity by his eldest son, W. H. Suttor, in which William, surrounded by Windradyne and his warriors, talked his way out of harm.

W. H. Suttor left a lasting monument to the friendship between his father and Windradyne in his *Australian Stories Retold and Sketches of Country Life*, published in 1887, compiled from short pieces written for *The Daily Telegraph* over a number of years. His 'stories retold' were 'chiefly gathered from the press records of the day, and from the word of mouth of old colonial friends', whereas the 'sketches' were from his own experience.[48] Among the 'stories retold' is an account titled 'Western Rebellions: Black and White', in which Suttor coupled the story of the British–Wiradjuri conflicts of 1823–24 with a famous bushranger story. He described the exchange around the potato field as the breaking point in British–Wiradjuri relations. The main thrust of the story was the merciless pursuit of Wiradjuri lives under martial law, which Suttor noted was a legal construct incomprehensible to the Wiradjuri. The story climaxed in a massacre built on a deception; Wiradjuri people were tricked into thinking that the settlers were making peace, as the settlers laid out food in a semblance of generosity before shooting indiscriminately. For Suttor, the landscape, which appeared peaceful, 'secluded and very romantic-looking', was haunted by this 'dastardly massacre'. Here and elsewhere, he chastised the settlers for their treachery.[49]

W. H. Suttor employed a language of war that was slippery. In pairing the Wiradjuri conflicts with a bushranger story, he characterised the conflicts as civil, a 'rebellion' in which Wiradjuri men were as 'offensive' to good order as bushrangers. At the same time, he alluded to a great historical war, concluding:

---

47   For example see Nowra and Perkins, 'Episode 1: They Have Come to Stay'; Heritage Listing, Grave of Windradyne, State Heritage Register Database, Record Number 5051560, Heritage Branch NSW, accessed 9 February 2009, www.heritage.nsw.gov.au/07_subnav_01_2.cfm?itemid=5051560. Debra Jopson, 'Grave a Symbol of 180 Years of Friendship', *The Sydney Morning Herald*, 20 April 2002.
48   Suttor, *Australian Stories Retold*, preface.
49   Ibid., 44–45. This is the theme of at least one of his other stories in the volume: 'Vengeance for Ippitha', in which a massacre is also perpetrated, showing the treachery of white men to be far greater than that of the Aboriginal people, an ironic rejoinder to his century's assessment of Aboriginal warfare as 'treacherous', because it is unpredictable and inexplicable in terms of British rules of engagement, see for example, Curthoys, 'Indigenous Subjects', 87.

> When martial law had run its course, extermination is the word that most aptly describes the result. As the old Romans said, 'They made a solitude and called it peace'. The last effort of a doomed race was thus ended.[50]

Roman historian Tacitus had put those words into the mouth of a Caledonian chief about to take on the Romans.[51] Suttor's reference was, perhaps, intended to make readers aware that Aboriginal people were in the same position as their own British ancestors had been. Yet, at the same time, the classical reference committed this heroism to the distant past. Suttor's story arraigned the protagonists (and European migrants to Australia more generally) for their part in destroying Aboriginal life, but did so in the romantic tradition of the late nineteenth century in which the Aboriginal 'race' was already extinct and the suitable sentiment was regret. Indeed, when he published his book, there would have been few of the original settlers of Bathurst still alive to have their consciences impugned. Yet, though the sting was taken out, his story nevertheless preserved ambivalence about the success of the pioneers and a vestige of the dilemmas of the 1820s.[52]

In the second part of the book, W. H. Suttor narrated his family's migration across the range. In 'A Cattle Muster in the Hills', he told the dramatic story of the surrounding of the hut by Windradyne and his men in the night. 'Fully equipped for war', the Wiradjuri were ready to enact a 'reprisal' in response to the hostile acts of the settlers, including the poisoning of dampers left where Wiradjuri people would find and eat them. William Suttor is the hero of the story, meeting the warriors 'fearlessly' and courteously talking them down in their own language. A pre-existing friendship is briefly and enigmatically invoked: 'They never

---

50   Suttor, *Australian Stories Retold*, 45–46. A similar admixture characterised contemporary responses to the conflicts. An editorial in *The Sydney Gazette* referred to the engagement of the Bathurst district in 'an exterminating war' (14 October 1824, 2) and also made whimsical allusions to the Battle of Waterloo. One of Windradyne's contemporaries, likewise engaged in action against the colonists, was admiringly referred to as 'Blucher' after a much celebrated Prussian general who, alongside the Duke of Wellington, defeated Napoleon only a decade earlier—an identification that could equally dignify or mock. In the same issue of *The Sydney Gazette* in which the death (in combat with settlers) of this Wiradjuri man was reported, an article recounting the Battle of Waterloo also appeared. *The Sydney Gazette*, 30 September 1824, 2, 4.

51   Tacitus's Galgacus rallied his fighters with an assessment of the Roman character: 'plunderers of the earth these, who in their universal devastations finding countries to fail them, investigate and rob even the sea … To spoil, to butcher and to commit every kind of violence, they style by a lying name, *Government*; and when they have spread a general desolation, they call it *Peace*' ('Ubi solitudinem faciunt, pacem appellant'). Tacitus, 'The Life of Agricola', 284.

52   Foster, Hosking and Nettelbeck, *Fatal Collisions*, 26–28.

molested man or beast of my father's. He had proved himself their friend on previous occasions'.[53] The meaning of this encounter cannot now be recovered. Perhaps, in surrounding the hut, Windradyne's party meant to warn William and scare him into contracting his pastoral operations; alternatively, the Wiradjuri men may have gathered to remind William of his ongoing mutual obligation in this rapidly developing conflict.[54]

Although the events were not strictly within his own experience, W. H. Suttor told this story among his 'sketches'. A private story made public, it set his own family apart from other Bathurst settlers and provided insights into Wiradjuri decision-making that were not explicable in British terms. The glimpse of the relationship between William and the Wiradjuri men involved in the encounter is radically different from the kind of friendship described in the first half of the book. There, a situation of goodwill persists between Windradyne and the settlers-in-general after the cease of conflict:

> He is said to have been really a fine specimen of the manly savage. For some time before his death he lived in peace with the whites and stories are told of his goodnatured and affectionate conduct towards the children of his former foes.[55]

This brief and formulaic description of Windradyne as a 'manly savage' echoes press accounts of his visit to the annual feast at Parramatta in 1824, in which he was celebrated as 'without doubt the most manly black native we have ever beheld', rather than family memories.[56]

W. H. Suttor was born five years after Windradyne's death, in 1834; therefore, he was not one of the children who had felt Windradyne's affection. He did not document any other stories of his father's or grandfather's relationships with Wiradjuri people in the 1820s. Instead, he wrote of his own diverse friendships with another generation of Aboriginal people in his 'sketches', including his childhood admiration for 'Maria'

---

53   Suttor, *Australian Stories Retold*, 65.
54   Shayne Breen demonstrated this in the central Tasmanian context, in which he found (on close examination of European accounts of similar events) that the Pallittorre people, in conflict with scattered outstations in the late 1820s and 1830s, often meant to create fear through the threat of violence (surrounding huts, demonstrating that they were armed and dangerous), rather than using violence itself. In a series of events in June 1827, the Pallittorre surrounded and plundered a number of outstations, and killed one man who had repeatedly attacked them, and spared another, who was presumably innocent of such crimes, when he was at their mercy. Breen, 'Human Agency'.
55   Suttor, *Australian Stories Retold*, 45.
56   *The Sydney Gazette*, 30 December 1824, 2.

and her skills as a swimmer and verbal sparring partner, and his affection for 'Laughing Billy', who he grew up alongside and later buried in a way that attempted to pay respect to his culture.[57] W. H. Suttor depicted these people in short anecdotes; he did not link them to place or to family, and their identity within Wiradjuri networks, if he knew of these connections, was not recorded.

Brucedale was one of the Bathurst Plains stations notable for its continued employment of Aboriginal people into the late nineteenth century. It may have provided sanctuary to local Wiradjuri people in the way that Hermannsburg did for Arrernte people, or Weilmoringle did for the Muruwari—that is, requiring or prompting them to change in significant ways, while enabling them to maintain links to family and country.[58] However, facing his reading public, W. H. Suttor wrote as if he understood his friendships with Aboriginal people as essentially belonging to the past. He was aged in his 40s and early 50s when he wrote *Australian Stories Retold*. Already a member of the Legislative Council and owner of several sheep stations in the Darling District,[59] he wrote as if he could not see a future for Wiradjuri people. He made poignant reference to traditional burial practices as the last sign of a Wiradjuri presence in the landscape:

> These people who fill my early memories of the 'Great Plain' with kindest reflections are nearly all gone. A mound of earth here and there slowly and surely sinking to the common level, with adjacent trees scarred over with deep-cut markings … are all that remain to remind us that they ever were.[60]

Under such circumstances, extending his friendship towards the Wiradjuri people seemed a commemorative act.

It was in this spirit too that Mr and Mrs Roy Suttor honoured Windradyne as the 'Last Chief of the Aboriginals' in 1954. The oral traditions of the Suttor family seem to have merged with, and emerged from, W. H. Suttor's small volume across the twentieth century. David Suttor told me that he grew up thinking that the stories about Windradyne were all family oral tradition, and was surprised when he found much of it in his great–great uncle's book. John Suttor (Roy Suttor's son) was proud to see his son

---

57 Suttor, *Australian Stories Retold*, 81–97, 145–48.
58 Papers of P. J. Gresser, AIATSIS MS21/3/a, 73; Gill, *Weilmoringle*.
59 Ruth Teale, 'Suttor, William Henry (1834–1905)'.
60 Suttor, *Australian Stories Retold*, 85–86.

David appear on *First Australians* telling the story as he had taught it to him.[61] When Wiradjuri man and ABC news anchor Stan Grant Jnr visited Brucedale sometime before 2002, John Suttor welcomed him with the family copy of *Australian Stories Retold* in his hand. He took Grant to Windradyne's grave and to the hut that Windradyne surrounded on that fateful night in 1823, reading aloud from the book.[62] W. H. Suttor may have written the extinction of the Wiradjuri, but his book has played a significant part in keeping the story of friendship alive.

At the close of World War Two, Anzac Day retained its significance in the definition of the Australian nation: 'the digger stood for freedom, comradeship, tolerance and the innate worth of man'.[63] As Joy Damousi observed, a complex dual loyalty—both to the nation and to the British Empire—endured through the 1950s, reinforced by that first visit by a reigning monarch in 1954. Australians continued to identify themselves closely with the empire's new incarnation, the Commonwealth of British nations, reinforced by Menzies proclamation that 'our nation is British in blood, tradition and sentiment'.[64] Did the Suttor family and the Bathurst Historical Society recognise Windradyne as a fallen patriot? Did they mean to extend the spirit of Anzac to this long-dead Aboriginal man? W. H. Suttor's reference to a classical war—the Caledonians versus the Romans—may have allowed room for a war memorial of sorts, but one to a hero of distant and different times. It may have been possible to pay tribute to Windradyne as a great leader no longer partisan in defeat, and embodying universally recognised virtues that could be recruited to local national pride. Certainly, 10 or 15 years later, Roy Suttor did imagine Windradyne as a wounded hero at the time of his death as he recounted the family story of Windradyne escaping from the hospital at Bathurst, where he had been taken to have wounds tended, throwing off his bandages and returning to his people at Brucedale, where he died and was buried.[65]

---

61   David Suttor, in conversation with the author, 20 January 2009; John Suttor, in conversation with the author, 20 January 2009.
62   Grant, *The Tears of Strangers*, 64–67.
63   White, *Inventing Australia*, 136–37.
64   Damousi, 'War and Commemoration', 303–05. Menzies's speech at the opening (by the Queen) of the Australian–American War Memorial in Canberra in 1954, quoted in Damousi, 'War and Commemoration', 304.
65   Roy Suttor's contribution of this story to Salisbury and Gresser's history (published 1971) is discussed further below. By this time, Roy had been discussing the Aboriginal history of the district with Gresser for more than a decade, Papers of P. J. Gresser, AIATSIS, MS21f, 34.

As Ashton and Hamilton have observed, postwar memorial culture was greatly influenced by war commemoration. Ironically, it was perhaps the very commemorative culture of Anzac, which drew much of its strength from the feeling that the nation was forged through bloodshed and sacrifice at Gallipoli and elsewhere (as the conflicts with Aboriginal nations across Australia 'were deemed not to have happened'), that reflected heroic patriotism back onto Windradyne in 1954. Those who landed at Gallipoli had failed spectacularly in a military sense, but had proved that nothing could be found wanting in Australian manhood.[66] Those gathered around Windradyne's grave in 1954 may have been paying tribute to a similar integrity and virility. Still, given how difficult, even impossible, it was for white Australians to be 'mates' with Aboriginal people during this era, the Suttor family and the Bathurst Historical Society's desire to embrace Windradyne in this way remains 'unexpected'.[67] Their memorial has aged; its stark claim that Windradyne was the 'Last Chief of the Aboriginals' no longer represents the Suttor family or the Bathurst Historical Society's commemorative ideas as they engage in continuing dialogue with Wiradjuri people about their history. Yet, Windradyne's designation as a 'patriot' and the Anzac-like notion that Wiradjuri manhood and courage remains intact in heroic defeat has had enduring appeal for Wiradjuri history-makers.

It was, perhaps, a combination of symbolic flexibility, the assumption that the Wiradjuri were no longer a political force and the erection of the memorial on private land that rendered it uncontroversial, despite being unusual.[68] When Ken Colbung, chairman of the Aboriginal Lands Trust, proposed a memorial statue to Yagan in the heart of Perth as the 150th anniversary of white settlement approached in 1978, he met with stiff opposition. Sir Paul Hasluck, recently retired from the post of governor general, strongly opposed the monument. His wife, Dame Alexandra, who had written a biography of Yagan, declared that he had been a thief and certainly no patriot. Despite support from other quarters, the statue did not go ahead until some years later.[69] However, on private

---

66   Ashton and Hamilton. 'Places of the Heart', 1; Damousi, 'War and Commemoration', 290–97; Seal, 'Digger', 122–24.
67   Smith, 'The Spectre of Truganini', 14–15.
68   Read, 'The Truth that Will Set Us All Free', 36.
69   Ironically, Dame Hasluck had been eager to credit Yagan with patriotism when she had not felt there was a risk of Aboriginal people taking ownership of the term. Hasluck, 'Yagan the Patriot', 33–48. Bulbeck, 'Aborigines, Memorials and the History of the Frontier', 173–74. A statue was finally set up in 1984. It was beheaded in 1997 when Yagan's own head was repatriated, and then again when repaired. It has been surrounded by ongoing controversy, many preferring that Yagan be clad rather than naked in this public space. Batten and Batten, 'Memorialising the Past', 99–100.

land at Brucedale no public justification was necessary. If the Suttor family thought Windradyne worthy of commemoration, that was all that was needed.

This commemoration may not have helped contemporary Wiradjuri people in any practical way; yet, in signifying a reaching out on the part of the Suttor family, it served a positive purpose. Windradyne's story was a part of the Suttor family's history; the commemoration signalled the family's desire to make sure that it stayed that way. John Suttor, aged in his early teens in 1954, remembered that when the memorial was to be erected, his father Roy followed instructions provided by his father and one of his uncles years earlier to identify which of the tumuli on the hill above Winburndale Rivulet was Windradyne's grave. There was a moment of anxiety as Roy wondered whether he had chosen the correct grave. He eventually rested certain in his decision. Already, Roy had made an even more significant decision—to act on the story handed down to him by his father and uncle, H. C. and Horace Suttor, who were convinced that Windradyne was buried at Brucedale.[70]

'Colo', announcing Windradyne's death in March 1829, had reported that Windradyne was wounded in the knee during a night skirmish, on the banks of the Macquarie River, with a tribe from the south, and that the wound 'mortified', leading swiftly to his death and a respectful burial near the Bathurst hospital:

> He continued talking to his countrymen till life was extinct, in the hospital at Bathurst, near which place he was buried, his body being wrapped in his mantle, and his weapons deposited in the grave.[71]

In line with this account, W. H. Suttor, William Suttor's eldest son, believed that Windradyne was 'buried, wrapped in his opossum cloak, in the grounds of the old hospital at Bathurst'.[72] However, a strong

---

70  John Suttor, in conversation with the author, 20 January 2009. Roy Suttor had also told Percy Gresser he was not sure 'which of the graves is Windradyne's but he was certainly buried in the close vicinity'. Papers of P. J. Gresser, AIATSIS, MS21/3/a, 120; Salisbury and Gresser, *Windradyne of the Wiradjuri*, 42–43.
71  *The Sydney Gazette*, 21 April 1829, 3. It is not known whether 'Colo's' account informed the discussions between the three Suttor brothers (H. C., Horace and W. H. Suttor) 60 years later. Grace Hendy-Pooley closely paraphrased 'Colo's' account and replicated his unusual spelling, 'Windrodine', in a short history of Bathurst published in 1905 (though she did not explicitly refer to the letter). Subsequently, though, it seems to have fallen below the horizon for tellers of Windradyne's story. Hendy-Pooley, 'Early History of Bathurst', 230–36.
72  Suttor, *Australian Stories Retold*, note to page 45.

counter-tradition arose within the Suttor family that Windradyne had returned to Brucedale and had died and been buried there. H. C. and Horace Suttor's story, which Roy Suttor recounted to Percy Gresser, held that Windradyne died in 1835 after being badly wounded in a tribal fight. He was taken to the old Bathurst hospital where Dr Busby dressed his wounds. However:

> To be confined in hospital was too much for Windradyne, so he tore off the bandages and made his escape, making his way to *Brucedale*, where there were a number of his own people. Gangrene supervened and he died, and was buried, wrapped in his o'possum mantle, by his fellow Aborigines in the sacred tribal cemetery on *Brucedale*.[73]

When W. H. Suttor was writing his book *Australian Stories Retold* in the 1880s, energetic debate apparently sprang up between the three brothers. However, as their father, William Suttor, had died in 1877, no more light could be shed on the divergent traditions and their relationship to one another. Roy Suttor's 1954 memorial represented a decision to claim Windradyne's burial for Brucedale. As the grave mound sunk further into the surrounding earth, the family drew Windradyne to its bosom.

In the mid-1990s, John and David Suttor started to feel that they should do more to protect Windradyne's grave, prompted partly by reflection on the recent Wik and Mabo land rights decisions. Tom Griffiths wrote of the wave of hysteria, fanned by the media, that swept across the nation as land owners worried they might be 'Mabo-ed'. One man in Victoria told Griffiths that 'you'd have to be stark raving mad' to admit to having special sites on your property. John Suttor was bothered by the fragile state of Windradyne's grave, and a second grave mound nearby, which both sat in his paddock with cattle wandering over them. Aware of a local native title claim that made reference to Windradyne's grave, he decided to take the initiative.[74] Encouraged by Wiradjuri elder John Bugg and others, he approached the National Parks and Wildlife Service (NPWS) to negotiate

---

73  Salisbury and Gresser, *Windradyne of the Wiradjuri*, 42–43 (original emphasis).
74  Johnson, *Lighting the Way*, 48. The Coe sisters filed a native title writ in mid-1993. One of their objectives was to gain free access to important sites, including Windradyne's grave, or at least to draw attention to the fact that, at that time, land owners' permission was needed to visit these sites. Tony Hewett, 'Wiradjuri People's Writ Immortalises a Warrior', *The Sydney Morning Herald*, 7 June 1993, 8; Griffiths, *Hunters and Collectors*, 230. David Roberts noted a reluctance of the Sofala community (about 20 kilometres north of Brucedale) in the mid-1990s to acknowledge Aboriginal sites identified by the National Parks and Wildlife Service, and found an atmosphere of caution among landholders about the potential presence of Aboriginal artefacts and evidence pointing to massacre sites on their land. Roberts, 'Bells Falls Massacre', 616.

a Voluntary Conservation Agreement that would protect the cultural significance of the grave site into the future. The family's cordial and mutually respectful relationship with Dinawan Dyirribang, the National Parks and Wildlife cultural sites officer with whom they negotiated the agreement, developed through this process.[75]

A 2002 article in *The Sydney Morning Herald* referred to 'a friendship of almost 180 years and six generations' between the local Wiradjuri and the Suttor family, and linked the completed Conservation Agreement with the friendship displayed by Windradyne towards William on that fateful night in 1823:

> It is an association [that] saved one Suttor's life and has now saved Wyndradyne's grave from being wrecked by cattle that like to scratch themselves on a cairn [that] the Bathurst Historical Society erected beside it 47 years ago.[76]

This comment attempts to capture a century and a half of relationships within a journalistic flourish. How do we reconcile it with W. H. Suttor's certainty that the family's association with a living Wiradjuri community closed with the nineteenth century? Contact between the Suttor family and the Wiradjuri community was interrupted. Dinawan Dyirribang says that two local Wiradjuri clans left the Bathurst area shortly after Windradyne's death—one went to Wellington where they were documented by the missionary Reverend Gunther, and the other, Peneegrah's people, went to Cowra—but some people stayed too.[77] John Suttor stated that he did not know of any family relationships with Wiradjuri people after Windradyne's generation until he found an old box containing a photograph of an Aboriginal couple who had taken on the family name.[78] Peter Read concluded that the friendships between Wiradjuri people and European farmers during the mid and late nineteenth century could be fragile, as constant change in the white world

---

75  Johnson, *Lighting the Way*, 48.
76  Debra Jopson, 'Grave a Symbol of 180 Years of Friendship', *The Sydney Morning Herald*, 20 April 2002. Interpretive signage installed by the National Parks Service at Brucedale in 2010 makes a much more circumspect claim to continuity, stating that Windradyne's 'grave has been protected by seven generations of the Suttor family'. Entry sign installed at the gate of Brucedale, Peel Road, NSW National Parks and Wildlife Service (Bathurst), 2010.
77  Dinawan Dyirribang, in conversation with the author, 8 July 2011. The Suttor family's close connection with Brucedale was interrupted at this time as well. In the 1840s, as William purchased land and established stations on the Lachlan and Darling Rivers, and as far afield as Moreton Bay, Brucedale was let to tenants for a number of years. Teale, 'Suttor, William Henry (1805–1877)'.
78  John Suttor, in conversation with the author, 20 January 2009.

put pressure on the life ways of the Wiradjuri. The need to move, or marry out, or the death of a Wiradjuri person could result in an absence of Wiradjuri people from a locality for decades, breaking contact with even the most sympathetic Europeans. Compared with the 'bi-cultural community' at Weilmoringle on the New South Wales – Queensland border—where Muruwari and migrant families have lived alongside each other, worked together and shared land, knowledge and childcare across the decades—the Brucedale friendship has been, for much of its history, a symbolic rather than an intimate, involved and practical one.[79]

Yet, this notion of continuity may contain some truth for the present. In her 2002 book, Dianne Johnson drew on W. H. Suttor's accounts of friendship with Aboriginal people as evidence of the Suttor family's continuing relationship with the Wiradjuri.[80] However, as we saw above, W. H. Suttor himself was not able or willing to represent his family's relations with the Wiradjuri as ongoing. Believing that no Wiradjuri people survived in the present, his generation had considered the friendship to be one-sided. Yet, the responsibility to not only preserve the story, but also to actively reaffirm the friendship and share it with a wider public, whether or not it could be reciprocated, was passed from generation to generation. The continuity of this friendship has been rediscovered via the reconciliation era; looking back from a position in which the Wiradjuri have survived, a two-way relationship has now been renewed.

---

79 Read, *A Hundred Years War*, 25–28; Gill, *Weilmoringle*.
80 Johnson, *Lighting the Way*, 57–58.

# 8

# At the Confluence of Two Stories

The Bathurst Historical Society produced two local histories in the early 1960s. One of them did not refer to Wiradjuri people. In the other, the conflicts of the 1820s were depicted as a mere flicker of the district's candle; Bathurst began 'as a stronghold ... against a foe who virtually did not exist'.[1] The society appeared to have forgotten its commemoration of Windradyne the patriot. At the same time, Percy Gresser was writing a very different history. On his retirement to Bathurst in 1953, Gresser began to donate his large collection of carefully documented stone tools to the Australian Museum and to write a history of the local Aboriginal people. He attended the 1954 ceremony at Windradyne's grave, leaving a brief account of the day in one of his fastidiously organised notebooks. Embedded in the concrete memorial at Brucedale is a piece of carefully worked stone that Gresser described as a 'remarkably good specimen of a large Aboriginal axe head'; he had probably donated the axe head, which had been found in the bed of nearby Clear Creek.[2]

Gresser's understanding of this memorial was very different from that of some of the Bathurst Historical Society members. His intimate engagement with the landscape kept an Aboriginal presence in the forefront of his mind. For example, he knew that, all over the region,

---

1  Bathurst District Historical Society, *A Short History of Bathurst*, 1–8; Taussig, 'How Bathurst Began', 15. See also the work of J. P. M. Long, held in the Historical Society archives, in which continued action by Aboriginal people is described as one of the 'most conspicuous discomforts and dangers of life in the district throughout this period'. Long, 'Bathurst 1813-1840', 51.
2  Mulvaney, 'The Gresser Papers', 86–88; Papers of P. J. Gresser, AIATSIS, MS21/51/a, 28; MS21/51/c, 167; MS21/3/a, 120; John Suttor, in conversation with the author, 20 January 2009.

'ploughing or water erosion reveals that practically every low ridge adjacent to a creek or a spring was a former campsite of the Aborigines'. Further, he knew that Windradyne was one man among many—a local leader of one generation in a long line of generations; Gresser perceived a history of some 20,000 years in the hand-shaped stones he found on the surface of the land.[3] Gresser rightly considered his work to be very different from that of the Bathurst Historical Society. In the early 1960s, the society's secretary, Bernard Greaves, attempted to divert part of Gresser's collection from the Australian Museum to the society's local museum. Gresser rebuffed his approaches by making a distinction between disciplines; the local museum, he pointed out, somewhat indignantly, was a folk museum with no aspirations to serious anthropological or geological knowledge—a collection of Aboriginal stone tools (especially a good collection) had no place there.[4] Greaves had his own version or vision of 'accurate' history, authenticated by a basis in documents and their sincere interpretation by Bathurst's citizenry.[5] For him, Windradyne and his memorial were a kind of 'exception' to history, best acknowledged in situ in Bathurst's hinterland, marked with an axe head that signalled a pre-historic context—a different place and time entirely to the Bathurst Historical Society's tidy civic histories.

Gresser's history, 'The Aborigines of the Bathurst District', was published as a daily serial in *The Western Times* across the latter half of August 1962. It began with the crossing of the range by Europeans and their first observations of Aboriginal people to the west, and also made suggestions about how those Aboriginal people may have understood the Europeans. Gresser gave an account of good relations between exploratory parties, early settlers and Aboriginal groups, and the role of Aboriginal people in guiding Europeans to Mudgee and other areas. Then, referencing Colonel Mundy's explanation of the possession of the country via 'gradual eviction … without treaty, bargain or apology', he charted the beginnings of their

---

3   Papers of P. J. Gresser, AIATSIS, MS21/6, 'Articles Relating to the Aborigines' (1963), 37; *The Western Times*, 31 May 1962, 2, 10. Griffiths observed that, as the discipline of history became increasingly professionalised, and as historians focused increasingly on the analysis of documents, it was often amateur historians and collectors who remained interested in the connections of their local landscapes with the past and who were constantly reminded of an Aboriginal presence and history in those places. Griffiths, *Hunters and Collectors*, 5.
4   Papers of P. J. Gresser, AIATSIS, MS21b, 16–28.
5   Greaves, *The Story of Bathurst*, editor's preface. This citizenry was presumably comprised of the 'Bathurstians' who had written the chapters of this book, and the circles in which they moved.

dispossession.[6] Gresser's Windradyne—a man 'of strong personality, shrewdness and courage'—became an 'implacable enemy to the whites' after the shooting of his companions while gathering potatoes. Gresser noted the role of the district's settlers in advocating for the declaration of martial law, and the brutalities that had been committed under it, including the massacre described by W. H. Suttor. He canvassed the official account, that peace had been achieved without bloodshed, and asked the reader to consider whether Governor Brisbane was in ignorance of the reality or whether he condoned it.[7] He gave an account of early missionary activities in the region, followed by an in-depth consideration of Aboriginal religious beliefs. In this he was guided by Katie Langloh Parker's maxim that, 'if we cannot respect the religion of others, we deny our own'; Parker had translated and published legends told to her by Aboriginal people of central and western New South Wales in the late nineteenth century. Gresser admonished those who would call Aboriginal languages 'gibberish' for having no knowledge of grammar in any tongue.[8]

Overall, though, Gresser was writing a history of 'decimation, decay and death'. He catalogued the deaths of the last Aboriginal men, and referred to the absorption of the women into white society, concluding his history at the graves of Yuranigh and Windradyne.[9] His explanation for the decline of the local Aboriginal population was the breaking of their close associations with the landscape, and hunger, disease and demoralisation. These complex historical explanations for the continued poor social and economic position of Aboriginal people were cutting edge at the time. The Aborigines Project of the Social Sciences Research Council of Australia (1964–67) sought (on a much larger scale than Gresser's project) to develop a historical understanding of Aboriginal disadvantage to replace

---

6   Percy Gresser, 'The Aborigines of the Bathurst District', *The Western Times*, 15 August 1962, 9. Gresser absorbed Mundy's indignantly ironic tone as he pointed out the double standard upheld by the Europeans; that justice was 'deaf, dumb, lame and blind' when it came to protecting Aboriginal people and 'in full possession of all her faculties' when protecting the whites. Mundy, 'Our Antipodes' (1852), quoted in Gresser, 'The Aborigines of the Bathurst District', *The Western Times*, 22 August 1962, 7–8, 10. Mundy had visited Brucedale, and documented his interactions with Aboriginal people there. Papers of P. J. Gresser, AIATSIS, MS21/3/a, 122–31.
7   Gresser, 'The Aborigines of the Bathurst District', *The Western Times*, 18 August 1962, 3 and 20 August 1962, 3. As Barker noted, W. H. Suttor did not claim that Windradyne was present at the potato field massacre; it was Gresser who explicitly involved Windradyne in this part of the narrative. Barker, *A History of Bathurst*, vol. 1, 73.
8   Muir, 'Stow, Catherine Eliza Somerville (Katie) (1856–1940)'. Gresser, 'The Aborigines of the Bathurst District', *The Western Times*, 24 August 1962, 9.
9   Gresser, 'The Aborigines of the Bathurst District', *The Western Times*, 17 August 1962, 9; 29 August 1962, 10; 31 August 1962, 7.

the common wisdom, which underpinned policy and public opinion, that Aboriginal society was a static one of inferior character. Gresser also repeated the explanation that some Wiradjuri people had given Parker—namely, that they were being punished for not abiding by Biami's laws.[10]

The serial was addressed to a white audience. Frederick McCarthy, archaeologist and curator at the Australian Museum, on hearing that Gresser's history was to be published in the local paper, observed archly, 'it should make most interesting reading to the locals whose ancestors had so much to do with the extermination of the unfortunate Aborigines'.[11] However, by Gresser's own account, it was warmly received. He noted 'tributes of appreciation from various residents of Bathurst', including the Bathurst Naturalist Society, which complemented him on his thorough research and clear exposition on a 'subject … of universal interest'. As challenging as Gresser's history was, it was not out of sympathy with the Naturalist Society's interest in the 'customs, legends and languages of the Aborigines' or with their ostensibly regretful refrain that it was 'now too late' to learn any more from Aboriginal people themselves.[12] As he reworked his history over the next few years, Gresser became strongly persuaded that W. H. Suttor had exaggerated his account of the brutalities of the 1820s; certainly there were many and unjust killings, but there were also few Europeans and many places to hide. Instead, Gresser traced the extinction of the Wiradjuri people of the Bathurst district to the 1880s and 1890s. Yet, even in the mid-1960s, 'a few families of mixed blood are to be found throughout the district', though they were in imminent danger of 'becoming completely absorbed into the white population'. Like W. H. Suttor, Gresser wrote of his own Aboriginal acquaintances in a nostalgic register that did not seek to connect them to the *longue durée* of their peoples' histories.[13] Just a few years later, Dinawan Dyirribang's family, having maintained the knowledge of their family connection to Windradyne, moved into Bathurst town under the new 'salt and pepper' philosophy of the assimilation policy. The local council notified their neighbours-to-be that an Aboriginal family was moving in and a petition

---

10   Rowley, *The Destruction of Aboriginal Society*, 1–9; Gresser, 'The Aborigines of the Bathurst District', *The Western Times*, 27 August 1962, 3.
11   Papers of P. J. Gresser, AIATSIS, MS21d, 19, McCarthy to Gresser, 18 July 1963.
12   Papers of P. J. Gresser, AIATSIS, MS21e, 23; MS21f, 38; MS21h, 21.
13   Papers of P. J. Gresser, AIATSIS, MS21j, 4–5; MS21/3/a,102–03; MS21/6, 'Aborigines in the Shearing Sheds'; MS21/35, 'Little Part Aborigine Girl I met at Pambula'.

was raised in objection. The mayor, who knew Dinawan Dyirribang's parents well, refused to respond to the petition, but it was years before Dinawan Dyirribang's family were embraced by their neighbours.[14]

Across the 1960s, Gresser continued to add to his history and to correspond with a network of other amateurs with a serious interest in Aboriginal archaeology and culture.[15] Tom Salisbury, of the Bankstown Historical Society, had developed an interest in Windradyne and, frustrated by meagre findings in the Mitchell Library, travelled to Bathurst in 1966. The Bathurst Historical Society directed him towards Gresser, who pointed him towards the sources he had found, and to Roy Suttor, who took him to see Windradyne's grave. On his return to Sydney, Salisbury read Gresser's newspaper serial and wrote in amazement that, despite his long interest in Australian history, '"The Aborigines of the Bathurst District" was as a completely new world to me'. He felt this history should be published as a book. On the one weekend in four that Salisbury had to himself, he continued his research in the Mitchell Library, updating Gresser on his findings. In March 1967, he uncovered a pair of notices offering a reward for Windradyne's capture, with the proviso 'alive' omitted from the second.[16] Old and tired, Gresser was concentrating on 'getting his house in order'; he had no objection to Salisbury compiling a book, but did not wish to take an active part in co-authorship.[17]

The correspondence between the two men, as David Roberts has noted, shows the shifting historiographical 'sympathies' that transformed Gresser's serial into Salisbury's history in the making. Salisbury reached towards the activist impulse that would drive historians to expose the terrible violence of the frontier in the early 1970s and 1980s, quite distinct from Gresser's restrained (if excoriating) historical moralism. In mid-1967, Salisbury wrote: 'I am struck by the similarities which existed in Bathurst in 1824 and the present day situation in Vietnam …

---

14   Dinawan Dyirribang, in conversation with the author, 8 July 2011.
15   Gresser had Ted Suttor of *The Rocks*, Bathurst, collecting any stones that looked like they might have been worked by Aboriginal people as he moved around his property. He corresponded with Brian Fillery of Narromine, photographing and analysing commemorative carved trees, and Brian Woolley in Nowra, studying the use and distribution of ochres in his area. Papers of P. J. Gresser, AIATSIS, MS21i, 10; MS21d, 32, McCarthy to Gresser; MS21g, 14, 30.
16   Papers of P. J. Gresser, AIATSIS, MS21f, 34; MS21f, 36–37; MS21h, 1–4. The proclamations were issued 18 and 25 August 1824, respectively, quoted in Salisbury and Gresser, *Windradyne of the Wiradjuri*, 34.
17   Papers of P. J. Gresser, AIATSIS, MS21h, 45, Gresser to McCarthy, October 1967; MS21i, 31–32.

our own dreadful participation today'. Salisbury was alarmed to find that the 1961 history of Bathurst edited by Greaves gave the conflicts of the 1820s such short shrift. Gresser, perhaps attempting to divert him from charging the authors with a conspiracy of silence, explained simply that the book had been written before his own serial was published.[18]

Salisbury had fixed on Windradyne and the power of his life story to convey the Bathurst story. In August 1968, breathless with excitement after giving a presentation before the Wild Colonial Society, he addressed Gresser:

> You who have lived … in Windradyne's country and have … been brought up in the knowledge of Windradyne's history and importance, may not realise that there are many people, here in Sydney, who are greatly interested in Australian History, but have only a vague, indefinite knowledge of someone known as 'Saturday' and are amazed … to hear of Windradyne as he really was.[19]

The result of Salisbury's endeavours was published in 1971 as *Windradyne of the Wiradjuri: Martial Law at Bathurst in 1824*. This small book has been a touchstone for subsequent storytellers; most have relied heavily (or solely) on the extracts from primary sources reproduced therein, and Salisbury's and Gresser's interpretations of them.[20] Foregrounding the primary documentary sources, and adding 'ethnographic' insights into the Wiradjuri perspective when possible, it traces the 'dispossession' of the great Wiradjuri 'Nation'.[21] Windradyne is portrayed as a leader whose strength and daring captured contemporary imaginations. The friendship between Windradyne and the Suttor family is touched upon via the dramatic episode in which William's hut was surrounded in the night, and his life saved by his language skills and prior friendship with the Wiradjuri. Salisbury consulted with Roy Suttor and his family in compiling the short chapter on Windradyne, and a sense of warm regard

---

18   Roberts, 'Bells Falls Massacre', 628–29; Papers of P. J. Gresser, AIATSIS, MS21h, 27; MS21f, 34, 36–37.
19   Papers of P. J. Gresser, AIATSIS, MS21i, 31–32.
20   Most of the more recent renditions of the story I have been discussing refer almost exclusively to Salisbury and Gresser's 1971 work for the events of the early 1820s (or to other histories that have already stood on their shoulders), including the work of Coe, Elder, Grassby and Hill, and others, such as Lowe, *Forgotten Rebels*.
21   Salisbury and Gresser, *Windradyne of the Wiradjuri*, 9. Salisbury added to Gresser's explanation of the potato incident, for instance, that for the Wiradjuri, helping themselves to a few potatoes on their own land would not have been considered theft, as the emphasis in Wiradjuri law was on the owner's responsibility to protect their possessions. Salisbury and Gresser, *Windradyne of the Wiradjuri*, 22.

pervades it.²² Salisbury's enthusiasm for his project remains palpable in his letters, and it is possible that his interpretation of Windradyne's story helped to reshape the Suttor family's engagement with it.

One of Salisbury's most significant acts in shaping the story was his treatment of the traditions about Windradyne's death and burial. He understood the two stories—that Windradyne died at the Bathurst hospital and was buried nearby, and that he died and was buried at Brucedale—as parallel oral traditions passed down through the third generation of Suttors on Australian soil, W. H. Suttor and his brothers H. C. and Horace.²³ Like Gresser, he seems to have missed 'Colo's' 1829 letter to the Sydney papers.²⁴ In compiling the book, Salisbury favoured the Brucedale story. He told W. H. Suttor's story first, and undercut it, reminding the reader that, although it was a written account, it was penned 'more than 50 years after that event'. He pointed out that W. H. Suttor was not to be counted entirely reliable—he had made errors in his book, such as his statement that Windradyne visited Governor Darling at the Parramatta feast (when, of course, he met with Governor Brisbane). Salisbury then went on to tell H. C. and Horace Suttor's story of Windradyne's escape from the hospital and his death and burial at Brucedale. He affirmed this version with the use of the 1954 memorial's epithet, 'A True Patriot', as the title for his final chapter, and a meditation on the peaceful and timeless landscape that forms a setting for the Brucedale grave.²⁵ Salisbury's explicit evaluation of the two stories gave them equal weight, but it seems that he found the story of Windradyne's burial at Brucedale more fitting and appropriate than the idea that he had been buried near the Bathurst hospital. Perhaps the convictions of Percy Gresser and Roy Suttor also helped to sway him in that direction. As in other respects, Salisbury's history has been highly influential on later storytellers.

---

22   Papers of P. J. Gresser, AIATSIS, MS21f, 34.
23   Salisbury and Gresser, *Windradyne of the Wiradjuri*, 42–43. Gresser, in his 1962 serial, reported that Windradyne had left the hospital and died and was buried at Brucedale. However, Salisbury noted that W. H. Suttor gave Windradyne's place of death and burial as the old hospital at Bathurst. He determined to trace both versions to their source. Gresser, 'The Aborigines of the Bathurst District', *The Western Times*, 31 August 1962, 7; Papers of P. J. Gresser, AIATSIS MS21h, 20–21, Salisbury to Gresser, 20 April 1967.
24   His interpretation of Hendy-Pooley's 1905 article is revealing—her version of the story is seen as representing an independent oral tradition, partly because of her outlying transliteration of 'Windrodine'—which, as noted above, is identical to George Suttor's spelling in his 1829 letter. Salisbury and Gresser, *Windradyne of the Wiradjuri*, 41–42; *The Sydney Gazette*, 21 April 1829, 3; Hendy-Pooley, 'Early History of Bathurst', 230–31.
25   Salisbury and Gresser, *Windradyne of the Wiradjuri*, 42–43; Suttor, *Australian Stories Retold*, note to page 45.

In spite of the more urgent politics pervading his history, Salisbury did not anticipate a Wiradjuri readership any more than Gresser had; his story of dispossession was also one of extinction. Even as activists Isobel and Paul Coe and their colleagues conceived the Aboriginal Tent Embassy, established on the lawns of Parliament House in January 1972, Salisbury wrote: 'They had been plundered and despoiled and country taken from them, so what had they to live for … Wiradjuri people of the Bathurst area gradually disappeared and have finally vanished'.[26]

The Coe siblings grew up on the Erambie Mission at Cowra, where Windradyne had sent his surviving son, Wirrarai, after his other children were killed in the 'potato field massacre'; according to Dinawan Dyirribang, they are, like himself, direct descendants of Windradyne. Mary Coe, Isobel and Paul's sister, read Salisbury's book while researching a history project at school, and saw in the story great potential for connecting the present and the past. In 1986, she published *Windradyne—A Wiradjuri Koorie*, which tells the story of Wiradjuri resistance to invasion led by the 'great warrior' Windradyne, a struggle that continued in the fight for land rights in the present.[27] When Isobel lodged a native title writ in 1993, effectively claiming Wiradjuri sovereignty over Wiradjuri country as a whole, Mary told *The Sydney Morning Herald*, 'we are trying to finish what Windradyne began'.[28] Mary drew on Salisbury's and Gresser's work to reclaim the story for Wiradjuri readers, shifting the gaze so that Wiradjuri people saw Evans crossing the mountains, though he failed to see them, and *they* interpreted *his* behaviour. In her book, Windradyne is reclaimed from the descriptions of *The Sydney Gazette* as a manly man, strong, courageous and wise; a man that all Wiradjuri people can identify with. Mary dedicated the book to her father, a 'Wiradjuri warrior'. By explicitly linking Windradyne's fight with that of 'Pemulwoy and all the other Koories who resisted the invasion', her book offered Windradyne to all Aboriginal people as a hero.[29] Windradyne

---

26  Watson, 'The Aboriginal Tent Embassy'; Foley, 'Black Power'; Salisbury and Gresser, *Windradyne of the Wiradjuri*, 44. The main narrative is bookended by extracts of Dame Mary Gilmore's poem 'Waragery Tribe': 'We are the lost who went, / Like the birds, crying; / Hunted, lonely and spent, / Broken and dying'.

27  Dinawan Dyirribang, in conversation with the author, 8 July 2011; Coe, *Windradyne—A Wiradjuri Koorie* (1986), vi, 19–29, 35–36, and back cover. The second edition of Coe's book concluded with photographs of Aboriginal protesters linking Aboriginal fighting with war and war-commemoration, one group of painted, headbanded men marching behind a banner: 'Veterans of the 200 year War'. Coe, *Windradyne—A Wiradjuri Koorie* (1989), 88.

28  Tony Hewett, 'Wiradjuri People's Writ Immortalises a Warrior', *The Sydney Morning Herald*, 7 June 1993, 8; Nettheim, 'Isobel Coe on Behalf of the Wiradjuri Tribe', 14.

29  Coe, *Windradyne—A Wiradjuri Koorie* (1989), iv, 4–10, 15, frontispiece.

joined a growing pantheon of Aboriginal men recognised inter-regionally as warriors who had brought together forces far more extensive than their clan groups to fight the British, and whose stories became entwined with the radical politics and pan-Aboriginal activism of the 1980s. Pemulwuy and Sandawarra both starred in novels centred on resistance and the rebuilding of history from an Aboriginal point of view. Yagan, as we have seen, was honoured with a statue in 1984, following a five-year campaign by Nyoongar communities in Perth.[30]

Mary Coe felt that Windradyne's story was a part of her people's history that had been neglected. For her, reading Salisbury's book 'was the first time [she] had ever seen anything about Wiradjuri people fighting a war'.[31] Yet, it was partly her own work, following on from Gresser's and Salisbury's, that reframed Windradyne's story as one of *war* in terms that were comprehensible in the late twentieth century. Nevertheless, her claim invites questions about the nature of Windradyne's story, handed down through Wiradjuri generations across the century-and-a-half between Windradyne's death and the 1980s. Peter Read, making enquiries about Windradyne in the early 1980s, found no traditions within the Wiradjuri community that added distinctive new information to Gresser's and Salisbury's stories. He asked of Windradyne's mysterious appearance at Parramatta:

> Was he ever in real danger or did he, like Jimmy Governor seventy years later, lead the whites in a mocking and exhausting dance through the recesses of the Hill End Plateau? Nobody knows.

Read argued that this knowledge, like so much else, did not survive the 'great dispersals' set in train by the New South Wales *Aborigines Protection Act 1909*, which regulated Aboriginal life on a minute scale, separating children from parents, and parents from grandparents, interrupting cycles of teaching and learning.[32] Today, Windradyne is significant as part of local Wiradjuri knowledge, in which he is a figure linking cultural traditions, history, teaching and learning, and the landscape. This tradition adds little detail to a history of Windradyne's campaigns or his friendship with the Suttor family. However, it points towards his continued importance for his descendants and other Wiradjuri people. Wiradjuri family and oral

---

30   Perkins, 'Political Objectives', 235; Johnson, *Long Live Sandawara*; Willmot, *Pemulwuy*; Batten and Batten, 'Memorialising the Past', 99–100.
31   Coe, *Windradyne—A Wiradjuri Koorie* (1986), back cover.
32   Read, *A Hundred Years War*, 11, 54–55.

traditions have been enhanced by the research and writings of Gresser, Salisbury and others, and have reshaped the meanings of these written traditions in turn.

When I asked local Wiradjuri Elder Dindima Gloria Rogers whether the story of Windradyne was among the stories she had been told as a child, she replied in the affirmative:

> I had an old Auntie, she used to call us kids together ... you would sit around, close to her, and she would never speak until there was complete silence. And then she'd start in with the stories, and Windradyne's story was one of them, and of course with any story there was always a message ... But as a kid you think it's just a story, it's only when you get older and you have better understanding that you get the message.[33]

Like Rogers, Dinawan Dyirribang remembered being taught about his connection with Windradyne as a child, and he is gradually teaching his own grandchildren about this connection. However, his knowledge of Windradyne as a leader in war is a result of his reading and asking around as an adult.[34]

Dinawan Dyirribang and Rogers were engaged to advise on, and teach in, a learning program about connection to country at Kelso Public School. Known as 'high five', the program incorporated five symbols, one of which was the message stick. This was linked with the story of Windradyne, his resting place at Brucedale, and an ethic of being proud of Aboriginal culture and identity in a strong but non-aggressive way. As Gloria Rogers explained, it was about 'finding the strength within to be able to resolve, rather than to, you know, knuckle up ... [for both] boys and girls'. In this way, Windradyne's story has become part of a re-mapping of Bathurst and its hinterland in combination with the other four symbols: Platypus Dreaming, Wahluu (Mt Panorama), Wambool (the Macquarie River) and Blackfellows Hand (a meeting and learning site near Lithgow that has been recognised as an Aboriginal place under the *National Parks and Wildlife Act*). One of the Aboriginal teachers at the school created a 'high five' artwork in which children walk between stepping stones, creating conceptual relationships between Dreaming stories and the historical past, and between people, places and stories.[35]

---

33   Gloria Rogers, in conversation with the author, 15 June 2010.
34   Dinawan Dyirribang, in conversation with the author, 8 July 2011.
35   Ibid.; Gloria Rogers, in conversation with the author, 15 June 2010. Blackfellows Hand Aboriginal Place was gazetted in 2008, see *NSW Government Gazette* 88 (18 July 2008): 7252.

## 8. AT THE CONFLUENCE OF TWO STORIES

The landscape of Windradyne's story remains dominated by European land use, boundaries, buildings and businesses. The streets of Bathurst run in a grand grid pattern, with public spaces dominated by monuments to the history of European foundation and exploration. It is a landscape of past and present dispossession and segregation, but, at the same time, conversations about making Wiradjuri culture and history more visible are gradually changing the way in which this landscape can be understood and inhabited by local residents. For the most part, the Wiradjuri presence takes intangible form as journeys and stories, knowledge and memory, infusing the fabric of the town even as its architecture and the surrounding roads, paddocks and fences visually and physically deny it.[36] A long campaign for the dual naming of Bathurst's defining geographical features has borne some fruit with the approval by the New South Wales Geographical Names Board for the dual naming of Mt Panorama – Wahluu in April 2015. The commemorative furniture of the town is under public review. The Evans Monument, dedicated in 1920 to the surveyor who reached the site of the present Bathurst in 1814, has a prominent place in the centre of town, in view of the massive classical bulk of the courthouse. George Evans strikes an imperial pose on top of a large stone plinth while an Aboriginal man, said by some locals to be Windradyne, crouches in front, both men looking intently to the west. Interpretations of the sculpture have multiplied alongside debate about whether the monument should be remodelled, or removed to make way for a different memorial, perhaps a monument honouring Windradyne.[37]

In collaboration with the local branch of the National Trust, Dinawan Dyirribang organised a ceremony marking the 193rd anniversary of the 1824 declaration of martial law, which is intended to inaugurate an annual gathering. It was held in the Peace Park, part of the Macquarie River Bicentennial Park on the northern side of town—a prominent commemorative and recreational space thought to be in the vicinity of the potato field where Wiradjuri people faced the unexpected wrath of an armed settler in 1824. Not far away is Bathurst's flagstaff, reinstated on

---

36  Macdonald, 'Master Narratives and the Dispossession of the Wiradjuri', 164–66; Byrne, 'Nervous Landscapes: Race and Space in Australia', 177.
37  'Bathurst's Bicentenary 2015: Photos', *Newcastle Herald*, 8 May 2015; 'Bathurst's Evans Statue—Should it Stay or Should it Go?', *Western Advocate*, 8 March 2016; 'Welcome to Wahluu: Mount Panorama officially has a second name', *Central Western Daily*, 14 April 2015. Siobhan Lavelle has given a comprehensive account of the changing contexts of commemoration of the crossing of the Blue Mountains and argues that the sites and monuments located in the Blue Mountains themselves are a 'critical moment of uncertainty'. Lavelle, *1813. A Tale That Grew in the Telling*, 213.

the bicentennial anniversary of the founding of Bathurst by Governor Macquarie, which now incorporates Wiradjuri Dreaming stories and intends to recognise the Wiradjuri people as traditional owners of the land, alongside the story of Bathurst's foundation.[38]

John Bugg, Dinawan Dyirribang's uncle, has worked closely with a number of local institutions to make the Wiradjuri presence more visible. One of these was the local Macquarie Rivercare group, which erected a large interpretive installation in the Macquarie River Bicentennial Park in the 1990s or early 2000s. The installation sets out the environmental and cultural values of the river, Wambool, casting it as a central feature of Wiradjuri life before 1813. Like the 'high five' program, the panels recognise a Wiradjuri cartography that reaches across the city, past the Macquarie Memorial Cairn on the other side of the park, to connect the river with Mt Panorama – Wuhluu. Windradyne is the key figure in Bugg's story of the coming of the Europeans and the period of martial law and its aftermath. His story spans from the time before European arrival, across the Wiradjuri wars of the Bathurst area, and into the period of accommodation and adaptation that began in the late 1820s, attesting to continuity in the Wiradjuri story.[39]

One of the great Wiradjuri educationists, Stan Grant Snr, told a story for young readers that began with a group of Wiradjuri boys approaching an old man and asking: 'who created our great Wiradjuri land and people; why [are] we no longer being put through the Burbang (Initiation)?' After telling the boys a creation story and explaining what the Burbang involved, the old man addressed the important matter of why it was no longer practised—a council of Elders resolved that 'there would have to be changes if we were to survive'. A vital part of the old man's teaching, focused on Murrumbidgee Wiradjuri country, was the

---

38   Sonia Feng and Melanie Pearce, 'Scars of Bathurst's Declaration of Martial Law Laid Bare at Commemoration 193 Years On', *ABC Central West*, 15 August 2017, accessed 18 July 2018, www.abc.net.au/news/2017-08-15/scars-of-martial-law-laid-bare-in-bathurst/8804586.
39   Macquarie Rivercare interpretive panels, Macquarie River Bicentennial Park, Bathurst. These panels were erected sometime in the late 1990s or early 2000s, and have been renewed once during that period. Wayne Feebrey, Greening Bathurst, in conversation with the author, 13 March 2012.

history of the arrival of Europeans following Sturt's expedition in 1829. The Wiradjuri extended customary hospitality to these guests before declaring 'war on the invaders' once it was clear that they would not leave. 'Fearless fighters from beyond the Murray and Lachlan rivers' came to help, but, eventually, the Wiradjuri were forced to compromise.[40] The old man concluded:

> We were defeated and humiliated but we could never be made to become white men, which is evidenced here by you young men wanting to know more about your traditions … It is a different battle we fight today … for recognition and the rights to our land. This can only be brought about by you young people getting educated in the white man's way. Do not forget your heritage. Be proud of who you are … Do not be angry and point the finger of blame … for humility is part of our tradition. Do this and one day we will win.[41]

The narrative connects the listening children to a past before and outside Western knowledge and institutions, as well as orientating them in their learning, both within and against the dominant structures. The tensions of this position are made bearable by a sense of integrity and pride.

Windradyne's story performs a similar function, connecting past and present, and providing a proud connection to Wiradjuri history and knowledge. Linda Burney, a distinguished member of the Wiradjuri diaspora from the Murrumbidgee area and former New South Wales minister for community services, often introduces herself with a brief description of the Wiradjuri nation and the British invasion of Wiradjuri country, against which Windradyne led the resistance.[42] Told in public spaces, Windradyne's story suggests the parity of Aboriginal history with European history and all the 'big men' who appear in that story. As Bill Murray observed in a 1993 film, *Windradyne: Wiradjuri Resistance, the Beginning*:

---

40  Grant, *Stories Told by My Grandfather*, 21–24, 28–33. Stan Grant Snr received an OAM for his work in collaboration with John Rudder in bringing together the linguistic knowledge held by many different Wiradjuri people to create the *Wiradjuri Dictionary*, published in 2005, and a number of children's books based around Wiradjuri grammar, songs and stories.
41  Ibid., 33.
42  For example, Burney, 'Speech To Teachers Federation Conference'.

> I see him as a hero to the Aboriginal people—what he done was equal to any other general or whatever you see in a white society, what kids learn about in their history books and … he should be honoured as such.[43]

Windradyne embodies a strength that provides a resounding answer to depictions of Aboriginal weakness and to the weakness experienced by the Wiradjuri as a colonised people. Stan Grant Jnr wished that he had had the example of Windradyne, and his warriors before him, at school, for he believed as he was taught—that Aboriginal people were 'cowardly and dim witted'. The story of the Wiradjuri wars was integral to his growing pride in his heritage: 'I know now that my people were not passive, we did not drop our weapons and flee. We were warriors and there's pride in that'.[44] A correspondent to the *First Australians* online guestbook similarly identified wholeheartedly with Windradyne's standing as a leader in resistance, introducing himself as 'a strong & powerful wiradjuri black warrior man'.[45]

The figure of the warrior has been critiqued for encouraging a mentality of perpetual combat and sacrifice, endangering any regenerative impetus, and leaving room only for a defensive 'survival' and a narrow definition of self and community.[46] Importantly, Windradyne is not merely a figure of resistance who provides a point of opposition to the dominant culture. Like Stan Grant Snr's story, Windradyne's story provides a model of integrity in a state of conflict. It is important to Dinawan Dyirribang that Windradyne fought in a Wiradjuri way, rejecting the opportunity to use firearms, and killing only those who had harmed the Wiradjuri, not engaging in wholesale slaughter. For Dinawan Dyirribang, Windradyne was a leader who was strong in his culture and who kept his people together in a time of crisis—a leader like Braveheart, who (particularly

---

43  Pearson, *Windradyne: Wiradjuri Resistance*. Windradyne appears in educational tools and curriculum materials as an identifiably Wiradjuri figure and strong male role model. See, for example, 'Caring for Place, Caring for Country' (education kit); 'Making a difference: Windradyne', referred to by 'Indigenous Students Connect with Blogs', The Learning Place, *Education Views*, 6 June 2007, 17. The Windradyne Scholarship was established at the Mitchell College of Advanced Education in 1987, and a Windradyne Lecture inaugurated in 2000. *Pemulwuy Newsletter* 13 (1987–88): 6; Adam Motsokono, 'Social Justice Commissioner to Give Windradyne Lecture', *Western Advocate*, 22 October 2001.
44  Grant, *The Tears of Strangers*, 63–64, 87.
45  'Mr Kevin May [Jnr] from Marrickville', 21 October 2008, SBS First Australians, Your Comments, accessed 16 December 2008, www.sbs.com.au/firstaustralians/.
46  De Souza, 'Maoritanga in Whale Rider', 23. Mark McKenna followed Ghassan Hage in observing that imagining ourselves as cultural warriors, in the way that Australians have been encouraged to as participants in the War on Terror (and the History Wars), is an essentially defensive position, which 'pushes us to define our society more narrowly, more aggressively'. McKenna, 'Australian History and the Australian "National Inheritance"', 8–9.

in the wake of Mel Gibson's 1995 film) is understood to have been not only a militarist, but also someone with 'a concern for civil rights, equity and self-determination', the stuff of contemporary political discourse for a people seeking recognition and independence.[47]

Conversely, Dennis Foley, having interrogated Windradyne's leadership style, argued that he (and Pemulwuy and Musquito) operated in a 'most uncharacteristically Indigenous mode'. Foley asked whether Windradyne's journey to Parramatta was anything more than a capitulation, after which Windradyne spent his final years in the service of the colonisation of the Western Plains; if he was a 'patriot' as the 1954 memorial suggested, 'was he a true patriot to … colonial conquest … and stealing of land, or a patriot to the Aboriginal cause?'[48] Yet, it was Windradyne's negotiation of this self-same tension that has made him an inspiring figure for others. Chief executive officer of the Bathurst Local Aboriginal Land Council (LALC), Warwick Peckham, told me that he thought of Windradyne most days, because Windradyne's dilemmas, in judging how far to accommodate the whites, how long to fight and when to compromise, were mirrored in his own work.[49] Since the mid-1980s, Aboriginal communities have developed working relationships with government and other institutions. Constant effort is required to maintain trust. The potential always exists for these institutions to reproduce social and economic inequalities and to 'manage Aboriginal resistance' to state rule using the very same joint initiatives that ostensibly aim to support Aboriginal aspirations. This is a situation somewhere between war and friendship, in which Aboriginal leadership, and its basis in a combination of local Aboriginal

---

47   Dinawan Dyirribang, in conversation with the author, 8 July 2011; Edensor, 'Reading Braveheart', 147. As well as a fighter and 'crusader', Bill Murray characterised Windradyne as a 'saviour of the Aboriginal people', a figure not just of survival but of deliverance. Pearson, *Windradyne: Wiradjuri Resistance*.
48   Foley, 'Leadership', 184–85. This may partly reflect the nature of the tradition within Foley's own family, in which stories of heroic Irish insurgents were brought together with those of the British–Wiradjuri conflicts of the 1820s. The details of the Irish stories were forgotten, while the reshaped stories focused on 'Wiradjuri accomplishments on the battlefield and Windradyne's leadership'. Coe also charted a transition from the waging of a traditional Wiradjuri conflict against the British, to a war to defend land, a kind of war that was unprecedented, but which the Wiradjuri, under Windradyne's leadership, realised was necessary as they were steadily driven into the back country away from water and food sources. Coe, *Windradyne—A Wiradjuri Koorie* (1989), 24.
49   Warwick Peckham, in conversation with the author, 17 June 2010. Peckham does not have a family connection with Windradyne. He came to Bathurst from Dubbo in the 1990s and subsequently learned about Windradyne's story. The portrait hung in the Bathurst LALC office is a print of J. W. Lewins's lithograph, 'A native chief of Bathurst' (1815), which is widely believed to be a portrait of Windradyne.

and governmental structures and traditions, is a continuously contested matter.[50] Windradyne's example as a more-than-warrior with political vision, diplomatic skills, strong cultural knowledge and commitment to family, held together by a hard-won (and at times contested) integrity, can provide a stabilising and inspiring centre, as well as grist for the mill of continued deliberation on what Wiradjuri leadership is, or could be, in the future.

Local and regional identifications are contested as well as confirmed around Windradyne's story. The Wiradjuri community in Bathurst is somewhat fragmented today; it coexists with Aboriginal families from other language groups who were resettled or who settled in Bathurst, Orange and Dubbo over the past 30 or 40 years. Thus, marking public places with local Wiradjuri history involves sharing with Aboriginal people from other parts of the Wiradjuri nation, as well as from other language groups.[51] The Bathurst LALC was originally named after Windradyne.[52] In Dinawan Dyirribang's account, there has been a transition from the management of the LALC by local traditional owners, to management by Wiradjuri people from other localities. In the mid-1990s, when there was a risk of the LALC going into receivership, John Bugg (Dinawan Dyirribang's uncle) took responsibility for resolving many of the problems before officially removing Windradyne's name from the organisation, so that his reputation could not be tarnished in the future.[53]

According to Paul House, a Ngambri man from the Queanbeyan area, Windradyne's father was Wiradjuri but his mother was a member of one of the Ngunnawal–Gundangarra groups. House claimed that Windradyne's mother went home to the Lake George area north of Canberra to give birth to Windradyne and that later, when Windradyne was a young man, he returned to Wiradjuri country to fight the resistance. Like the leader

---

50  Dodson, 'The End in the Beginning', 9; Lambert-Pennington, 'What Remains?', 320–32; Peters-Little, 'The Community Game', 14–15.
51  Gloria Rogers, in conversation with the author, 15 June 2010; Warwick Peckham, in conversation with the author, 17 June 2010.
52  Macdonald, *Two Steps Forward*, 25.
53  Dinawan Dyirribang, in conversation with the author, 8 July 2011. Gaynor Macdonald documented the forging of a strong pan-Wiradjuri feeling in the early 1980s in the lead-up to the Land Rights Bill, under which the Wiradjuri Land Council, which Wiradjuri leaders had formed through their own networking ahead of the Act, was registered as a Regional Land Council. Pan-Wiradjuri feeling and action through the land council system was put under great pressure over the following decade by the underfunding of the entire system, and by the limited opportunities that existed for the claiming of Wiradjuri lands. Macdonald, *Two Steps Forward*, 10–11, 29–57.

Onyong (or Alynyonga), who the Gundangarra look to for inspiration as a resistance leader, Windradyne was born at one of the special waterholes, Lake George and Rose Lagoon, that were known to produce warriors. Today, Lake George is known as Wirriwa, but the non-Aboriginal owners of the property have called it Windradyne.[54] Gloria Rogers told me that Windradyne had a Gamilaroi father and Wiradjuri mother (the Wiradjuri tradition being matrilineal) making another, incompatible, set of links with the Wiradjuri people's powerful northern neighbours.[55] Dinawan Dyirribang related a number of stories about Windradyne's travels across the range to King's Tableland and to northern New South Wales, where he has a number of Dunghutti descendants (Dunghutti country is centred on Kempsey).[56] Today, as overlapping interests in land and story are presided over by government and legal authorities administering heritage, encouraging tourism and adjudicating native title claims, stories about family connections, exchanges and travels are brought into conflict and competition with each other by modern cartography, linear time and the demand for a single true (as well as plausible) story. In this context, the vast and fluid family histories that have lived through the memories of individuals are increasingly coming into conflict with the recognised authority of linear, European-style family trees and other documentary sources.[57]

Yet, at the same time, these written histories have helped Wiradjuri people to reclaim Windradyne's story via writing and talk. As Vivienne Mason of Narooma, on the south coast of New South Wales, told Mark McKenna:

> It was actually the white people who saved our history for us … not our culture but our history … The white man has taken our culture and history away from us but he has actually given it back in what he has recorded.[58]

---

54   Paul House, in conversation with the author, 12 July 2010. Dinawan Dyirribang refuted this story; he stated that there was a man who came from the south to assist the Wiradjuri in fighting the British known as 'Big Bull'. Dinawan Dyirribang, conversation, 8 July 2011.
55   Gloria Rogers, in conversation with the author, 15 June 2010.
56   Dinawan Dyirribang, in conversation with the author, 8 July 2011.
57   For example, Heather Goodall argued that Aboriginal people were being 'forced to reconceptualise their stories about family and land' so that they could 'meet the demanding set of criteria defined by the white-Australian legal and bureaucratic system' and regain access to land. Goodall, 'Telling country', 181–84.
58   McKenna, *Looking for Blackfellas' Point*, 222. Tom Griffiths, writing about the successful protection of Mumbulla Mountain, near Bega on the New South Wales south coast, from logging by the Yuin community, and reclamation of its sacred history for the contemporary community in the face of scepticism by the government, logging interests, and the local white community, observed that 'places can be reclaimed by writing and talk … continuity of occupation is not the only measure of possession'. Griffiths, *Hunters and Collectors*, 234.

Peter Read remembered visiting Windradyne's grave with Mary and Isabel Coe in 1979, and, from about 1990, John Bugg began to visit Brucedale regularly to talk with the Suttor family about maintaining and protecting Windradyne's grave.[59] In the early 1990s, a film funded by the New South Wales Department of Education, *Windradyne: Wiradjuri Resistance, the Beginning*, featured members of the Coe family, John Suttor, Theo Barker from the Bathurst Historical Society and Rob MacLaughlin from Charles Sturt University.[60] The film emerged from an exchange of traditions. It was closely based on Mary Coe's book in which she (perhaps expanding on Salisbury's tentative statements with regard to Wiradjuri knowledge) explained that, in keeping with the Wiradjuri way of being hospitable to guests:

> Windradyne and the Wiradjuri people accepted small numbers of white settlers coming to their lands and they acted as guides for the settlers taking them to the areas away from their camping and hunting grounds and their sacred sites.[61]

In the film, John Suttor related how Wiradjuri people had guided his forebears to the place where Clear Creek and Winburndale Rivulet met, which is where they established Brucedale.[62] This part of the story, illustrating friendly relations between the Wiradjuri and the Suttor family soon after their arrival in Wiradjuri country, had apparently been preserved in Suttor family oral tradition; however, until the film's release, it had not formed part of the public story.[63] Talking with the Coe family had probably confirmed the veracity and importance of this part of the story for John Suttor. It is unlikely that either party had preserved an 'independent' tradition about the friendship to the present. The Suttor

---

59  Peter Read, in conversation with the author, February 2012; Gloria Rogers, in conversation with the author, 15 June 2010.
60  Mary Coe and John Bugg advised on the film, and family members including John Coe, Jenny Munro and Bill Murray appeared in the film. Barker had just completed his history of Bathurst, which examines the period of martial law in detail.
61  Coe, *Windradyne—A Wiradjuri Koorie* (1989), 19. See also Salisbury and Gresser, *Windradyne of the Wiradjuri*, 16–17. Warwick Peckham also emphasised that Wiradjuri people first directed the Europeans in how and where to settle. War broke out when the increasing numbers of livestock began to have a serious effect on food sources, while at the same time providing a readily accessible food source that was protected with firearms. Warwick Peckham, in conversation with the author, 17 June 2010. Stan Grant Snr also explained that hostilities had broken out on the Murrumbidgee after Wiradjuri hospitality had been outworn by the newcomers. Grant, *Stories Told by My Grandfather*, 28–32.
62  Pearson, *Windradyne: Wiradjuri Resistance*.
63  John Suttor, in conversation with the author, 20 January 2009.

family and other non-Aboriginal tellers of this story, just as much as Wiradjuri people, have, in some senses, rediscovered this story of friendship in the latter part of the twentieth century.

The coming together of these streams of history-making has profoundly reshaped the story and a much more consistent emphasis on friendship has emerged. Before the reconciliation decade, when William Suttor and Windradyne featured in pioneer stories or histories of the Wiradjuri wars, their friendship was not a necessary or central element of the story. In a *Daily Mirror* special feature of 1956, William starred as a gallant, yet earthy giant of history—a quintessential Australian, pursuing bushrangers and becoming wealthy, yet always answering his own front door: someone who could speak the native language fluently and move through the bush like an Aboriginal man. It was implied that Wiradjuri people looked up to him as much as the reader was encouraged to; however, no Aboriginal people were named.[64] Bruce Elder's bloody and shaming anti-bicentennial history, *Blood on the Wattle*, features Windradyne as a 'martyr', a warrior and, finally, a 'broken man'. The Wiradjuri war and massacres of the 1820s form a damning episode in the armed conquest of the continent, and the story of Windradyne and his people is complicated neither by friendship nor by the survival of the Wiradjuri people.[65]

An emphasis on the *particular* friendship between the Suttor family and Windradyne and his family has also developed. Hand in hand with this shift, the timing of the friendship has also changed in emphasis, with great importance being placed on the friendship being established before war broke out and enduring through the conflicts. 'Colo's' 1829 obituary for Windradyne, W. H. Suttor's story of 'western rebellions' and the plaque on the 1954 memorial represent a situation of friendly relations between Windradyne and the settlers-in-general *after* the acute conflicts of the 1820s. In his letter to *The Australian* in 1826, as well as trying to

---

64  'Pioneer Who Farmed at 16 Owned 10,000 Acres at 30', *Daily Mirror*, 24 May 1956, 27. See also Archdeacon Oakes, 'Story of the Bathurst Pioneers, No. 2—the Suttor Centenary', *The Daily Telegraph*, 4 November 1922, in which George Suttor received acclaim as a fine upstanding man: loyal (to Bligh), pious, and principled amid great treachery and upheaval in the colony. A family history published in 1994 followed suit in its focus on the 'character, personality and style' of William Suttor as a 'Pioneer of the West'. Aboriginal people were most often referred to as 'hostile' or dangerous, though Windradyne received brief coverage as an 'Aboriginal Warrior-Hero'. See Norton and Norton, *Dear William*, x, 29, 31, 33, 37.
65  Elder, *Blood on the Wattle*, 44–53. See also 'The Black War: When Aboriginals Were Hunted, Poisoned and Shot in Order to Be Taught a Lesson', *Living Australia* 40 (1985): 19–21; Grassby and Hill, *Six Australian Battlefields*, 134–68.

encourage all settlers to adopt a friendly attitude after the wars, 'Colo' had set himself apart as a constant friend to the Wiradjuri. However, until recently, it probably was not politic to harp on this distinction, as William led the family to growing success in the region.[66]

Debra Jopson's 2002 article in *The Sydney Morning Herald* typifies the recent emphasis on the singularity of the relationship of the Suttor family with local Wiradjuri people, in the past and the present:

> In an area where some landholders—fearful of land claims—often bar access to such sites, [Dinawan Dyirribang] can [visit Windradyne's grave] because of a friendship of almost 180 years and six generations between local Aborigines and one white family—the Suttors of Brucedale.[67]

Similarly, a sign erected at the entry to Brucedale in the latter months of 2010 states that Windradyne 'led his warriors in a bloody campaign against white settlers, and yet one white family continued to respect and befriend him'.[68] Two story elements that began to circulate more widely as part of the main stream of the story from the 1980s helped to shape this shift.

The first of these is the story that John Suttor told in the film, *Windradyne: Wiradjuri Resistance, the Beginning*—namely, that Wiradjuri people helped George and William Suttor find the place where they settled and have been ever since: Brucedale. This act of guidance illustrates the agency of Wiradjuri people in a way that friendliness after their 'defeat' in 1824 cannot, hinting at the complexity of the Wiradjuri response to the arrival of the Europeans and the way in which Wiradjuri people may have been able to take the initiative in peaceful and warlike relations across the early 1820s. By the turn of the twenty-first century, it was being interpreted in a number of ways, including as an offer of 'coexistence' to the Suttor family soon after their arrival in Wiradjuri country.[69] A history produced

---

66   Barker noted his involvement in the Holy Trinity Church, the Turf Club and Agricultural Association, and his election as the first member of the New South Wales Legislative Council for the counties of Roxbury, Phillip and Wellington in 1843. Barker, *A History of Bathurst*, vol. 1, 177 and vol. 2, 138.
67   Debra Jopson, 'Grave a Symbol of 180 Years of Friendship', *The Sydney Morning Herald*, 20 April 2002.
68   Entry Signs to be erected at Brucedale, NSW National Parks and Wildlife Service (Bathurst).
69   Dianne Johnson interpreted this advice from the Wiradjuri: 'It appears in hindsight, that the local Wiradjuri were offering co-existence to the Suttors'. Johnson, *Lighting the Way*, 51.

## 8. AT THE CONFLUENCE OF TWO STORIES

by another branch of the Suttor family tells the story of the Brucedale selection as if the Wiradjuri recommendation of this spot endowed the family with special rights of possession:

> When ordered to move elsewhere the Suttors remembered the glowing accounts of rich alluvial flats and grazing hill country further out that friendly Aborigines had related to them 'where the creeks join' they said. Suttor went, saw and was convinced … This time their right to the land was secure.[70]

It was Governor Brisbane's more open policy of settlement that allowed the family to cross the range as they had long hoped to do. Yet, some recent versions of the story imply that George and William Suttor were part of an early trickle of strangers, which the Wiradjuri could more or less accommodate, the friendship being one of the few remaining legacies of a peaceful period of migration and settlement before Brisbane's opening of the floodgates.[71] In this scenario, the family's settlement in Wiradjuri country seems more a 'taking-up' of land than a taking of land from Aboriginal people, echoing, perhaps, some of 'Colo's' desires to have taken land in a benevolent way.[72] Conversely, David Suttor, appearing on *First Australians*, was emphatic in his acknowledgement that his family had taken Wiradjuri land; the governors were giving out land to white settlers, he explained, and 'we just took it … there [weren't] any treaties or … recognition of prior ownership'.[73]

The incident in which Windradyne and his warriors surround William's hut in the night has also played a pivotal role in the changing shape of the story. Where W. H. Suttor separated this incident from his wider story of the conflicts of the 1820s, Gresser integrated it into the main narrative of his 1962 serial. Salisbury, for his part, signposted the dramatic potential of this 'encounter … between the enraged natives

---

70 Norton and Norton, *Dear William*, 31.
71 For example, in *First Australians*, William and George Suttor's friendly contact with the Wiradjuri is established in the narrative before 'the country is opened up to anyone who can pay to settle there by the new Governor Sir Thomas Brisbane'. Nowra and Perkins, 'Episode 1: They Have Come to Stay'. See also Grassby and Hill, *Six Australian Battlefields*, 148. However, George Suttor expressed frustration with Governor Macquarie and his strict control of migration over the mountains. Suttor, *Memoirs of George Suttor*, 58. This has remained part of the family story, see Suttor, *Australian Stories Retold*, 63–64; Norton and Norton, *Dear William*, 23, 33.
72 Adam Gall critiqued this persistent idea of the 'good' settler as animated in Kate Grenville's novel, *The Secret River*, in which this figure is conceived as 'taking up' land, rather than taking land from Aboriginal people. Gall, 'Taking/Taking Up'.
73 Nowra and Perkins, 'Episode 1: They Have Come to Stay'.

and one lone white settler'.[74] Indeed, the immediacy of this incident of cross-cultural frisson and resolution has had great appeal for storytellers, particularly in telling stories of friendship and reconciliation following the negotiation of the Conservation Agreement over Windradyne's resting place, for it is via this incident that we learn that William had a pre-existing, friendly relationship with the Wiradjuri, and that he spoke the Wiradjuri language. This revelation is both potent and inarticulate. Storytellers typically reproduce or paraphrase W. H. Suttor's account, and then leave it to 'speak for itself'.[75] The story probably originated with William Suttor himself, but nothing of the all-important conversation with Windradyne is preserved. Subsequent generations have been left to speculate, as Dinawan Dyirribang did on *First Australians*, imagining that William might have said:

> He had nothing to do with the killings, and he probably would have said that he was appalled with what was going on … [and] Windradyne probably would have accepted that.[76]

The significance of William's fluency in Wiradjuri language, the sustained closeness required to learn the language and the commitment on the part of the Wiradjuri people involved to teach him, is seldom explored.[77] At the same time, William's language skills are provided with the ultimate reference; they saved his life.

What shape did the relationship take *during* the conflicts? If the Suttor family were friends to the Wiradjuri before the outbreak of hostilities, did they not attempt to restrain the violence of other settlers, or hide

---

74  Gresser, 'The Aborigines of the Bathurst District', *The Western Times*, 18 August 1962, 3. He told both versions of this story discussed below. Salisbury and Gresser, *Windradyne of the Wiradjuri*, 22. Of course, William was not alone in the unprovenanced version of the story reproduced on the following page, in which he was in the company of Peneegrah, and probably at least one shepherd.

75  See for example, Heritage Listing, Grave of Windradyne, State Heritage Register Database, Record Number 5051560; Johnson, *Lighting the Way*, 52–53; Norton and Norton, *Dear William*, 37; Jordan Baker, 'Heritage Listing Keeps Proud Memories Alive', *The Sydney Morning Herald*, 24 January 2006, 7.

76  Nowra and Perkins, 'Episode 1: They Have Come to Stay'. For a similar account from the Suttor family, see also Joel Gibson, 'Friendship across Time and Place', *The Sydney Morning Herald*, 11 October 2008, 4.

77  One of the few renditions that seeks to explain how William came to speak Wiradjuri language fluently claims, ahistorically, that 'the lad had been brought up with the Aboriginals, possibly with Saturday, spoke their language and respected their customs'. 'The Black War: When Aboriginals Were Hunted, Poisoned and Shot in Order to Be Taught a Lesson', *Living Australia* 40 (1985): 21. Interpretive panels at Windradyne's grave state simply: 'William must have spent time with Wiradyuri friends to learn their language'. NSW National Parks and Wildlife Service (Bathurst), 'A Shared History' panel in Windradyne's grave conservation area, 2010.

Wiradjuri people as Thomas Foley, Dennis Foley's grandfather's great-grandfather, hid the Wiradjuri woman he later married?[78] A correspondent to the SBS *First Australians* guestbook probed:

> I have been told by Bathurst locals that the Suttor family actually physically protected first Australians when under attack from white people—do you have any stories or records of this?[79]

When I asked John Suttor whether he had heard any such stories, he replied in the negative, and was anxious to ensure that new, unsubstantiated elements not be added to the story.[80] Apart from the tensions inhering in 'Colo's' letters to the press, no insights have been gained by this historian into the battles that may have raged in Suttor hearts as philanthropic ideas came up against loyalty to the colonial regime and interests in land, and as friendships with neighbouring settlers and local Aboriginal people became a scarcely navigable thicket. That this story of confrontation could so easily have had a different ending in this time of violent confusion, fear and retaliation, is clearly part of its appeal. However, it also illustrates how little the Suttor family were set apart from some of the other property owners, such as the Hassall family and their staff, who faced each other in court in August 1824 over the deaths of three Aboriginal women after one of their stockmen was wounded on the family's property at O'Connell Plains.[81]

A second version of the story of the night encounter, perhaps a parallel oral tradition within the family (which seems to have appeared in the written record for the first time in 1957), populates the events with a number of other figures. Here, William was surrounded while 'visiting one of his outlying shepherds', rather than at the main hut near today's Brucedale homestead, and he was in the company of Peneegrah, with whom he had 'explored the rough country between Bathurst and Mudgee'. As in W. H. Suttor's version, Windradyne and his men seemed poised to attack, and William quickly defused the situation by opening the door and speaking to

---

78  Foley, 'Leadership', 184.
79  'Jess from Bathurst', 20 October 2008, SBS First Australians, Your Comments, accessed 16 December 2008, www.sbs.com.au/firstaustralians/.
80  John Suttor, in conversation with the author, 20 January 2009.
81  The Hassall case is discussed in detail in Barker, *A History of Bathurst*, vol. 1, 67–69. Karskens found such a thicket of relationships on the Hawkesbury frontier, in which different Aboriginal groups and families were aligned with different settler families who did not automatically 'combine as a group, for mutual benefits and governance', but needed to be ordered to do so. Karskens, *The Colony*, 466–73.

Windradyne in Wiradjuri language.[82] According to Dinawan Dyirribang, Peneegrah was Windradyne's cousin, so his presence may have influenced the course of events in William's (or his shepherd's) favour that night—or perhaps it was Peneegrah who Windradyne had come to see.[83]

As Peter Read observed, Windradyne 'towers over the events' of the 1820s.[84] His historical stature has perhaps eclipsed a more extensive web of relationships between members of the Suttor family and other Wiradjuri people. The friendship is projected consistently as a masculine affair. Barbara Dawson examined stories of European and Aboriginal women coming together around children, adornment and an appreciation of local plants and animals.[85] No such associations emerge as part of this story, though 'Colo' referred to women talking and laughing together at Brucedale and visiting the house in which Sarah Maria Suttor and (perhaps) some of her daughters were living.[86] A brief and wonderful vignette involves Charlotte, who married William Suttor at 16 years of age, fresh off a ship from England:

> [Charlotte] was sitting in the lounge when a native appeared down the chimney, badly cut about and with a spear in his hand. She rushed to help him and was considered the friend of the Aboriginals for many years.[87]

---

82  'Pastoral Prosperity', *Parade* (August 1957): 20; Salisbury and Gresser, *Windradyne of the Wiradjuri*, 23. Later retellings almost invariably followed W. H. Suttor's version of the story. Exceptions include Dianne Johnson, who included both versions, and Grassby and Hill, *Six Australian Battlefields*, 156.

83  Dinawan Dyirribang, in conversation with the author, 8 July 2011. As Dianne Johnson pointed out, in this version of the story, the events take place at a hut in which Windradyne may not have known William was staying. Johnson, *Lighting the Way*, 52–53.

84  Read, *A Hundred Years War*, 10. William Suttor also towers over these events. It is generally overlooked that two of his brothers, probably Thomas Charles (b. 1804) and John Bligh (b. 1809), had also helped their father to establish Brucedale, and would also have interacted with Wiradjuri people. Suttor Family Papers, ML, MSS 2417, item 3 (correspondence 1800–40), George Suttor to his wife, undated, 119. Percy Gresser mentioned 'Penneegrah' as a companion and guide to George Suttor Jnr, William's eldest brother, who was also in Bathurst in the early 1820s. Papers of P. J. Gresser, AIATSIS, MS21c, loose leaf.

85  Dawson, 'Sisters under the Skin?'.

86  *The Australian*, 14 October 1826, 3–4; Suttor, *Memoirs of George Suttor*, 59.

87  Colleen Knights, 'Brucedale: The Family Home', *The Sunday Telegraph*, 6 May 1973, 122. Knights referred to this as a 'family legend'. Charlotte Suttor's surviving diaries are a terse record of health, weather, the weekly sermon, and meetings with friends and acquaintances. A close reading of entries March–April 1850 indicated that Aboriginal people at Brucedale would likely only be mentioned as servants, and referred to by first names that I lack the requisite knowledge to identify. Suttor Family Papers, ML, MSS 1520/2, Diary of Charlotte Augusta Anne Suttor, kept at Brucedale, Bathurst, March 1850 – September 1852, 1853, viewed on microfilm reel MAV/FM4/1390.

The loss of glimpses of other relationships is perhaps one we feel now more than ever, as historians and readers of history become increasingly interested in encounters and connections apart from part-defensive, part-formal man-to-man exchanges.[88]

The powerful image of the two men face to face in the intimacy of a life-and-death situation resonates strongly with a discourse of fraternity that took root in the trenches in World War I. Parts of this discourse have remained central to understandings of friendship across the late twentieth and early twenty-first centuries as a symmetrical relationship between individuals of equal power, bound together by affection. As well, these fraternal friendships under the extreme pressure of war were understood to have a strong thread of moral fibre running through them, with friends together maintaining 'values such as self-control, honor, and courage'. If we have sometimes come to worry that friendship is frivolous or selfish, and somehow erodes the wider structures of community and family, then this is a model for friendship that seems to be fortified by a degree of formality, and to have the greater good at its core.[89] Perhaps this slightly 'old-fashioned' model of masculine friendship (looking back from the centenary of WWI) provides one of the lenses through which we understand William and Windradyne.

Friendship since the mid-twentieth century has increasingly come to mean a relationship that has been freely chosen by the friends, and is understood to be quite distinct from relationships of proximity and obligation with kin, neighbours and in places of work. In *First Australians*, the viewer's focus on Windradyne and William is accentuated by their introduction as they draw nearer to each other, making their meeting predestined within the narrative. The night encounter forms a dramatic fulcrum and Windradyne and William's relationship is mirrored with the telling of the story by Dinawan Dyirribang and David Suttor.[90] It seems we now want to witness Windradyne and William choosing friendship across the battlelines.

---

88  Paul Carter found in Lieutenant Dawes' notebooks traces of intimacy and humour as he met with Pattyegarang to talk about language, the record utterly different from the dry logbooks of words that appear in so many anonymous Aboriginal vocabularies collected in the first decades of the colony. Carter's 1996 sound installation, *The Calling to Come* (for the Museum of Sydney) was partly inspired by it. Carter, 'Repetitions at Night', 81–82; Carter, 'Speaking Pantomimes', 95.
89  Kaplan and Yanay, 'Fraternal Friendship', 127–28; Cole, *Modernism*, 4, 138; Peel, Reed and Walter, 'The Importance of Friends'.
90  Peel, Reed and Walter, 'The Importance of Friends, 316–28; Nowra and Perkins, 'Episode 1: They Have Come to Stay'.

Whereas, in the nineteenth and mid-twentieth centuries, the Suttor family sought to draw others into a circle of cross-cultural friendship by generalising that friendship, today it is the magic of the particular (and even exclusive) friendship that holds the power to include and inspire us. Perkins acknowledged that the 'character-based' approach of *First Australians* was 'narrow but we tried to make the series engaging by making it personal'.[91] Similarly, Dianne Johnson, in *Lighting the Way: Reconciliation Stories*, focused closely on the interaction of individuals meeting, apologising and forgiving. However, Johnson's focus on individuals was not only aimed at heightening the emotional effect or persuasive power of her reconciliation stories, but also was an instance of the 'grass roots' reconciliation taking place across the nation despite the Howard Government's inaction on the recommendations of the Council for Aboriginal Reconciliation's final report, handed down in December 2000. The government had failed to make a meaningful reconciliation with Aboriginal people and her stories of 'ordinary' Australians going ahead with personal, local and family reconciliations both shamed the government and showed that government inertia could not stop this process.[92]

Stories of friendship played an important role in *First Australians*, tempering what producer Rachel Perkins described as 'a brutal and devastating history' with a little 'salvation and hope'. Perkins and co-producer Darren Dale were aware that viewers might approach the program gripping the historical 'balance sheet' championed by former Prime Minister John Howard, a tool of moral objectivity and realism that prevents us from dwelling too much on 'negative' aspects of history. In an interview with *The Canberra Times*, Dale attested to the team's efforts to bring moral 'complexity' to the screen and not make it just a simple 'goodies and baddies story'.[93] For viewers, the notion of balance was pervasive and was intimately connected with a concern that the settlers, no matter what sufferings they ultimately caused Aboriginal

---

91  George, '[Re]Writing History', 20. Marcia Langton's introduction to the book *First Australians* declares that the work seeks to communicate the passions and personalities of particular people, rather than the impersonal 'dust, rock and debris' of archaeology. Perkins and Langton, *First Australians*, xxvi.
92  Johnson's book brings the spirit of Reconciliation to the reader through the stories of ordinary people such as John and David Suttor, and the descendants of the perpetrators and victims of the Myall Creek Massacre who have come together in public reconciliation activities. Johnson, *Lighting the Way*, 72–74. Johnson and Linda Burney expressed these sentiments in the two prefaces to the volume.
93  Perkins, quoted in, Sacha Molitorisz, 'The Story of Black Australia', *The Age*, 9 October 2008, Green Guide, 12; 'Unearthing Our First Voices', *The Canberra Times*, 14 October 2008. On the historical 'balance sheet' see Crotty and Roberts, *The Great Mistakes of Australian History*, 2–3.

people, did not, or did not *all*, deliberately set out to do so.[94] On one level, this concern—played out repeatedly across the 'history wars'—is part of a defensive response to the enormity of the history of Aboriginal dispossession that white Australians have been asked to recognise; it is linked to widespread public understanding of the importance of intent and totality in definitions of genocide. However, at the same time, as Alan Atkinson has observed, 'the moral judgement of European Australians is crippled so long as they are convinced that their own past is nothing more than shameful'.[95] The appearance of the friendship of Windradyne and William Suttor in *First Australians* as one of those shining beacons of shared humanity in a dark past is characteristic of the contemporary struggle to accept this history. As one viewer commented: 'My ancestors were land grabbers so I found the story of Brucedale inspirational as this young man proved diplomacy could have prevented much violence and suffering'.[96]

A *Sydney Morning Herald* article introduced the *First Australians* series via the friendship between Windradyne and William Suttor, stating:

> The makers of the nation's most important piece of indigenous television are hoping that [this] 200-year-old relationship and others like it will finally inspire a new, collaborative approach to Australian history.[97]

It was as if this particular friendship could help to heal the rifts between Indigenous and non-Indigenous Australians more generally, and that this healing process might take place through history-making itself. As friendship became firmly associated with equality from the mid to late twentieth century, friendship indeed gained a new political potential

---

94   The *First Australians* 'guest book' on the SBS website included over a thousand comments by December 2008. Many evaluated the series according to notions of 'balance'. One admirer found 'the first episode to be very well balanced … I was concerned that the doco may persecute the early settlers … but rather it just painted the facts without judgement or bias'. Another contributor protested: 'This show is "wrong" if its intention is to make some young Australians feel ashamed or guilty of their history … I'd like to think the future is more positive for all Australians, aboriginal and non aboriginal [sic]'. 'Ben from The Fleurieu' and 'Alison from Ryde', 13 October 2008, SBS First Australians, Your Comments, accessed 16 December 2008, www.sbs.com.au/firstaustralians/.

95   Dirk Moses showed how genocide is commonly associated with totality, a central 'Plan' of extermination that results in the complete disappearance of a race (concepts that are not in line with the UN definition of genocide), a definition that seems to provide 'proof' that genocide cannot have happened in Australia. Moses, 'Moving the Genocide Debate', 255–70. Alan Atkinson, *The Commonwealth of Speech* (2002), quoted in Cowlishaw, 'On "Getting It Wrong"', 199.

96   'Debbie Jagoe from Brunswick', 13 October 2008, SBS First Australians, Your Comments, accessed 16 December 2008, www.sbs.com.au/firstaustralians/.

97   Joel Gibson, 'Friendship Across Time and Place', *The Sydney Morning Herald*, 11 October 2008, 4.

as a 'model for a new kind of world and a way of bringing it about'. Friendships across lines of race and class could now form a public assertion of equality and respect, against laws, economies and wider social discourses that enforced inequality.[98] The friendship between poets and activists Oodgeroo Noonuccal and Judith Wright—which was both a private relationship of great importance and a public performance of sisterhood via which the friends sought to inspire others and work together to achieve change—is one Australian example of this kind of 'friendship of conviction'.[99] The relationships formed around Windradyne's grave, like Johnson's reconciliation stories and the friendships featured in *First Australians*, could be said to bear out this notion. Yet, the war has continued.

Soon after the Conservation Agreement over Windradyne's grave was signed in 2000, signifying a legal and bureaucratic recognition of Wiradjuri history and heritage in Bathurst's hinterland, Keith Windschuttle launched an attack on the First Australians gallery of Canberra's newly opened National Museum of Australia. The exhibit telling the story of the Bells Falls Gorge massacre, closely connected with Windradyne's story, presented Dinawan Dyirribang's account of the way in which this event is remembered in his community, concluding, 'our people still hear the echoes of the women and children who died here'.[100] Windschuttle sought to demolish truth claims surrounding the massacre, partly by pointing out that:

> Although [the massacre story] is now claimed as part of an ancient Aboriginal tradition, Aboriginal activists only learnt about it from an article … written by a white amateur historian in 1962.[101]

Indeed, the massacre at Bells Falls is not a precisely documented event. In 1995, David Roberts found there was a strong feeling within the Bathurst community on the whole that a massacre had occurred, but specific details had been lost. He concluded that the story had become connected with the dramatic local landform of Bells Falls Gorge through the processes of local oral tradition.[102] Windschuttle could not countenance the combination of oral and written tradition, a lack of precision linking

---

98 Peel, Reed and Walter, 'The Importance of Friends', 328–32.
99 See Dortins, 'Apology and Absolution'.
100 Attwood, 'Contesting Frontiers', 103–14.
101 He was presumably referring to Percy Gresser. Windschuttle, 'Social History', 30–31.
102 Roberts, 'Bells Falls Massacre', 615–33.

the events to time, place and agents, and the labile nature of the story, changing and responding to present concerns. The interconnected story of Windradyne's friendship with the Suttor family presents a similar historiographical terrain in some respects, and it seems to be precisely these qualities that have allowed the story to remain robust and relevant, and to embrace a two-way friendship once more. Yet, in Windschuttle's view, history itself should not have a history. His insinuation that 'ancient Aboriginal tradition' had been invented in the First Australians gallery taps into a persistent valorisation of recognisably 'ancient' Aboriginal stories in public thinking and in scholarship, and a corresponding suspicion of the unfolding cultural knowledge of living Aboriginal traditions.[103] Windschuttle was not only attacking the Bells Falls massacre story, but also the prerogative of Wiradjuri people to continue to develop understandings of their history. Taking a long view, Wiradjuri people's use of the written historical record as part of their historical tradition is part of a Wiradjuri regeneration that began in the 1920s. Windschuttle's challenge of the legitimacy of this history-making is part of a longer history of European–Wiradjuri relations across the nineteenth and twentieth centuries, incorporating patterns of combat and accommodation, which continues into an unknown future.[104]

Mary Coe touched on Wiradjuri people's friendly relationship with the Suttor family only in passing. William was spared because he had not committed crimes against the Wiradjuri, who acted according to their law; by contrast, the British engaged in indiscriminate killing. Otherwise, the distinction between friendly and unfriendly settlers is not important to her story. She explained Windradyne's meeting with Governor Brisbane as a deeply ironic rapprochement:

> Windradyne tried to end the slaughter of his people by going to the Governor to make 'friends'—make friends with people who had invaded his lands, had stolen his country and in cold blood had slaughtered hundreds of his people.[105]

---

103 Macdonald, 'Master Narratives and the Dispossession of the Wiradjuri', 170–72; Attwood, 'Contesting Frontiers', 110. Macdonald developed a definition of 'tradition' that seeks to shift these preconceptions. Traditions are 'meanings and practices moving through time, dynamic ... [they] have histories ... full of tension, change and contradiction'. Further, traditions do not have to be old to be important in a community's history and self-understanding. Macdonald, 'Does "Culture" Have "History"?', 188.
104 Read, *A Hundred Years War*, xiii–xiv.
105 Coe, *Windradyne—A Wiradjuri Koorie* (1989), 22, 46.

Gloria Rogers's interpretation of the story is very different. She understood Windradyne's journey to Parramatta to see the governor as:

> The first act of reconciliation ... he could see that there was no good coming out of the conflict between the Wiradjuri people and the whitefellas because there was killings on both sides, and that solves nothing. So something had to be done ... We do believe that was the first act of reconciliation in Australia when he went down to hold out the olive branch, to make peace and to come to a place of understanding.[106]

Although Rogers expressed her deep appreciation of a strong positive relationship with the Suttor family in the past and the present, like Coe, she insisted that the more significant relationship was a general and formal one—with the government—which mirrors the general and official nature of the warfare that preceded it.[107] A friendship with one family cannot heal the wrongs committed between two peoples.

---

106  Gloria Rogers, in conversation with the author, 15 June 2010.
107  Similarly, Wiradjuri artist Julie Dowling, for whom Windradyne has provided inspiration, said: 'He represents to me the hundreds of elders who actively engaged with wudjulahs, in good faith, only to have their authority ignored, disrespected and diminished by the invading colonial forces. This continues on into the present day, where the authority and wisdom of the elders goes largely unrecognized by white society'. Julie Dowling, Widi Boornoo (Wild Message), 1–12 August 2006, exhibition notes, Brigitte Braun Art Dealer, current exhibition pages, accessed 24 April 2012, www.artplace.com.au/exhibscurrent/Dowling_0806/storytext.html.

# 9

# Friendship and the Grave

Windradyne's grave sits on a low rise above Winburndale Rivulet in a broad valley overlooked by Big Flat and Mt Wiagdon. The grave is raised into a mound or 'tumulus' and rests alongside a second grave mound. This form of grave is particular to the Western Plains and to Wiradjuri burial practices. Surveyor General John Oxley, leaving the Lachlan River to return to Bathurst in July 1817, documented a burial tumulus under which a man's body was buried in a sitting position, wrapped in a possum skin cloak, facing east. Two of the nearby trees were stripped of bark on the side facing the grave and marked with 'curious characters deeply cut upon them'. Jane Piper, whose family lived on a property neighbouring Brucedale, also described the burial of Wiradjuri people in a seated position, wrapped in a cloak with their own tools and weapons, under an ant nest–shaped tumulus presided over by carved trees.[1] Commemorative carved trees, had they once marked the graves at Brucedale, no longer stood there in the 1960s. A ground-penetrating radar survey carried out in 2010 detected signs that the remains of at least three people lie within the two graves. A third burial tumulus rests beside an ancient, and now

---

1   The party disturbed the grave out of curiosity, after which 'the whole was carefully re-interred, and restored as near as possible to the station in which it was found'. Oxley, *Journal of the Two Expeditions*, 138–41. Papers of P. J. Gresser, AIATSIS, MS21/2, 1–2. A.W. Howitt noted the Wiradjuri practice of wrapping the body of the deceased in a skin rug, depositing some of the deceased's belongings in the grave and covering it over with sticks and bark and then earth, as Oxley had described. He did not mention the burial mound, but noted the marking of surrounding trees. Howitt, *The Native Tribes*, 466.

deceased, yellow box tree nearby. The area may be a Wiradjuri burial ground from pre-contact times, or a burial place for Wiradjuri people who worked on Brucedale.[2]

The low mound of Windradyne's grave is easily hidden by the grass when it grows long, as it was when I visited in January 2009. More prominent are the concrete memorial (dedicated by Mr and Mrs Roy Suttor and the Bathurst Historical Society in 1954) and the young eucalypt trees, which frame the grave in the traditional diamond pattern, and were planted by the local Wiradjuri community in 2000.[3] It is a tranquil place, suffused with the solemnity of death and memory. I signed the visitors' book and headed off with John Suttor to talk somewhere cooler.

The Voluntary Conservation Agreement over Windradyne's grave, initiated in 1995, was signed by New South Wales Minister for the Environment, Bob Debus, in May 2000, and sent to Brucedale. The Suttor family and members of the local Wiradjuri community gathered at the grave. Dinawan Dyirribang performed a cleansing smoking ceremony, and he and Gloria Rogers spoke of the importance of the site for the Suttor family, local Wiradjuri people and for the nation. About 50 people gathered on the verandah of the old Brucedale homestead where John Suttor signed the agreement.[4] As a *Sydney Morning Herald* article put it:

> Yesterday, the friendship between the Suttor family and the Wiradjuri warrior was formally recognised. His gravesite was given formal preservation status with the signing of a Voluntary Conservation

---

2   Gresser recorded in 1964 that there was 'not a tree standing' in the vicinity of the graves; they had all been used for firewood many years earlier. Papers of P. J. Gresser, AIATSIS MS21/3/a, 119–20. Gresser believed there was more evidence that the small burial ground was for Wiradjuri workers on Brucedale. Papers of P. J. Gresser, AIATSIS, MS21/3/a, 119–20. Interestingly, the other burials and their relationship with Windradyne's grave is often overlooked. For example, the heritage listing of Windradyne's grave mentions the adjacent grave in its description of the site, but not in its assessment of the place's significance. Wiradjuri Elder Dinawan Dyirribang told me that the grave beside the yellow box tree may be where Windradyne's father is buried. Dinawan Dyirribang, in conversation with the author, 8 July 2011; Heritage Listing, Grave of Windradyne, State Heritage Register Database, Record Number 5051560.
3   Debra Jopson, 'Grave a Symbol of 180 Years of Friendship', *The Sydney Morning Herald*, 20 April 2002; John Suttor, in conversation with the author, 20 January 2009.
4   A Voluntary Conservation Agreement is an agreement between the government and landowner. See Community Based Conservation, Voluntary Conservation Agreements, Brucedale–Suttor, Bathurst District, VCA075, Department of Environment, Climate Change and Water File: F/2030 (hereafter Voluntary Conservation Agreement, Brucedale, 2000), 'Signing of the Suttor VCA Near Bathurst, Speech Notes' and associated photographs; Gloria Rogers, in conversation with the author, 13 July 2010.

Agreement by John Suttor, William's great-grandson. 'There was a sense of co-operation and co-existence', Mr Suttor said of the relationship. 'We have cemented that here today. That spirit still exists.'[5]

The Conservation Agreement covers just under one-third of a hectare, taking in the three grave mounds and the 1954 memorial.[6] The agreement is highly unusual; such agreements have overwhelmingly been made to protect natural values, with the protection of cultural values incidental.[7] The agreement recognises the complex history of the place and its many layers of cultural significance today: as an Aboriginal burial site and burial place of Windradyne; as a part of the 'first war arena between Aboriginal people and settlers on the Western Plains'; as part of 'Brucedale', one of the original settlements in the area still in the ownership of the Suttor family; as a property that was not attacked by Windradyne and his warriors; and as a site of commemoration, via the erection of the memorial in 1954. It specifies that Wiradjuri people and members of the Bathurst LALC 'shall be permitted access to the conservation area provided that at least 24 hours' notice has been given to the Owner', and directs the property owner to consult with and coordinate with these parties in undertaking works and maintenance within the site.[8] The agreement 'runs with the land'—that is, it binds not only John Suttor, and now his son David, but any future owner.

Isabel Coe's 1993 native title writ had a different vision. In claiming the whole of Wiradjuri country (whether claimable under native title or not), its aim was 'to contribute to a political settlement of claims made by the Aboriginal people of Australia or by the Wiradjuri who constitute part of that people'.[9] It was one of a series of cases that sought to 'articulate through legal avenues the relationship between Aboriginal people and their land' and to show that the ongoing alienation of Aboriginal people from their land was 'a continuing act of genocide'.[10] A *Sydney Morning Herald* report on the proceedings sketched the geographical oppression

---

5   Nick Leys, 'Black Warrior's Spirit Preserved', *The Sydney Morning Herald*, 27 May 2000, 9.
6   As noted above, a third visually identifiable grave is located outside the area covered by the agreement, which Dinawan Dyirribang claimed was Windradyne's father's grave. Dinawan Dyirribang, in conversation with the author, 8 July 2011.
7   Sally Ash, state co-ordinator Conservation Partners Program Department of Environment, Climate Change and Water, in conversation with the author, 23 June 2010.
8   Voluntary Conservation Agreement, Brucedale, 2000, section 2.3 and sections 2.2.4, 2.2.5, 3.1.
9   Solicitor General for New South Wales, Keith Mason QC, quoted in Nettheim, 'Isabel Coe on Behalf of the Wiradjuri Tribe'.
10  Walker and Bhuta, 'Upholding the Law', 15–18.

of Wiradjuri people, their confinement on the reserve at Cowra, the prohibition of hunting and fishing on private land, and the impossibility of visiting important cultural sites without permission from private land holders, citing Windradyne's grave as such a place.[11] The Conservation Agreement, in formalising the right of local Wiradjuri people to visit the grave and their right to have a say in future management decisions, returned Windradyne's grave to Wiradjuri people in a way that could never have been achieved under native title (seeing as it is situated on private property), but in a way that also requires ongoing cooperation with the land owners.

John Suttor was aware of the parallel tradition that places Windradyne's burial near the old hospital. Diane Johnson, engaging closely with those who care most for the grave, acknowledged both stories about Windradyne's death and burial in her book *Lighting the Way*. Dinawan Dyirribang, Gloria Rogers and Warwick Peckham of the Bathurst LALC were also aware of the hospital story; it is included in Windradyne's entry in the *Australian Dictionary of Biography*, written by David Roberts.[12] However, there is a very strong consensus among those who care for the grave at Brucedale that Windradyne died there and is buried there in the Wiradjuri way.

In seeking to make my own contribution to Windradyne's story, I inadvertently tested the strength of this consensus early in my study of the story. I had noted that the State Heritage Register listing of the grave at Brucedale did not refer to the parallel story of Windradyne's burial near the hospital. I wrote to the New South Wales Heritage Branch about the possibility of revising the register's listing of Windradyne's grave to include this additional information. I was anxious that, in leaving out part of the story, the listing left room for a whistleblower (such as a future owner of the property not committed to the conservation of this important place) to burst onto the scene with the 'new' evidence contained in 'Colo's' 1829 letter and attempt to have the place delisted. In taking this action, I was not entirely comfortable; I worried whether, in doing what I felt was my job as a historian, I was threatening to disturb Windradyne's remains. Apart from the removal of the carved trees around the graves at Brucedale,

---

11   Tony Hewett, 'Wiradjuri People's Writ Immortalises a Warrior', *The Sydney Morning Herald*, 7 June 1993, 8.
12   John Suttor, in conversation with the author, 20 January 2009; John Suttor, letter to the author, 4 February 2009; Johnson, *Lighting the Way*, 56. David Roberts seems to have brought 'Colo's' 1829 letter, with its statement that Windradyne was buried alongside the old hospital, back to light. Roberts, 'Windradyne (1800–1829)'.

the remains had been allowed to rest in peace, unlike the remains of so many Aboriginal people, which have been exhumed, collected, measured and classified, to produce knowledge that further disempowered their descendants.[13] The ancestors buried at Brucedale appear to have been neither exhumed nor threatened with exhumation, yet the fear that they might have been is never far off. For example, Mary Coe wrote: 'It is rumoured that even Windradyne's body was disturbed by these grave robbers and his head shipped to England'.[14] Notwithstanding my conviction that the wider acknowledgement of both stories would help to protect his grave into the future, I worried that my attempt to complicate the connection between the story and the grave (within one of the very mechanisms that supports its conservation) might be disrespectful. The people I consulted on the matter reassured me that they knew about the hospital story—it was no secret—and that knowing that a member of the Suttor family had written it down in 1829 did not shake their conviction of Windradyne's burial at Brucedale or the robustness of their commitment to care for his grave and share his story. Warwick Peckham told me that he had consulted with a number of people on receiving my letter, and it was his own view and theirs that I should leave the State Heritage Register listing as it is. Many people believe very strongly that Windradyne rests at Brucedale. It is better to let it rest.[15] Gloria Rogers told me:

> We have heard that story of him supposedly dying up there at the hospital ... and that he was buried there near the hospital. *But* ... we think it was just a story ... If he was buried there, why take him from that resting place back to Brucedale? Certainly Aboriginal people would not have done that, once a person is laid to rest, that is where they stay ... Because the Suttor family had a good relationship with Wiradjuri people ... we could not see [them] agreeing to Windradyne being taken ... from the hospital grounds out to their place ... So that is why I believe he died out there [at Brucedale] and that was his last resting place.[16]

Rogers's conviction that Windradyne's remains now rest at Brucedale was so strong that the only alternative she could conceive of was that he was buried at the hospital, and then moved to Brucedale later on—a scenario that she did not find credible.

---

13   Byrne, 'The Ethos of Return', 73–77; Griffiths, *Hunters and Collectors*, 25–31.
14   Coe, *Windradyne—A Wiradjuri Koorie* (1989), 73.
15   Warwick Peckham, in conversation with the author, 17 June 2010.
16   Gloria Rogers, in conversation with the author, 15 June 2010.

When I visited Brucedale for the first time in 2009, I noticed that 'Colo's' 1829 letter, with its striking obituary of Windradyne (as well as the statement he was buried at the hospital), was not among the sources in the family file. I sent John Suttor a number of copies of this letter, asking him to forward one to Dinawan Dyirribang, whom I had not yet met. John replied with great enthusiasm, saying he was looking forward to showing it to a group of Wiradjuri visitors the following day.[17] When I wrote a few months later proposing to amend the State Heritage Register listing, John told me about the current works at the site, hoping that the national parks service's interpretation panels—then being drafted—might answer my concerns about the evidence for the hospital story being included.[18] The panels, right at the graveside itself, acknowledge that 'there has … been some doubt about exactly where Windradyne's grave is—and even if he was buried here at all'. An explanation is offered in an effort to combine the two stories into one, in a way that is supported by the circle of people who care for the grave:

> In his recently discovered letter of 1829, George Suttor wrote at length about 'Windrodine', and his death. He says the warrior died 'in the hospital at Bathurst, near which place he was buried …' Was Suttor being deliberately vague to protect Windradyne's resting place? We may never know the answer to these and other questions.[19]

At the same time, the panels, installed by the NPWS later that year, affirm the visitor's understanding that Windradyne is buried at Brucedale. The panels refer to the 1954 memorial as a 'gravestone', subtly changing its status from memorial to memorial marker, linking it intrinsically to the grave. The panels cite the burial of Windradyne at Brucedale (along with William's knowledge of the Wiradjuri language, the fact that the Suttor property was not attacked when others were and George Suttor's 1826 letter) as a key piece of evidence for the friendship. Dinawan Dyirribang is quoted as saying that 'Windradyne formed a close friendship with this white man culminating in him being buried on the Suttor family property'.[20]

---

17  John Suttor, letter to the author, 4 February 2009.
18  John Suttor, letter to the author, 17 June 2010.
19  NSW National Parks and Wildlife Service, 'A Shared History' panel and 'Two Centuries Later' panel.
20  Ibid.

In the meantime, I went to the NPWS offices to look at the Voluntary Conservation Agreement documents. Although they do not include the hospital story either, the wording of the agreement links the significance of the site to the ongoing relationship between the Wiradjuri people and the Suttor family and the commemorative value of the site as much as the believed presence of Windradyne's remains, making it a robust conservation document in any eventuality.[21] Reassured by this, and accepting the consensus that I should leave the heritage listing as it is, I wrote to the Heritage Branch retracting my inquiry.

At the same time that layers of commemoration honouring Windradyne's memory have been laid down at Brucedale, the old Bathurst hospital site, on the corner of Bentick and Howick streets, has been transformed into a hectic supermarket precinct with little open space and constant car traffic. It is not a place that invites reflection or commemoration. When I met Dinawan Dyirribang in Bathurst in early 2011, he pointed out the site of the old hospital and explained that Windradyne had left there, tearing off his bandages, and returned to Brucedale.[22]

Dinawan Dyirribang has brought many local school groups to the grave site, and Gloria Rogers and others occasionally 'bring some people out' or just 'come and sit'. As well as creation stories, the landscape around Bathurst is rich with historical associations, including places associated with the 'sorry business' of the 1820s. Bill Murray, narrating Windradyne's story in 1993, said there were 15 massacre sites known to the community within a 10 mile radius of Bathurst. The LALC had acquired small blocks of land close to two of these significant places, at Wattle Flat and on the banks of the Macquarie River, but these were sold again in the 1990s. These sites, though very much in mind, remain unmarked and are seldom visited.[23] By contrast, over the past two decades (at least), Windradyne's grave, situated at the confluence of Windradyne's own importance in Wiradjuri heritage and the generous amicability of the Suttor family,

---

21  Voluntary Conservation Agreement, Brucedale, 2000, 2, clauses A–H and Plan of Management, section 6, 'Cultural Conservation Values'.
22  Dinawan Dyirribang, in conversation with the author, 8 July 2011.
23  Pearson, Windradyne: Wiradjuri Resistance. Dinawan Dyirribang, in conversation with the author, 8 July 2011; Gloria Rogers, in conversation with the author, 15 June 2010. The site of the potato farm where Wiradjuri people were killed in 1823 or 1824 is thought to be on the Macquarie River near the Japanese Gardens. There has been some discussion about extending the river parklands to commemorate Elizabeth Macquarie. However, the proposal to locate this new garden on the site of the potato farm has been highly controversial. Wayne Feebrey, in conversation with the author, 13 March 2012.

has become a place of reflection and refuge. When I asked Gloria Rogers whether Windradyne's grave was a place where people go to think about 'sorry business' as well as Windradyne himself, she replied:

> Yes, of course ... we're always made to feel welcome, and treated very respectfully. So when we do go out there, it is all those things that you mentioned. We go out there to sit, to reflect, to evaluate and get strength from it I suppose, and to remember ... those Elders past and present.[24]

Dinawan Dyirribang told *The Sydney Morning Herald* that visiting the grave gives him access to a past in which all the country was Aboriginal country, and that this enables him to draw strength for the present. He explained: 'I look back to when he was alive and think of what the country would have been like and the values he and his family had'.[25] Dinawan Dyirribang also visits the grave with a men's group that maintains the area by weeding and cleaning up fallen branches, providing an opportunity for visiting and caring for this important part of local Wiradjuri country. A research project discussing kinship with the natural world involving Aboriginal people from various parts of New South Wales found that the opportunity to visit special places and to care for them regularly was extremely important to participants. For example, Phil Sullivan, a Ngiyampaa man based in Bourke, explained how caring for rock art at Gundabooka as part of his role as an Aboriginal Sites Officer with the national parks service connected him to significant places right across the Manara Hills, and with his own ancestors, who may have been among those who placed their hands on the rock walls to create the stencils he cares for today.[26] In the same way, caring for Windradyne's grave is an activity that can help Wiradjuri people to connect with country much more broadly.

For a decade, John and David Suttor continued to accompany many of the grave's visitors, opening and closing gates to keep the cattle in, and conveying those without a four-wheel-drive vehicle along the rough track to Windradyne's resting place.[27] Discussions with the NPWS about

---

24   Gloria Rogers, in conversation with the author, 15 June 2010.
25   Debra Jopson, 'Grave a Symbol of 180 Years of Friendship', *The Sydney Morning Herald*, 20 April 2002.
26   Dinawan Dyirribang, in conversation with the author, 26 July 2011; Bird, James and Watson, *Indigenous Kinship*, 61.
27   John Suttor, in conversation with the author, 20 January 2009. This number included some local visitors, but many from further afield as well. John was particularly impressed by a group of Aboriginal visitors from Western Australia and the strength of their respect for the place, so far from their own home. One young man was left under a tree at some distance from the burial ground, as he had been forbidden to approach the grave by his elders, due to a wrong committed at home.

improving access to the site bore fruit in late 2010 and, as well as cattle grids en route to the grave, new interpretation panels have been installed, joining the traditional grave mounds, the 1954 memorial and the tree memorial planted by the Wiradjuri community in 2000. Making the place all the richer, these tributes of different eras to Windradyne combine with an occasional, invisible curdling of the air as they refuse to align.[28]

The 1954 memorial still sits quietly beside the grave with commemorative sediment from an earlier age embedded in its cement. In 1986, Mary Coe addressed its inscription:

> The Historical Society did not understand Windradyne and his people. The Society called him 'the last chief' but this is wrong. There have been a great many Wiradjuri leaders since the days of Windradyne, right up to the present … 'First a terror and then a friend to the settlers'—Windradyne was trying to defend his land, his people, his culture against the invading forces and in the end, if he had continued his armed resistance against them, the whites would have surely killed all his people … Windradyne is a true patriot to the Koorie people of Australia.[29]

For Coe, the memorial's first two epithets were inept and unjust. However, the affinity of the 1954 memorial to a war memorial appealed to her. Her re-bestowal of the epithet 'a true patriot' on Windradyne resonated with the discourse developed by Kevin Gilbert and others around the Aboriginal patriot as a person of rare courage, vision and commitment, who could truly advance the Aboriginal 'nation'.[30] Commemorating Windradyne in 2000, the Wiradjuri community did not place a priority on 'correcting' the 1954 memorial. In fact, the Voluntary Conservation Agreement documents suggest that the memorial is embraced by the Wiradjuri people involved because of the vital role it has played in attesting to the grave and marking its presence. Drawing on Dinawan Dyirribang's comments on the initial site recording form, the final agreement includes a clause stating that both the Aboriginal burial sites and the 1954 memorial are of 'special significance to the Wiradjuri people'.

---

28   Frances and Scates discussed the way in which 'a dialogue in which one perspective [on] history challenges another' can be achieved by the addition of a memorial alongside pre-existing commemorative material. The conversation they referred to was between the La Grange memorial standing in Esplanade Reserve, Fremantle, commemorating the deaths of a group of explorers at the hands of Aboriginal people, and a new memorial, proposed in 1988, which was to give the Aboriginal side of the story, and affirm 'the right of Aboriginal people to defend their culture and their land'. Frances and Scates, 'Honouring the Aboriginal Dead', 78–79.
29   Coe, *Windradyne—A Wiradjuri Koorie* (1989), 62.
30   See Gilbert, *Because a White Man'll Never Do it*, 191–92; Gilbert, 'Pearl Gibbs', 4–9.

The management plan specifies that the memorial be conserved. Rogers feels that John Bugg's collaboration with the Suttor family to protect the grave was so important because 'it was just a stone in the middle of a paddock' at that stage, but also because the 'stone' itself was beginning to weather.[31] The Conservation Agreement documents, as overseen by Dinawan Dyirribang, and the recently commissioned interpretive material, also make prominent references to Windradyne as a 'patriot', as well as a leader and warrior. This creates a certain solidarity with the 1954 memorial and with Coe's story, even though the epithet looks somewhat archaic as Aboriginal commentators continue to modify the pan-Aboriginal nationalism championed by Gilbert, Michael Anderson and others in the 1970s.[32]

Dinawan Dyirribang's notes reveal that the erection of a statue of Windradyne was considered; however, by 1997, the idea had been abandoned.[33] Instead, the memorial chosen by the Wiradjuri community in 2000 was a reinstatement of the traditional diamond pattern of eucalypts around the grave, which observes and honours the rising and setting sun. According to Rogers, because Windradyne's age and personal and clan totems are not known, there is no plan to carve the trees in the traditional Wiradjuri way. Rogers talked about Windradyne's trees in conjunction with the trees planted around the remains of an unknown 'old fella' recently repatriated from the Australian Museum.[34] The planting of trees around Windradyne's grave was, in a sense, a reclamation of Windradyne and his resting place for Wiradjuri culture and history.

---

31   Voluntary Conservation Agreement, Brucedale, 2000, 2; Gloria Rogers, in conversation with the author, 15 June 2010.
32   Julia Martinez found that Aboriginal people increasingly articulated multiple layers of identification through the 1980s and 1990s, not necessarily repudiating the pan-Aboriginal model, but rendering it secondary to family networks and local identifications. Martinez, 'Problematising Aboriginal Nationalism, 133–46. One of the few changes Gloria Rogers would have liked to see to the National Parks Service brochure (2011) was that its title describe Windradyne as 'warrior' rather than 'patriot'. Gloria Rogers, in conversation with the author, 15 June 2010.
33   Voluntary Conservation Agreement, Brucedale, 2000, Dinawan Dyirribang, National Parks and Wildlife Service site recording form, 12 July 1995. The Draft Plan of Management, dated December 1995, in the same location, includes a reference to the statue which is crossed out and replaced in handwriting with 'a cairn on the site will be maintained' (p. 4). The Draft Plan of Management, 1997, includes no reference to a statue.
34   Gloria Rogers, in conversation with the author, 15 June 2010. Wiradjuri people have also undertaken more general plantings of local species around the graves 'in memory of Windradyne and the Wiradjuri nation'. See 'Brucedale—site of Windradyne's grave—caring for our cultural heritage', *Bush Matters* (National Parks and Wildlife Service NSW) (Spring 2002), 3.

Figure 6: Windradyne's grave conservation area in 2018.
Source: Photograph taken by author.

The trees will grow and mature and eventually die, in contrast to the concrete and brass memorial, which was intended to remain the same for all time and to give out the same message. The tree memorial is also a memorial with meanings chiefly accessible to the Wiradjuri people who planted the trees and continue to maintain them. As National Parks Ranger Gavin Newton put it, it looked like 'just a block of land'—the story was not visible to the visitor unless he or she was accompanied by a knowledge holder. The trees do not spell out a new version of history for the visitor, or directly address their relationship with the 1954 memorial or the graves themselves. In that sense, the commemorative work carried out in 2000 could be seen as 'unfinished'.[35]

---

35   The plantings are in some ways an 'anti-memorial' in the sense that Sue-Anne Ware developed—they will change, grow and die along with memory, instead of attempting to freeze memory in time. Sue-Anne Ware, 'Contemporary Anti-Memorials and National Identity in the Victorian Landscape' (2004), quoted in Ashton and Hamilton, 'Places of the Heart', 8. Batten and Batten, 'Memorialising the Past', 107–12; Gavin Newton, National Parks Bathurst Area, in conversation with the author, 31 May 2010.

The interpretive material prepared under the auspices of the NPWS in 2010 takes on the task of articulating the story of Windradyne and his grave in a way that educates the new visitor and supports the memory work of regular visitors. The panels within the conservation area tell a broader story of Wiradjuri life in the three rivers country before invasion and, in answer to the 1954 memorial, point to the survival of the Wiradjuri as a 'strong people … proud of their heritage and how they have adapted to massive changes in their way of life'. The panels give an account of Windradyne's life in the context of the wars, and support the site's function as a de facto commemorative place for massacre and sorry business, by telling the story of the mutual bloodshed of 1823–24. The signs installed at the entrance to Brucedale prepare the intending visitor to be embraced by a shared place of memory; they welcome the visitor to Windradyne's grave—'a special place for two cultures'—on behalf of the 'Wiradyuri people and the Suttor family'. The panels develop the theme of shared history and shared knowledge by quoting extensively from Dinawan Dyirribang and Coe, along with 'Colo' and W. H. Suttor.[36]

The friendship between Windradyne and William is honed to a fine point, focused on the night encounter of 1824. This dramatic fulcrum looks back to the advice of George Suttor to his son to 'treat the Wiradyuri with respect', and forward to the ongoing good relations that saw Windradyne buried at Brucedale. Meditating on this 'unique' encounter, the visitor is asked to consider whether 'a different history might have been possible', presumably one in which mutual respect and compromise prevented bloodshed. While this is a viewpoint from amid the conflicts themselves, it is also a point of stillness, a moment of calm amid the storm. The panels depict the Suttor family as a neutral party in the conflicts of the 1820s, claiming 'although the Wiradyuri wars boiled around the Suttors, they were unscathed'.[37] As much as this suggests a 'liberal fantasy' (i.e., that goodwill might have prevented dispossession), it is also in keeping with the meaning of Windradyne's grave as a place of rest. As visitors approach Windradyne's grave, they are informed that they are entering a 'quiet place'. The Voluntary Conservation Agreement has created an island of calm among the landscape of ownership and

---

36 NSW National Parks and Wildlife Service, panels titled 'People of the Three Rivers—Wiradyuri life'; 'Wiradyuri Wars' and 'Windradyne, a Wiradyuri patriot'; entry sign installed at the gate of Brucedale, Peel Road, 2010.
37 NSW National Parks and Wildlife Service, 'A Shared History' panel.

dispossession. As a place where a range of voices can be heard on an equal footing, Windradyne's grave is also a place of calm amid the storm of history-making.

David Roberts described the Bells Falls Gorge massacre story as a 'nut without a kernel'—so much of its detail has been lost over time that it cannot be fleshed out and it remains on the threshold between myth and history.[38] Though this story of friendship is comparatively well documented, it too has lost much of its meat. The story's substance could almost be said to exist in the *feeling* between the sparse constellation formed by the mercy extended to the Suttor family and their property by the Wiradjuri warriors, William's language skills, George Suttor's 1826 letter and Windradyne's burial at Brucedale, as much as in these factual pillars themselves. In recent years, the friendship has chiefly been in the telling. John and David Suttor, Dinawan Dyirribang, Gloria Rogers and others tell Windradyne's story, and the story of his good relations with the Suttor family, with a conviction based in history, but which extends beyond history. The feeling at this place, Windradyne's grave, is significant to the story whether or not Windradyne's remains lie there or elsewhere. Who taught William the Wiradjuri language and how proficient was he? To what extent was William adopted into Wiradjuri networks and ways of thinking? What did William and Windradyne say to each other on that fateful night in 1824? How did Windradyne and other Wiradjuri people understand this friendship? How much did the relationship change when William married and as European settlement on the Bathurst Plains became more established and more populous across the late 1820s and 1830s? Did some local Wiradjuri people maintain links with country at Brucedale beyond the Suttor family's understanding? These and many other questions about the overlapping histories of the Suttor family and the local Wiradjuri people are hushed at Windradyne's grave. They are not silenced; instead, as William and Windradyne look into each other's eyes through the thick air of a dangerous night, and as Windradyne and his companions lie in the earth, they are calmed.

---

38   Roberts, 'Bells Falls Massacre', 626.

# Conclusion: Living Histories, Living Stories

Inga Clendinnen, returning to Bennelong's story, found the two centuries' worth of public and popular history about him oppressive or at least distracting. She used the less common spelling 'Baneelon' (Watkin Tench's transliteration), hoping a small dose of unfamiliarity might help her 'escape the freight of banalities time has placed on the word Bennelong'.[1] Clendinnen's remark helped to crystallised my project—I was setting out to explore this very same 'freight of banalities'. The terrain turned out to be varied, exciting and confronting, as much as it was banal. Much of the popular, public, official, local, family and academic history-making I engaged with was commonplace, in the sense that it was everyday history work, but it was not predictable. The retellings of these stories were repetitive, but not stale. Cliché abounded, but it was not necessarily unimaginative. Far from being a deadweight of 'freight' carried along by history, the retellings of Bennelong's, Morrill's, and Windradyne's and William's stories seemed to help many vital conversations about the past to progress.

When I set out, I was on the alert for change; I wanted to hear the new interpretations and fresh perspectives on these old stories that I felt would flow from their retelling in changing social and political climates. Initially, characterisation of the differences between versions came more easily to me than plumbing the meanings of the many layers of continuity that had been maintained through repetition. I was most flummoxed by a story that had not changed when I expected that it would have. However, I gradually came to see that the patterns of repetition and familiarity

---

1   Clendinnen, *Dancing with Strangers*, 103–04. Clendinnen's second reason for using this unusual transliteration was to remind herself and the reader about the 'complex store of social meanings stored within' Bennelong's five names, meanings which are often 'swept aside'.

told their own story. Film theorist Kara Keeling develops the idea of the 'cliché' as a repository of shared meaning with the potential for creative use. In Gilles Deleuze's account, 'cliché' is the usual human response to stimuli. When we come upon a new situation, a reflex of memory quickly supplies us with something that is familiar, something that can reconcile the new experience with 'commonsense'. Occasionally, when we reach out for a helpful memory, nothing familiar can be found. Deleuze valorised this moment, in which no cliché can be grasped and commonsense is out of reach, as a moment when original thought must occur. However, Keeling found the cliché itself full of possibility as a starting point of shared understanding, from which new meaning might be created even as common meanings are consolidated, and called this 'positive unoriginality'.[2] She described this kind of repetition as not simply naive or unthinking, but as an affirmation of 'commonsense'.[3] For her, the pattern created by this constant activity is 'a record of a group's survival'.[4]

Critical histories, revisiting the sources, questioning accepted understandings of the past and investigating afresh the relationships of people to place have been vital in the recognition of Aboriginal dispossession and survival, and in the ongoing process of reconciling 'Australia and its Aboriginal history', as Lorenzo Veracini put it.[5] Yet, critical history is not the only kind of history-making that can be a rallying point for change, and for ending the 'silences and denial' that are a barrier to thinking about Aboriginal people's claims to the places in which non-Indigenous Australians also live. Particularly on a local scale, a transformed 'commonsense' may also come about through the affirmative retelling of the stories with which people are already familiar

---

2    Keeling, *The Witches' Flight*, 14–21.
3    Meghan Morris developed this term in response to the myth that Australians are 'positively unable to originate', destined forever to feebly imitate American and European cultural innovations (citing Jessie Ackerman (1914), an American who visited Australia as an organiser for the Women's Christian Temperance Union). Morris, via an analysis of *Crocodile Dundee* (1986), transformed this supposed tendency to be 'positively unoriginal' into a capacity for 'positive unoriginality', a term intended to capture the innovation inherent in reuse and imitation, and the distinctive and assertive nature of the statements that can be made thereby. Morris, 'Tooth and Claw', 105–27.
4    Keeling, *The Witches' Flight*, 21.
5    Providing an account of the effect on the public sphere, and in legal decisions, of historians working to bring together apparent oppositions in Australian history (e.g., 'invasion' and 'settlement', 'resistance' and 'accommodation', 'genocide' and 'survival', and 'colonial' and 'contemporary' pasts), Veracini argued that this conceptual 'incorporation' of oppositions through the examination of regional and thematic histories (that are both 'critical' and 'synthetic'), has gradually ushered a basic recognition of Aboriginal pasts, presents and futures beyond debate and into public consciousness. Veracini, 'Of a "Contested Ground"', 224–39.

in the changing contexts created by critical histories and social activism, as well as law, policy and local economies. As Mark McKenna has observed, it is not enough for a new kind of history to be made and told once; rather, it is necessary to 'retain and repeat' histories that recognise the presence of Aboriginal people and open opportunities for dialogue in conversation after conversation.[6]

I experienced the power of repetition first-hand when I told Windradyne's story at a forum focused on the approaching bicentenary of the 'crossing of the Blue Mountains', organised by Lithgow City Council in March 2011. I went with Kath Schilling, a senior colleague at the New South Wales Office of Environment and Heritage, and a Wiradjuri woman with links to the Darlington Point area of south-western New South Wales, who had been asked to run a workshop on Aboriginal histories. The day opened with a 'welcome to country' and many of the speakers acknowledged the traditional owners of the places they spoke about. However, the morning sessions had focused closely on the histories of Blaxland, Wentworth and Lawson, the surveying of roads by Evans and Cox, and the European–Australian heritage associated with the road makers. There were a number of Wiradjuri and Gundungurra people present, but there were few openings for connecting Aboriginal histories to these discussions.

A seasoned convenor, Kath had arranged the program so that I would open the afternoon session by telling the story of Windradyne and his crossing of the Blue Mountains west to east, and of his friendship with the Suttor family, before she opened the floor to discussion. Conscious that, for the first time, I would be telling this story back to Wiradjuri people on the western side of the mountain range, I focused on telling the story of war and friendship in brief, but from as many perspectives as possible. I knew it was beside the point to analyse its meanings or to emphasise my own interpretations, but I did not fully understand my role in telling the story in that place until after I had finished. Windradyne's story had opened

---

6   McKenna made recommendations for accessible, affirmative public history-making of this kind for the south-eastern corner of New South Wales, including dual naming of landscape features and the commemoration of some of the region's important Aboriginal residents. McKenna, *Looking for Blackfellas' Point*, 220–27. Public histories such as the City of Sydney's 'Barani/ Barrabugu (Yesterday/ Tomorrow)' walking tour, and The Australian National University's 'Deepening Histories of Place' project take this approach to communicating complexity with simplicity by bringing interconnected histories of place to life through innovative interpretation materials. *Barani/Barrabugu (Yesterday/ Tomorrow): Sydney's Aboriginal Journey*; description of the 'Deepening Histories of Place' research project, Australian National University, Australian Centre for Indigenous History, accessed 16 June 2018, www.deepeninghistories.anu.edu.au/.

up possibilities. Kath introduced Dinawan Dyirribang and a number of other Wiradjuri and Gundungurra people to the audience, and they took the stage to talk about language and history. There was no further need to demonstrate the relevance of Aboriginal histories to the crossing of the Blue Mountains—Windradyne's story had made the connection; the Wiradjuri and Gundungurra Elders were free to talk about the cultural and historical matters most important to them. The audience of mostly non-Indigenous history enthusiasts listened with warmth, possibly aided by the inclusive space opened up by the narration of the Suttor family's friendship with Windradyne.

The reconciliation movement has given a new intensity of life to stories of Aboriginal–settler friendship as beacons of hope, 'lighting the way' to a new future.[7] Each of these stories has been touched by the reconciliation zeitgeist, which has popularised the concept of sharing histories, and set up expectations about history's power to heal. The 'lives of stories' in this book, I think, help to demonstrate that there is no simple answer to the relationship between history and reconciliation. They illustrate how complex matters of remembering and forgetting are, and how interwoven the sharing of histories is with practices of history-making.

A fresh start in history-making is part of reconciliation rhetoric. Prime Minister Rudd, in his 'Apology to the Stolen Generations' speech in 2008, proposed a new start both in history and in history-making: 'Let us turn this page together: Indigenous and non-Indigenous Australians, government and opposition, Commonwealth and state, and write this new chapter in our nation's story together'.[8] The careers of the three stories retold here show an intricate relationship between fresh perspectives and old stories. As particular stories about the past, they have never been completely assimilated to the values or demands of the unfolding present. Across the 1990s and following decades, they continued to transmit a complex inheritance of genres formed and re-formed by many generations, symbols tinged with nineteenth-century ideas about race, and the flavour of ways of being friends that have faded from our social lexicon. A fresh start has not been possible, partly because the ways in which we explain the past have become part of our past too, and form part of the reservoir on which we draw to face the future. This is a strength

---

7   To quote the title of Johnson's book, *Lighting the Way*.
8   Rudd, 'Speech by Prime Minister Kevin Rudd to the Parliament'. For a discussion of these metaphors and impulses see Hamilton, 'Memory Studies', 95–96.

as well as a limitation. The heritage embodied in historical stories will not simply comply with the desired politics of the present and future, as it is not a completely consciously chosen heritage, like the canonical 'national inheritance' John Howard would have liked all Australians to subscribe to.[9] Rather, it is a 'commonsense' in which family, local and national concerns are combined; social, cultural and historical knowledge merges; and that is played out across local landscapes. A reconciliatory 'shared history' may be a hegemonic notion, not entirely different from a 'national inheritance', but it is also an unrealistic one; layer upon layer of smaller histories would precede and follow any such overarching narrative, slowly modifying and multiplying meaning.

Some of the history-makers featured in this book set out to prosecute an inquiry into the past, or to do so at the same time as revising the histories that have gone before; others engaged with the past to commemorate, to entertain or to invigorate political purpose. Yet, the 'stories' of Morrill, Bennelong, and Windradyne and the Suttor family have, to some extent, flowed between versions that have quite distinct aims, and measure themselves against quite different standards. Like the medium of water in Graeme Swift's novel *Waterland*, as much as human hands try to direct it into rivers, channels, sluices and dams, it cannot be completely or reliably separated; it trickles between, merges in the wet soil and will flow all together again when the banks break. Further, because they all make use of story (narrative, with its verbal images, sense of character and appetite for movement), meaning seems to leap across genres. In a sense, though all those busy with history work and storytelling have their own objectives, the story also has a life of its own. As long as it is still in the process of being told, events and their interpretation remain entangled.[10]

Heather Goodall called for 'open-ended' spaces in which matters of reconciliation, apology, shame and responsibility can be worked on in public. As these matters are complex and difficult to articulate, she observed that spaces of 'evocation' are acutely important.[11] The three stories of friendship, diplomacy and adoption examined here, and many more like them, can be understood as such open-ended spaces, in which history, understandings of landscape, public space and social relationships are negotiated and renegotiated in an ongoing way. Many local tellers

---

9   McKenna, 'Australian History and the Australian "National Inheritance"', 1–12.
10  Swift, *Waterland*; Nugent, *Captain Cook Was Here*, x–xi.
11  Goodall, 'Too Early Yet', 17–23.

of Morrill's story do not embrace Noel Loos's idea that they might stand together proud of a common ancestor. Yet, the storytelling of Aboriginal and non-Indigenous people in the Bowen–Townsville region interacts through telling this story in a mutually recognisable way, creating opportunities for diffuse, and diverse, personal exchanges, some of which are bound to be uncomfortable, and some imbricated with the perpetuation of a social, political and economic status quo, in which the recognition of Birri-gubba shares is not secure. The stories of Windradyne and William Suttor cross paths in an enigmatic but powerful way at Windradyne's resting place, forming the foundation for an agreement about the custodianship of land, an agreement that achieves much more than simply actualising reconciliation aspirations. At the same time, though, the meaning of this space of sharing for Wiradjuri people is much more complex than an affirmation of the past goodwill between William Suttor and Windradyne. The results of negotiations at Brucedale are inseparable from a chequered landscape of recognition and denial, sharing and segregation across Wiradjuri country. The story of Bennelong's friendship with the colony, and its consequences, functions as a space for an ongoing popular and public dialogue about the dangers of sharing pasts and histories. As a space of 'evocation', the story accommodates multiple and changing meanings, allowing for communication across a range of scales and on literal and metaphorical planes. Bennelong's story is often about Sydney and about the recognition and understanding of Aboriginal experiences of and claims to urban space; however, it also functions as a founding parable through which the dilemmas and tensions in cross-cultural relationships are continually played out in the telling, often on a national or even transnational scale.

Narratives, characters and symbols that seem quite incompatible sit down side by side around these three stories, as on Bill Ashcroft's 'verandahs' of meaning, where postcolonial stories (all stories since the foundation of a colony) look inwards as well as outwards. Each perspective creates its own verandah that joins it with, as well as delineates it from, others.[12] It is the activity of sharing stories, and working on their meanings, that can, at times, bring people together to enact social healing, and may also highlight different desired futures. It is the activity of sharing stories that continues to lay down strata of meaning about ancestors, past events and ancient places. These three stories are part of a conversation about the past in which there will be no last word.

---

12   Ashcroft, 'Excess: Post Colonialism', 33–44.

# Bibliography

## Articles, Essays, Book Chapters and Poems

Anderson, Ian. 'Black Bit, White Bit'. In *Blacklines: Contemporary Critical Writing by Indigenous Australians*, edited by Michele Grossman, 43–51. Carlton, Vic: Melbourne University Press, 2003.

Ashcroft, Bill. 'Excess: Post Colonialism and the Verandahs of Meaning'. In *De-scribing Empire: Post-colonialism and Textuality*, edited by Chris Tiffin and Alan Lawson, 33–44. London: Routledge, 1994. doi.org/10.4324/9780203203682.

Ashton, Paul and Paula Hamilton. 'Places of the Heart: Memorials, Public History and the State in Australia since 1960'. *Public History Review* 15 (2008): 1–29. doi.org/10.5130/phrj.v15i0.776.

Atkinson, Alan. 'The Charmed Circle: Review of *Dancing With Strangers* by Inga Clendinnen'. *Australian Book Review* 256 (2003): 9–10.

Attwood, Bain. 'The Past as Future: Aborigines, Australia and the (Dis)course of History'. In *In the Age of Mabo: History, Aborigines and Australia*, edited by Bain Attwood, vii–xxxviii. St Leonards, NSW: Allen & Unwin, 1996.

Attwood, Bain. 'Contesting Frontiers: History, Memory and Narrative in a National Museum'. *reCollections: Journal of the National Museum of Australia* 1, no. 2 (September 2006): 103–14.

Attwood, Bain. 'Aboriginal History, Minority Histories and Historical Wounds: The Postcolonial Condition, Historical Knowledge and the Public Life of History in Australia'. *Postcolonial Studies* 14, no 2 (2011): 171–86.

Batten, Bronwyn and Paul Batten. 'Memorialising the Past: Is There an "Aboriginal" Way?'. *Public History Review* 15 (2008): 92–116. doi.org/10.5130/phrj.v15i0.656.

Besley, Joanna. 'At the Intersection of History and Memory: Monuments in Queensland'. *Limina* 11 (2005): 38–46.

Bevernage, Berber. 'Writing the Past Out of the Present: History and the Politics of Time in Transitional Justice'. *History Workshop Journal* 69 (Spring 2010): 111–31. doi.org/10.1093/hwj/dbq008.

Birch, Tony. '"History is Never Bloodless": Getting it Wrong after One Hundred Years of Federation'. *Australian Historical Studies* 33, no. 118 (2002): 42–53. doi.org/10.1080/10314610208596178.

Blake, Thom. 'Deported … at the Sweet Will of the Government: The Removal of Aborigines to Reserves in Queensland 1897–1939'. *Aboriginal History* 22 (1998): 51–61.

Bolton, G. C. 'Morrill, James (1824–1865)'. *Australian Dictionary of Biography*, National Centre of Biography, The Australian National University. First published 1967. Accessed 14 June 2018, adb.anu.edu.au/biography/morrill-james-2484.

Bostock, Gerry. 'Colebe'. *Meanjin* 53, no. 4 (Summer 1994): 613–18.

Bradford, Vivian. '"A Timeless Now": Memory and Repetition'. In *Framing Public Memory*, edited by Kendall R. Phillips, 187–211. Tuscaloosa: University of Alabama Press, 1997.

Breen, Shayne. 'Human Agency, Historical Inevitability and Moral Culpability: Rewriting Black-White History in the Wake of Native Title'. *Aboriginal History* 20 (1996): 108–32.

Briscoe, Gordon. 'Review of Bain Attwood's *Telling the Truth about Australian History*'. *History Australia* 3, no. 1 (2006): 25.1–25.3.

Brodie, Marc and Barbara Caine. 'Class, Sex and Friendship: The Long Nineteenth Century'. In *Friendship: A History*, edited by Barbara Caine, 223–78. Oakville, CT: Equinox Pub., 2008.

Brook, Jack. 'The Forlorn Hope: Bennelong and Yemmerrawannie Go to England'. *Australian Aboriginal Studies* 1 (2001): 36–47.

Brooks, Barbara. 'Introduction'. In Eleanor Dark, *The Timeless Land*, vii–xviii. Pymble, NSW: HarperCollins Publishers Australia, 2002.

Broome, Richard. 'Historians, Aborigines and Australia: Writing the National Past'. In *In the Age of Mabo*, edited by Bain Attwood, 54–72. St Leonards, NSW: Allen & Unwin, 1996.

Bulbeck, Chilla. 'Aborigines, Memorials and the History of The Frontier'. In *Packaging the Past: Public Histories*, edited by John Rickard and Peter Spearritt, 168–78. Carlton South, Vic: Melbourne University Press, 1991.

Burrows, Victoria. 'The Ghostly Haunting of White Shame in David Malouf's *Remembering Babylon*'. *Westerly* 51 (November 2006): 124–132.

Byrne, Denis. 'Deep Nation: Australia's Acquisition of an Indigenous Past'. *Aboriginal History* 20 (1996): 82–107.

Byrne, Denis. 'The Ethos of Return: Erasure and Reinstatement of Aboriginal Visibility in the Australian Historical Landscape'. *Historical Archaeology* 37, no. 1 (2003): 73–86. doi.org/10.1007/BF03376593.

Byrne, Denis. 'Nervous Landscapes: Race and Space in Australia'. *Journal of Social Archaeology* 3, no 2 (June 2003): doi.org/10.1177/1469605303003002003.

Byrne, Denis. 'Archaeology in Reverse: The Flow of Aboriginal People and Their Remains Through the Space of New South Wales'. In *Public Archaeology*, edited by Nick Merriman, 240–54. New York: Routledge, 2004.

Carter, Paul. 'Repetitions at Night: Mimicry, Noise and Context'. In *Exchanges: Cross-Cultural Encounters in Australia and the Pacific*, edited by Ross Gibson, 59–88. Sydney: Historic Houses Trust of New South Wales, 1996.

Carter, Paul. 'Speaking Pantomimes: Notes on The Calling to Come'. *Leonardo Music Journal* 6 (1996): 95–98. doi.org/10.2307/1513328.

Casey, Maryrose. 'Referendums and Reconciliation Marches: What Bridges Are We Crossing?'. *Journal of Australian Studies* 30, no. 89 (2006): 137–48. doi.org/10.1080/14443050609388099.

Chadwick, Doris. 'Governor Phillip and the Natives'. *The New South Wales School Magazine of Literature for Our Boys and Girls* 40, no. 9, Part 1 (November 1955): 267–72.

Clark, Anna. 'The History Wars'. In *Australian History Now*, edited by Anna Clark and Paul Ashton, 151–66. Sydney: New South Press, 2013.

Claughton, S. G. 'Walker, William (1800–1855)'. *Australian Dictionary of Biography*, National Centre of Biography, The Australian National University. First published 1967. Accessed 28 November 2011, adb.anu.edu.au/biography/walker-william-2768/text3933.

Clendinnen, Inga. 'The Power to Frustrate Good Intentions: Or, the Revenge of the Aborigine'. *Common Knowledge* 11, no. 3 (Fall 2005): 410–31. doi.org/10.1215/0961754X-11-3-410.

Colley, Linda. 'Going Native, Telling Tales: Captivity, Collaborations and Empire', *Past and Present* 168 (August 2000): 170–93. doi.org/10.1093/past/168.1.170.

Collins, Felicity. 'Historical Fiction and the Allegorical Truth of Colonial Violence in the Proposition'. *Cultural Studies Review* 14, no.1 (March 2008): 55–71. doi.org/10.5130/csr.v14i1.2098.

Cowlishaw, Gillian. 'On "Getting It Wrong": Collateral Damage in the History Wars'. *Australian Historical Studies* 37, no. 127 (April 2006): 181–202. doi.org/10.1080/10314610608601210.

Curthoys, Ann. 'Expulsion, Exodus and Exile in White Australian Historical Mythology'. *Journal of Australian Studies* 23, no. 61 (1999): 1-18. doi.org/10.1080/14443059909387469.

Curthoys, Ann. 'Mythologies'. In *The Australian Legend and its Discontents*, edited by Richard Nile, 11–41. St Lucia, Qld: University of Queensland Press, 2000.

Curthoys, Ann. 'Cultural History and the Nation'. In *Cultural History in Australia*, edited by Richard White and Hsu-Ming Teo, 22–37. Sydney: University of New South Wales Press, 2003.

Curthoys, Ann. 'Indigenous Subjects'. In *Australia's Empire*, edited by Deryck M. Schreuder and Stuart Ward, 78–102. New York: Oxford University Press, 2008.

Curthoys, Ann. 'W. E. H. Stanner and the Historians'. In *An Appreciation of Difference: W. E. H. Stanner and Aboriginal Australia*, edited by Melinda Hinkson and Jeremy Beckett, 233–50. Canberra: Aboriginal Studies Press, 2008.

Darian-Smith, Kate. '"Rescuing" Barbara Thompson and other White Women: Captivity Narratives on Australian Frontiers'. In *Text, Theory, Space: Land, Literature and History in South Africa and Australia*, edited by Kate Darian-Smith, Liz Gunner and Sarah Nuttall, 99–114. London: Routledge, 1996.

Dark, Eleanor. 'Bennelong (1764–1813)'. *Australian Dictionary of Biography*, National Centre of Biography, The Australian National University. First published 1966. Accessed 28 April 2012, adb.anu.edu.au/biography/bennelong-1769/text1979.

Dawson, Barbara. 'Sisters under the Skin? Friendship: Crossing the Racial Gulf'. *Crossings (International Australian Studies Association)* 7, no.3 (2002).

De Souza, Pascale. 'Maoritanga in Whale Rider and Once Were Warriors: A Problematic Rebirth through Female Leaders'. *Studies in Australasian Cinema* 1, no. 1 (2007): 15–27. doi.org/10.1386/sac.1.1.15_1.

Dixon, Robert. 'What Was Travel Writing? Frank Hurley and the Media Contexts of Early Twentieth—Century Australian Travel Writing'. *Studies in Travel Writing* 11, no. 1 (March 2007): 59–81. doi.org/10.1080/13645145.2007.9634819.

Dodson, Michael. 'The End in the Beginning: Re(de)finding Aboriginality'. *Australian Aboriginal Studies* 1 (1994): 2–13.

Dortins, Emma. 'James Morrill: Shipwreck Survivor, Birri-gubba Adoptee and Explorer-in-Retrospect'. *History Australia* 9, no. 3 (December 2012): 65–86.

Dortins, Emma. 'Apology and Absolution—the Poetic and Public Dialogue of Judith Wright and Kath Walker'. In *Testimony, Witness, Authority: The Politics and Poetics of Experience*, edited by Tom Clark and Sasha Henriss-Andersse, 166–77. Cambridge Scholars Publishing, 2013.

Edensor, Tim. 'Reading Braveheart: Representing and Contesting Scottish Identity'. *Scottish Affairs* 21 (Autumn 1997): 135–58. doi.org/10.3366/scot.1997.0061.

Erdos, Renee. 'Leichhardt, Friedrich Wilhelm Ludwig (1813–1848)'. *Australian Dictionary of Biography*, National Centre of Biography, The Australian National University. First published 1967. Accessed 28 April 2012, adb.anu.edu.au/biography/leichhardt-friedrich-wilhelm-ludwig-2347/text3063.

Evans, Raymond. '"Steal Away": The Fundamentals of Aboriginal Removal in Queensland'. *Journal of Australian Studies* 23, no. 61 (June 1999): 83–95. doi.org/10.1080/14443059909387477.

Fitzpatrick, Kathleen. 'Burke, Robert O'Hara (1821–1861)'. *Australian Dictionary of Biography*, National Centre of Biography, The Australian National University. First published 1969. Accessed 28 April 2012, adb.anu.edu.au/biography/burke-robert-ohara-3116/text4633.

Foley, Dennis. 'Leadership: The Quandary of Aboriginal Societies in Crises, 1788–1830, and 1966'. In *Transgressions: Critical Australian Indigenous Histories*, edited by Ingereth Macfarlane and Mark Hannah, 177–92. Canberra: Aboriginal History Inc. and ANU E Press, 2007. doi.org/10.26530/OAPEN_459741.

Foley, Gary. 'Black Power in Redfern 1968—1972'. The Koori History Website. 5 October 2001. Accessed 4 July 2011, kooriweb.org/foley/essays/essay_1.html.

Fourmile, Henrietta. 'Who Owns the Past? Aborigines as Captives of the Archives'. In *Terrible Hard Biscuits: A Reader in Aboriginal History*, edited by Valerie Chapman and Peter Read, 16–27. Sydney: Allen & Unwin and Journal of Aboriginal History, 1996.

Fox, Ani. 'Dancing with Strangers: Europeans and Australians at First Contact, by Inga Clendinnen'. *Journal of World History* 17, no. 4 (2006): 456–58. doi.org/10.1353/jwh.2006.0055.

Frances, Rae and Bruce Scates. 'Honouring the Aboriginal Dead'. *Arena* 86 (1989): 72–80.

Frow, John. 'A Politics of Stolen Time'. *Meanjin* 57, no. 2 (1998): 351–67.

Furniss, Elizabeth. 'Timeline history and the Anzac Myth: Settler Narratives of Local History in a North Australian Town'. *Oceania* 71, no. 4 (June 2001): 279–97. doi.org/10.1002/j.1834-4461.2001.tb02754.x.

Gall, Adam. 'Taking/Taking Up: Recognition and the Frontier in Grenville's *The Secret River*'. *Journal of the Association for the Study of Australian Literature, Special Issue: The Colonial Present*, (2008): 94–104.

Garrioch, David. 'From Christian Friendship to Secular Sentimentality: Enlightenment Re-evaluation'. In *Friendship: A History*, edited by Barbara Caine, 165–214. Oakville, CT: Equinox Pub., 2008.

George, Sandy. '[Re]Writing History: First Australians Rewrite History Just by Telling It from an Indigenous Perspective'. *Storyline* 24 (Spring 2008): 20–22.

Gilbert, Kevin. 'Pearl Gibbs: Aboriginal Patriot: Three Tributes to Pearl Gibbs (1901–1983)'. *Aboriginal History* 7, no 1 (1983): 4–9.

Goodall, Heather. 'Telling Country: Memory, Modernity and Narratives in Rural Australia'. *History Workshop Journal* 47 (Spring 1999): 160–90. doi.org/10.1093/hwj/1999.47.160.

Goodall, Heather. 'Too Early Yet or Not Soon Enough?: Reflections on Sharing Histories as Process'. *Australian Historical Studies* 33, no.118, (2002): 7–24. doi.org/10.1080/10314610208596176.

Grieves, Vicki. 'Windschuttle's Fabrication of History: A View from the "Other" Side'. *Labour History* 85 (November 2003): 194–199. doi.org/10.2307/27515935.

Haebich, Anna. 'Imagining Assimilation'. *Australian Historical Studies* 33, no. 118 (January 2002): 61–70. doi.org/10.1080/10314610208596180.

Hamilton, Paula. 'Memory Studies and Cultural History'. In *Cultural History in Australia*, edited by Hsu-Ming Teo and Richard White, 81–97. Sydney: University of New South Wales Press, 2003.

Hasluck, Alexandra. 'Yagan the Patriot'. *Western Australian Historical Society* 5, no. 7 (1961): 33–48.

Healey, Sianan. '"Years Ago Some Lived Here": Aboriginal Australians and the Production of Popular Culture, History and Identity in 1930s Victoria'. *Australian Historical Studies* 37, no. 128 (October 2006): 18–34. doi.org/10.1080/10314610608601217.

Healy, J. J. 'A Most Tragic Theme'. *Hemisphere* 21, no. 5 (1977): 28–32.

Heiss, Anita. 'Barani: Sydney's Aboriginal History'. City of Sydney. Created 2002. Accessed 8 August 2009, www.cityofsydney.nsw.gov.au/barani/themes/theme7.htm.

Hendy-Pooley, Grace. 'Early History of Bathurst and Surroundings'. *Journal of the Royal Australian Historical Society* 1 (1905): 230–36.

Hill, Barry. 'Crossing Cultures'. *Meanjin* 62, no.4 (December 2003): 116–20.

Hinkson, Melinda. 'Exploring Aboriginal Sites in Sydney: A Shifting Politics of Place?'. *Aboriginal History* 26 (2002): 62–77. doi.org/10.1080/14443050903522069.

Hogan, Jackie. 'Gendered and Racialised Discourses of National Identity in Baz Luhrmann's *Australia*'. *Journal of Australian Studies* 34, no.1 (March 2010): 63–77. doi.org/10.1080/14443050903522069.

Hoorn, Jeanette. 'Julie Dowling's Melbin and the Captivity Narrative in Australia'. *Australian Cultural History* 23 (2004): 201–12.

Inglis, Ken and Jock Phillips. 'War Memorials in Australia and New Zealand'. In *Packaging the Past: Public Histories,* edited by John Rickard and Peter Spearritt, 177–91. Carlton South, Vic; Melbourne University Press, 1991.

Johnson, Miranda. 'Reconciliation, Indigeneity, and Postcolonial Nationhood in Settler States'. *Postcolonial Studies* 14, no. 2 (2011): 187–201.

Kaplan, Danny and Niza Yanay. 'Fraternal Friendship and Commemorative Desire'. *Social Analysis* 50, no.1 (Spring 2006): 127–46. doi.org/10.3167/015597706780886021.

Karskens, Grace. 'Red Coat, Blue Jacket, Black Skin: Aboriginal Men and Clothing in Early New South Wales'. *Aboriginal History* 35 (2011): 1–36.

Kinnane, Gary. '*Remembering Babylon* and the use of history'. *Agora* 36, no. 4 (2001): 7–12.

Kociumbas, Jan. 'Performances: Indigenisation and Post Colonial Culture'. In *Cultural History in Australia*, edited by Hsu-Ming Teo and Richard White, 127–41. Sydney: University of New South Wales Press, 2003.

Komunyakaa, Yusef. 'Bennelong's Blues'. *Callaloo* 20, no. 1 (Winter 1997): 35. doi.org/10.1353/cal.1997.0028.

La Nauze, J. A. 'The Study of Australian History 1929–1959'. *Historical Studies Australia and New Zealand* 9, no. 33 (1959): 1–11.

Lake, Marylin. 'On Being a White Man, Australia, circa 1900'. In *Cultural History in Australia*, edited by Hsu-Ming Teo and Richard White, 98–112. Sydney: University of New South Wales Press, 2003.

Lambert-Pennington, Katherine. 'What Remains? Reconciling Repatriation, Aboriginal Culture, Representation and the Past'. *Oceania* 77, no.3 (November 2007): 313–36. doi.org/10.1002/j.1834-4461.2007.tb00019.x.

Langton, Marcia. 'Rum, Seduction and Death: "Aboriginality" and Alcohol'. *Oceania* 63, no. 3 (March 1993): 195–206. doi.org/10.1002/j.1834-4461.1993.tb02417.x.

Loos, Noel. 'Koiki Mabo: Mastering Two Cultures, a Personal Perspective'. In *Lectures on North Queensland History 5*, edited by B. J. Dalton, 1–20. Townsville, Qld: Department of History and Politics, James Cook University, 1996.

McBryde, Isabel. '"Barter … Immediately Commenced to the Satisfaction of Both Parties": Cross-cultural Exchange at Port Jackson 1788–1828'. In *The Archaeology of Difference: Negotiating Cross-Cultural Engagements in Oceania*, edited by Robin Torrence and Anne Clarke, 238–77. London: Routledge, 2000.

McCann, Andrew. 'Unknown Australia: Rosa Praed's Vanished Race'. *Australian Literary Studies* 22, no.1 (May 2005): 37–50. doi.org/10.20314/als.d0884096f4.

McCann, Andrew. 'The Literature of Extinction'. *Meanjin* 65, no. 1 (March 2006): 48–54.

McCarter, James. 'They Began It'. In *These People Lived*, 2–19. Brisbane: 'The Worker' Newspaper Pty Ltd, 1944.

McCarthy, F. D. 'Bungaree (?–1830)'. *Australian Dictionary of Biography*, National Centre of Biography, The Australian National University. First published 1966. Accessed 28 April 2012, adb.anu.edu.au/biography/bungaree-1848/text2141.

Macdonald, Gaynor. 'Master Narratives and the Dispossession of the Wiradjuri'. *Aboriginal History* 22 (1998): 162–79.

Macdonald, Gaynor. 'Does "Culture" Have "History"? Thinking about Continuity and Change in Central New South Wales'. *Aboriginal History* 25 (2001): 176–99.

McGuanne, John. 'Bennelong Point and Fort Macquarie'. *Royal Australian Historical Society Journal Proceedings* 1, part 2 (1901, 2nd ed. 1911): 9–13.

McIntyre, Julie. '"Bannelong Sat Down to Dinner with Governor Phillip, and Drank His Wine and Coffee as Usual": Aborigines and Wine in Early New South Wales'. *History Australia* 5, no.2 (2008): 39.1–39.14.

McKay, Belinda. 'Writing from the Contact Zone: Fiction by Early Queensland Women'. *Hecate* 30, no. 2 (2004): 53–70.

McKenna, Mark. 'Australian History and the Australian "National Inheritance"'. *Australian Cultural History* 27, no. 1 (2009): 1–12. doi.org/10.1080/07288430902877841.

McKenna, Mark. 'Clark, Charles Manning (1915–1991)', *Australian Dictionary of Biography*, National Centre of Biography, The Australian National University, [2015]. Accessed 15 February 2017, adb.anu.edu.au/biography/clark-charles-manning-225/text29719.

McQueen, Humphrey. 'Introduction'. In Eleanor Dark, *The Timeless Land*, xix–xxiv. Pymble, NSW: HarperCollins Publishers Australia, 2002. First published 1990.

Martinez, Julia. 'Problematising Aboriginal Nationalism'. *Aboriginal History* 21 (1997): 133–47.

Mason, Brett. 'The Tragedy of Conspicuous Compassion'. *Party Room* 1 (Winter 2005): 6–9.

Maynard, John. 'Circles in the Sand: An Indigenous Framework of Historical Practice'. *The Australian Journal of Indigenous Education* (supplement) 36 (2007): 117–20.

Miller, Calvin. 'A Haven for Alcoholics Ditching their Addiction'. *Journal of the Australian Medical Association* 2, no. 12 (December 1982): 602–05.

Monypenny, Maria. '"Going Out and Coming In": Cooperation and Collaboration between Aborigines and Europeans in Early Tasmania'. *Tasmanian Historical Studies* 5, no. 1 (1995–96): 64–75.

Morris, Meaghan. 'Tooth and Claw: Tales of Survival and Crocodile Dundee'. *Social Text* 21 (1989): 105–27. doi.org/10.2307/827811.

Moses, Dirk. 'Moving the Genocide Debate Beyond the History Wars'. *Australian Journal of Politics and History* 54, no. 2 (June 2008): 248–70. doi.org/10.1111/j.1467-8497.2008.00497.x.

Muir, Marcie. 'Stow, Catherine Eliza Somerville (Katie) (1856–1940)'. *Australian Dictionary of Biography*, National Centre of Biography, The Australian National University. First published 1990. Accessed 8 March 2012, adb.anu.edu.au/biography/stow-catherine-eliza-somerville-katie-8691/text15205.

Muldoon, Paul. 'Thinking Responsibility Differently: Reconciliation and the Tragedy of Colonisation'. *Journal of Intercultural Studies* 26, no. 3 (August 2005): 237–54. doi.org/10.1080/07256860500153518.

Mulvaney, D. J. 'John Graham: The Convict as Aboriginal'. In *Irish Convict Lives*, edited by Bob Reece, 109–45. Sydney: Crossing Press, 1993.

Mulvaney, D. J. 'Stanner, William Edward (Bill) (1905–1981)'. *Australian Dictionary of Biography*, National Centre of Biography, The Australian National University [2012]. Accessed 12 December 2014, adb.anu.edu.au/biography/stanner-william-edward-bill-15541/text26753.

Mulvaney, Richard. 'The Gresser Papers'. *Australian Aboriginal Studies* 2 (1985): 86–88.

Nettheim, Garth. 'Isabel Coe on Behalf of the Wiradjuri Tribe v. Commonwealth of Australia and the State of New South Wales'. *Aboriginal Law Bulletin* 9, no. 3/66 (23 December 1993): 14.

O'Neill, Phillip. 'Putting the English in Drag: Bungaree's Theatre of Mimicry as a Response to Colonialism'. In *Aratjara: Aboriginal Culture and Literature in Australia*, edited by Dieter Riemenschneider and Geoffrey V. Davis, 69–86. Amsterdam: Rodopi, 1997.

Parsons, Vivienne. 'Suttor, George (1774–1859)'. *Australian Dictionary of Biography*, National Centre of Biography, The Australian National University. First published 1967. Accessed 28 April 2012, adb.anu.edu.au/biography/suttor-george-1270/text3813.

Peel, Mark, Liz Reed and James Walter. 'The Importance of Friends: The Most Recent Past'. In *Friendship: A History*, edited by Barbara Caine, 316–28. Oakville, CT: Equinox Pub., 2008.

Perkins, Charles. 'Political Objectives'. In *The Australian People: An Encyclopaedia of the Nation, Its People and Their Origins*, James Jupp, 233–39. North Ryde, NSW: Angus & Robertson, 1988.

Peters-Little, Frances. 'The Community Game: Aboriginal Self-definition at the Local Level'. AIATSIS Research Discussion Paper No. 10. Canberra: Aboriginal Studies Press, 2000.

Plomley, N. J. B. 'Book Review: Vivienne Rae Ellis: Trucanini: Queen or Traitor?' *Tasmanian Historical Research Association—Papers and Proceedings* 23, no. 2 (June 1976): 50–52.

Portelli, Alessandro. 'The Massacre at the Fosse Ardeatine: History, Myth, Ritual and Symbol'. In *Contested Pasts: The Politics of Memory*, edited by Katharine Hodgkin and Susannah Radstone, 29–41. London: Routledge, 2003. doi.org/10.4324/9780203391471.

Read, Peter. '"The Truth that Will Set Us All Free": An Uncertain History Of Memorials To Indigenous Australians'. *Public History Review* 15 (2008): 30–46. doi.org/10.5130/phrj.v15i0.810.

Reece, Bob. 'Inventing Aborigines'. *Aboriginal History* 11, no. 1 (1987): 14–23.

Reed, Liz. '"Mrs Bon's Verandah Full of Aboriginals": Race, Class, Gender and Friendship'. *History Australia* 2, no.2 (June 2005): 39.1–39.15.

Reynolds, Henry. 'Aborigines and European Social Hierarchy'. *Aboriginal History* 7 (1983): 124–33.

Roberts, David. 'Bells Falls Massacre and Bathurst's History of Violence: Local Tradition and Australian Historiography'. *Australian Historical Studies* 26, no. 105 (October 1995): 615–33. doi.org/10.1080/10314619508595986.

Roberts, David Andrew. 'Windradyne (1800–1829)'. *Australian Dictionary of Biography*, National Centre of Biography, The Australian National University. First published 2005. Accessed 28 April 2012, adb.anu.edu.au/biography/windradyne-13251/text4471.

Roberts, David and Hilary Carey. '"Beong! Beong! (More! More!)": John Harper and the Wesleyan Mission to the Australian Aborigines'. *Journal of Colonialism and Colonial History* 10, no. 1 (Spring 2009): n.p.

Rowe, C. S. 'Rowe's Memoranda'. In *The Townsville Book*, edited by W. J. Doherty, 105–15. Brisbane: Edwards, Dunlop & Company Limited, 1921.

Rowse, Tim. 'Historians and the Humanitarian Critique of Australia's Colonisation'. *Australian Journal of Anthropology* 14, no. 2 (2003): 253–58. doi.org/10.1111/j.1835-9310.2003.tb00234.x.

Ryan, Lyndall. 'The Struggle for Trukanini 1830–1997'. *Tasmanian Historical Research Association Papers and Proceedings* 44, no. 3 (September 1997): 153–73.

Sayers, C. E. 'Introduction'. In John Morgan, *The Life and Adventures of William Buckley, Thirty-Two Years a Wanderer amongst the Aborigines of the Then Unexplored Country around Port Phillip, Now the Province of Victoria*, vii–xvi. Melbourne: William Heinemann, 1967.

Seal, Graham. 'Digger'. In *Symbols of Australia: Uncovering the Stories Behind the Myths*, edited by Melissa Harper and Richard White, 121–28. Sydney: University of New South Wales Press and National Museum of Australia Press, 2010.

Smith, Keith. 'Bennelong: Ambassador of the Eora Part II'. *Australian Heritage* (Autumn 2006): 79–81.

Smith, Keith Vincent. 'Bennelong among His people', *Aboriginal History* 33, (2009): 7–30.

Spillman, Lyn. 'When Do Collective Memories Last? Founding Moments in the United States and Australia'. *Social Science History* 22, no. 4 (Winter 1998): 445–77.

Stanner, W. E. H. 'The History of Indifference Thus Begins'. *Aboriginal History* 1 (1977): 2–26.

Stockdale, Jacqueline. '"I Dreamed of Snow Today": Impediments to Settler Belonging in Northern Queensland as Depicted in a Selection of Recent Fiction'. *Proceedings of the Inaugural Tropics of the Imagination Conference*, *etropic* 9 (2010): 1–10.

Tacitus, Cornelius. 'The Life of Agricola'. In *The Annals of Tacitus*, edited by Arthur Galton. London: Walter Scott, c1890.

Taussig, J. C. 'How Bathurst Began'. In *The Story of Bathurst written by Bathurstians*, edited by Bernard Greaves, 1–16. Sydney: Angus & Robertson, 1961.

Teale, Ruth. 'Suttor, John Bligh (1859–1925)'. *Australian Dictionary of Biography*, National Centre of Biography, The Australian National University. First published 1976. Accessed 28 April 2012, adb.anu.edu.au/biography/suttor-john-bligh-4937/text7733.

Teale, Ruth. 'Suttor, William Henry (1805–1877)', *Australian Dictionary of Biography*, National Centre of Biography, The Australian National University. First published 1976. Accessed 15 June 2018, adb.anu.edu.au/biography/suttor-william-henry-1269/text7733.

Troy, Jakelin. 'Language Contact in Early Colonial New South Wales 1788–1791'. In *Language and Culture in Aboriginal Australia*, edited by Michael Walsh and Colin Yallop, 33–50. Canberra: Aboriginal Studies Press, 1993.

Tumarkina, Maria. 'First as a Tragedy, Second as a Farce: Traumascapes, Memory and the Curse of Indifference'. *Overland* 175 (Winter 2004): 22–26.

Tweg, Sue. 'Dream On: A "Reconciliation" Tempest in 2001'. *Contemporary Theatre Review* 14, no. 3 (August 2004): 45–52. doi.org/10.1080/1026716042000237612.

van Toorn, Penny. 'Indigenous Australian Life Writing: Tactics and Transformations'. In *Telling Stories: Indigenous History and Memory in Australia and New Zealand*, edited by Bain Attwood and Fiona Magowan, 1–20. Sydney: Allen & Unwin, 2001.

Veracini, Lorenzo. 'Of a "Contested Ground" and an "Indelible Stain": A Difficult Reconciliation between Australia and Its Aboriginal History during the 1990s And 2000s'. *Aboriginal History* 27 (2003): 224–39.

Veracini, Lorenzo. 'A Prehistory of Australia's History Wars: The Evolution of Aboriginal History during the 1970s and 1980s'. *Australian Journal of Politics and History* 52, no. 3 (2006): 439–54. doi.org/10.1111/j.1467-8497.2006.00428.x.

Veracini, Lorenzo. 'Historylessness: Australia as a Settler Colonial Collective'. *Postcolonial Studies* 10, no. 3 (September 2007): 271–85. doi.org/10.1080/13688790701488155.

Vincent, Eve. 'Who is Bennelong?' *Arena Magazine* 89 (June–July 2007): 46–48.

Walker, Melinda and Nehal Bhuta. 'Upholding the Law v. Maintaining Legality: Nulyarimma v. Thompson'. *Indigenous Law Bulletin* 4, no. 24/81 (1 September 1999): 15–18.

Willmot, Eric. 'The Dragon Principle'. In *Who Owns the Past?: Papers from the Annual Symposium of the Australian Academy of the Humanities*, edited by Isabel McBryde, 41–48. Melbourne: Oxford University Press, 1985.

Willmot, Eric. 'Beyond Contact'. In *The Pemulwuy Dilemma: The Voice of Koori Art in the Sydney Region* (exhibition catalogue). Emu Plains, NSW: Lewers Bequest and Penrith Regional Art Gallery, 1990.

Windschuttle, Keith. 'Social History and Aboriginal Legends: A Reply to Gary Morgan'. *Quadrant* 46, no. 4 (April 2002): 30–31.

# Books

Alexie, Sherman. *The Summer of Black Widows*. New York: Hanging Loose Press, 1996.

Anderson, Stéphanie. *Pelletier: The Forgotten Castaway of Cape York*. Melbourne: Melbourne Books, 2009.

Attenbrow, Val. *Sydney's Aboriginal Past: Investigating the Archaeological and Historical Records*. Sydney: University of New South Wales Press, 2002.

Attwood, Bain with Helen Doyle. *Possession: Batman's Treaty and the Matter of History*. Melbourne: The Miegunyah Press, 2009.

*Barani/Barrabugu (Yesterday/Tomorrow): Sydney's Aboriginal Journey*. City of Sydney with the City's Aboriginal and Torres Strait Islander Advisory Panel, June 2011.

Barker, Theo. *A History of Bathurst*, vols 1 and 2. Bathurst, NSW: Crawford House Press, 1992.

Barnard, Marjorie. *A History of Australia*. Sydney: Angus & Robertson, 1962.

Bathurst City Council. *Official Souvenir Programme of the Visit of Her Majesty Queen Elizabeth II … to Bathurst*. Bathurst, NSW: Bathurst City Council, 1954.

Bathurst District Historical Society. *A Short History of Bathurst*. Bathurst: Western Advocate, 1965.

Beatty, Bill. *Early Australia: With Shame Remembered*. Melbourne: Cassell & Co., 1962.

Binney, Judith. *Stories without End: Essays 1975–2010*. Wellington, NZ: Bridget Williams Books, 2010. doi.org/10.7810/9781877242472.

Bird, Deborah, Diana James and Christine Watson. *Indigenous Kinship with the Natural World in New South Wales*. Sydney: NSW National Parks and Wildlife Service, 2003.

Birmingham, John. *Leviathan: The Unauthorised Biography of Sydney*. Sydney: Random House, 1999.

Bond, George. *A Brief Account of the Colony of Port-Jackson in New South Wales: Its Native Inhabitants, Productions, &c. &c.* Vic: Edition Renard, 2005.

Bonwick, James. *The Wild White Man and the Blacks of Victoria*. Melbourne: Fergusson & Moore, 1863.

Bowen Historical Society. *The Story of James Morrill*. Bowen: The Bowen Independent, 1964.

Bowen Historical Society. *James Morrill: His Life and Adventures*. Bowen: The Bowen Independent, 2002.

Brantlinger, Patrick. *Dark Vanishings: Discourse on the Extinction of Primitive Races, 1800–1930*. Ithaca, NY: Cornell University Press, 2003.

Brayshaw, Helen. *Well Beaten Paths: Aborigines of the Herbert Burdekin District, North Queensland*. Townsville: Department of History, James Cook University of North Queensland, 1990.

Breslin, Bruce. *Exterminate with Pride: Aboriginal-European Relations in the Townsville-Bowen Region 1843 to 1869*. Townsville: James Cook University, Department of History and Politics, 1992.

Breslin, Bruce. *James Morrill: Captive of Empire*. North Melbourne: Australian Scholarly Publishing, 2017.

Brodsky, Isadore. *Bennelong Profile: Dreamtime Reveries of a Native of Sydney Cove*. Sydney: University Co-Operative Bookshop Limited, 1973.

Brooks, Barbara, with Judith Clark. *Eleanor Dark: A Writer's Life*. Sydney: Macmillan, 1998.

Carrington, Berenice and Pamela Young. *Aboriginal Heritage and Wellbeing*. Sydney: NSW Department of Environment, Climate Change and Water, 2011.

Carrington, George. *Colonial Adventures and Experiences, by a University Man*. London: Bell and Daldy, 1871.

Chenhall, Richard. *Benelong's Haven: Recovery from Drug and Alcohol Abuse within an Aboriginal Australian Residential Treatment Centre.* Melbourne: Melbourne University Press, 2007.

Cilento, Raphael and Clem Lack. *Wild White Men of Queensland.* Brisbane: W. R. Smith & Paterson for the Royal Historical Society of Queensland, 1959.

Cilento, Raphael and Clem Lack. *Triumph in the Tropics: An Historical Sketch of Queensland.* Brisbane: Smith and Paterson, 1959.

Clark, Anna. *Private Lives, Public History.* Melbourne: Melbourne University Press, 2016.

Clark, Manning. *History of Australia*, vol. 1. Carlton, Vic: Melbourne University Press, 1962.

Clarke, Marcus. *Old Tales of a Young Country.* Melbourne: Mason, Firth and McCutcheon, 1871.

Clendinnen, Inga. *Dancing with Strangers.* Melbourne: Text Publishing, 2003.

Clifford, Michael. *Political Genealogy after Foucault: Savage Identities.* New York: Routledge, 2001.

Coe, Mary. *Windradyne—A Wiradjuri Koorie.* Glebe, NSW: Blackbooks, 1986.

Coe, Mary. *Windradyne–A Wiradjuri Koorie.* Canberra: Aboriginal Studies Press, 1989.

Coetzee, J. M. *Foe.* Maryborough, Vic: Penguin, 2010.

Cole, Sarah. *Modernism, Male Friendship, and the First World War.* Cambridge: Cambridge University Press, 2003.

Collins, David. *An Account of the English Colony in New South Wales: With Remarks on the Dispositions, Customs, Manners, &C. of the Native Inhabitants of That Country, to Which Are Added, Some Particulars of New Zealand.* Adelaide: Libraries Board of South Australia, 1971.

Connor, John. *The Australian Frontier Wars, 1788–1838.* Sydney: University of NSW Press, 2002.

Conrad, Joseph. *The Heart of Darkness.* London: Penguin Books, 1991.

Crotty, Martin and David Andrew Roberts. *The Great Mistakes of Australian History.* Sydney: University of New South Wales Press, 2006.

Curthoys, Ann and John Docker. *Is History Fiction?* Sydney: University of New South Wales Press, 2006.

Dalziell, Rosamund. *Shameful Autobiographies: Shame in Contemporary Australian Autobiographies and Culture.* Carlton, Vic: Melbourne University Press, 1999.

Dark, Eleanor. *The Timeless Land.* Melbourne: Fontana Books, 1980.

*David Boyd: Retrospective 1957–1982: A Series of Seven Exhibitions Presented by the Wagner Art Gallery as a Contribution to the Festival of Sydney 1983.* Paddington, NSW: The Gallery, 1983.

Davison, Graeme. *The Use and Abuse of Australian History.* St. Leonards, NSW: Allen & Unwin, 2000.

De Foe, Daniel. *The Life and Adventures of Robinson Crusoe, to Which is Appended Howell's Life of Alexander Selkirk.* Edinburgh: Fraser & Co., 1837.

Dégh, Linda. *Narratives in Society: A Performer-Centred Study of Narration.* Helsinki: Suomalainen Tiedeakatemia, Academia Scientiarum Fennica, 1995.

Doherty, W. J. *The Bowen Book.* Townsville: T. Willmett and sons Ltd., 1920.

Doherty, W. J. *The Townsville Book.* Brisbane: Edwards, Dunlop & Company Limited, 1921.

Douglas, Mary. *Purity and Danger: An Analysis of the Concepts of Pollution and Taboo.* London: Routledge, 2002. First published 1966.

Ducharme, Leon. *Journal of a Political Exile in Australia.* Translated by George Mackaness. Sydney: D S Ford, 1944. First published 1845.

Duguid, Charles. *No Dying Race.* Rigby: Adelaide, 1963.

Egan, Ted. *The Aboriginals Songbook.* Richmond, Vic: Greenhouse Publications, 1987.

Elder, Bruce. *Blood on the Wattle: Massacres and Maltreatment of Aboriginal Australians since 1788.* Frenchs Forest, NSW: Child & Associates, 1988.

Ellis, Jean A. *Aboriginal Australians—Their Journey.* Penrith, NSW: Kaliarna Productions, 2006.

Endeavour Reading Programme. *Bennelong.* Milton, Qld: The Jacaranda Press, 1970.

Evans, Raymond. *A History of Queensland.* New York: Cambridge University Press, 2007.

Ferguson, John Alexander. *Bibliography of Australia*, vol. 6. Canberra: National Library of Australia, 1977.

Flood, Josephine. *The Original Australians: Story of the Aboriginal People*. Crows Nest, NSW: Allen & Unwin, 2006.

Foster, Robert, Rick Hosking and Amanda Nettelbeck. *Fatal Collisions: The South Australian Frontier and the Violence of Memory*. Kent Town, South Australia: Wakefield Press, 2001.

Foucault, Michel. *The Archaeology of Knowledge and the Discourse on Knowledge*. Translated by A. M. Sheridan Smith. New York: Pantheon Books, 1972.

Fox, M. J. *The History of Queensland: Its People and Industries*, vol. 2. Brisbane: Hussey and Gillingham for the States Publishing Co., 1923.

Garner, Alan. *Strandloper*. London: Harvill Press, 1996.

Garton, Stephen. *Medicine and Madness: A Social History of Insanity in New South Wales*. Sydney: New South Wales University Press, 1988.

Garton, Stephen. *Out of Luck: Poor Australians and Social Welfare, 1788–1988*. Sydney: Allen & Unwin, 1990.

Geeves, Philip. *Local History in Australia: A Guide for Beginners*. Sydney: Royal Australian Historical Society, 1967.

Gibbney, H. J. and Ann Smith. *A Biographical Register: Notes from the Name Index of the Australian Dictionary of Biography 1788-1939*. Canberra: The Australian National University, 1987.

Gibson, Ross. *Seven Versions of an Australian Badland*. St Lucia, Qld.: University of Queensland Press, 2002.

Gilbert, Kevin. *Because a White Man'll Never Do It*. Sydney: Angus & Robertson, 1973.

Gill, Merri. *Weilmoringle: A Unique Bicultural Community*. Dubbo, NSW: Development and Advisory Publications of Australia, 1996.

Goldsworthy, Peter. *Three Dog Night*. Camberwell, Vic: Viking, 2003.

Goodall, Heather. *Invasion to Embassy: Land in Aboriginal Politics in New South Wales, 1770–1972*. Sydney: Sydney University Press, 2008.

Grant, Stan (Jnr). *The Tears of Strangers: A Memoir*. Pymble, NSW: Harper Collins, 2002.

Grant, Stan (Snr). *Stories Told by My Grandfather and Other Old Men: A Collection of Short Stories*. O'Connor, ACT: Restoration House, 1999.

Grassby, Al and Marji Hill. *Six Australian Battlefields: The Black Resistance to Invasion and the White Struggle against Colonial Oppression*. North Ryde, NSW: Angus & Robertson, 1988.

Greaves, Bernard, ed. *The Story of Bathurst written by Bathurstians*. Sydney: Angus & Robertson, 1961.

Green, Martin. *The Robinson Crusoe Story*. London: The Pennsylvania State University Press, 1990.

Gregory, Edmund. *Sketch of the Residence of James Morrill among the Aboriginals of Northern Queensland for Seventeen Years; Being a Narrative of His Life, Shipwreck, Landing on the Coast, and Residence among the Aboriginals: Also an Account of the Natural Productions of Northern Queensland, and Manners, Customs Language, and Superstitions of its Inhabitants, By Edmund Gregory*. Brisbane: Courier General Printing Office, 1866.

Gregory, Edmund. *Narrative of James Murrell's ('Jemmy Morrill') Seventeen Years' Exile among the Wild Blacks of North Queensland, and His Life and Shipwreck and Terrible Adventures Among Savage Tribes; their Manners, Customs, Languages, and Superstitions; also Murrells' Rescue and Return to Civilisation, by Edmund Gregory*. Brisbane: Edmund Gregory, 1896.

Grenville, Kate. *The Lieutenant*. Melbourne: The Text Publishing Company, 2009.

Griffiths, Tom. *Hunters and Collectors: The Antiquarian Imagination in Australia*. Cambridge: Cambridge University Press, 1996.

Hancock, W. K. *Australia*. London: Earnest Benn Ltd., 1930.

Heaton, John Henniker. *Australian Dictionary of Dates and Men of the Time*. Sydney: George Robertson, 1879.

Hinkson, Melinda. *Aboriginal Sydney: A Guide to Important Places of the Past and Present*. Canberra: Aboriginal Studies Press, 2001.

Hirst, John. *Sense and Nonsense in Australian History*. Melbourne: Black Ink, 2006.

Horton, David, ed. *The Encyclopaedia of Aboriginal Australia*. Canberra: Aboriginal Studies Press, 1994.

Howard, Rod. *The Fabulist: The Incredible Story of Louis de Rougemont*. Sydney: Random House Australia, 2006.

Howitt, A. W. *The Native Tribes of South-East Australia*. London: Macmillan and Co., 1904.

Hubble, A. T. *Sydney Opera House Official Souvenir*. Sydney: Sydney Opera House Trust, 1973.

Hughes Turnbull, Lucy. *Sydney: Biography of a City*. Sydney, Random House, 1999.

Human Rights and Equal Opportunity Commission (HREOC). *Bringing Them Home: National Inquiry into the Separation of Aboriginal and Torres Strait Islander Children from Their Families*. Sydney: Human Rights and Equal Opportunity Commission, 1997.

Hunter, John. *An Historical Journal of Events at Sydney and at Sea 1787–1792*. Sydney: Angus & Robertson and the Royal Australian Historical Society, 1968.

Inglis, Ken. *Sacred Places: War Memorials in the Australian Landscape*. Melbourne: Melbourne University Press, 2008.

Johnson, Colin. *Long Live Sandawara*. Melbourne: Hyland House, 1987. First published 1979.

Johnson, Dianne. *Lighting the Way: Reconciliation Stories*. Annandale, NSW: Federation Press, 2002.

Karskens, Grace. *The Colony*. Crows Nest, NSW: Allen & Unwin, 2009.

Keeling, Kara. *The Witches' Flight: The Cinematic, the Black Femme and the Image of Common Sense*. Durham: Duke University Press, 2007. doi.org/10.1215/9780822390145.

Keneally, Thomas. *The Commonwealth of Thieves: The Sydney Experiment*. Sydney: Random House, 2005.

Keneally, Thomas. *Australians: Origins to Eureka*. Crows Nest, NSW: Allen & Unwin, 2009.

Kennedy, E. B. *Four Years in Queensland*. London: Edwards Stanford, 1870.

Kennedy, E. B. *Seventeen Years amongst Queensland Blacks*. London: W. R. Chambers Ltd, 1914.

Kenny, John. *Bennelong: First Notable Aboriginal*. Sydney: Royal Australian Historical Society, 1973.

Kerin, Rani. *Doctor Do Good? Charles Duguid and Aboriginal Advancement, 1930s–1970s*. North Melbourne: Australian Scholarly Publishing, 2011.

Kerr, John. *Black Snow and Liquid Gold: A History of the Burdekin Shire from First Contact of Europeans with the Aborigines, Analysing the Development of the Pastoral, Agricultural, Secondary and Service Industries Including Sugar Cane Growing and Milling from Inkerman to Giru on the Haughton River, Rice, Tobacco, Mango and Horticultural Production, Irrigation Schemes Leading to Construction of The Burdekin Dam, the Establishment of the Twin Towns of Ayr and Home Hill, Sea, Road, Rail and Air Transport, Local Government, Health Services, Social, Religious and Sporting Activities, and the Impact of Melanesian, Chinese, Japanese, Italian, Spanish and Other Immigrants*. Ayr, Qld: Burdekin Shire Council, 1994.

Kijas, Johanna. *Revival, Renewal and Return: Ray Kelly and the NSW Sites of Significance Survey*. Sydney: NSW Department of Environment and Conservation, 2005.

Langford, Ruby Giniby. *Don't Take Your Love to Town*. Ringwood, Vic: Penguin, 1988.

Larkin, John. *Dictionary of Australian History*. Sydney: Rigby, 1980.

Lavelle, Siobhan. *1813: A Tale That Grew in the Telling*. Blackheath, NSW: Siobhan Lavelle, 2013.

Learmonth, Andrew and Nancy Learmonth. *Encyclopaedia of Australia*. London: Frederick Warne and Co., 1968.

Levy, Michael. *Wallumetta: A History of Ryde and Its District 1792 to 1945*. Sydney: W. E. Smith, 1947.

London, Peter. *The Burdekin and the Burdekin Cultural Complex: A Short History Commemorating the Centenary of the Shire of Burdekin*. Ayr, Qld: Cane Toad Promotions, 1988.

Lowe, David. *Forgotten Rebels: Black Australians Who Fought Back*. Melbourne: Permanent Press, 1994.

Lumholtz, Carl. *Among Cannibals: An Account of Four Years' Travels in Australia and of Camp Life With the Aborigines of Queensland*. Canberra: The Australian National University Press, 1980. First published 1889.

McBryde, Isabel. *Guests of the Governor: Aboriginal Residents of the First Government House*. Sydney: Friends of First Government House Site, 1989.

McCalman, Iain. *The Reef: A Passionate History*. Melbourne: Victoria Viking, 2013.

Macdonald, Gaynor. *Two Steps Forward, Three Steps Back: A Wiradjuri Land Rights Journey*. Marrickville, NSW: Southwood Press, 2004.

McKenna, Mark. *Looking for Blackfellas' Point: An Australian History of Place*. Sydney: UNSW Press, 2002.

McKenna, Mark. *An Eye for Eternity: The Life of Manning Clark*. Carlton, Vic: Miegunyah Press, 2011.

McQueen, Humphrey. *Gallipoli to Petrov: Arguing with Australian History*. Sydney: Allen & Unwin, 1984.

Malouf, David. *Remembering Babylon*. Sydney: Random Books, 1993.

Maynard, John and Victoria Haskins. *Living with the Locals: Early Europeans' Experience of Indigenous Life*. Canberra: National Library of Australia Publishing, 2016.

Meston, Archibald. *Report on the Aboriginals of Queensland*. Brisbane: Edmund Gregory, Government Printer, 1896.

Mitchell, Susan. *The Matriarchs*. Ringwood, Vic: Penguin, 1987.

Moore, David. *Islanders and Aborigines at Cape York. An Ethnographic Reconstruction Based on the 1848–1850 'Rattlesnake' Journals of O. W. Brierly and Information He Obtained from Barbara Thompson*. Canberra: Australian Institute of Aboriginal Studies, 1979.

Moorhouse, Geoffrey. *Sydney*. Sydney, Allen & Unwin, 1999.

Morgan, John. *The Life and Adventures of William Buckley, Thirty-Two Years a Wanderer amongst the Aborigines of the Then Unexplored Country around Port Phillip, Now the Province of Victoria*. Melbourne: William Heinemann, 1967. First published 1852.

Morrill, James. *Sketch of a Residence among the Aboriginals of Northern Queensland for Seventeen Years; Being a Narrative of My Life, Shipwreck, Landing on the Coast, Residence among the Aboriginals, with an Account of Their Manners and Customs and Mode of Living; Together with Notices of Many of the Natural Productions, and of the Nature of the Country, by James Morrill*. Brisbane: Courier General Printing Office, 1863.

Morris, Alan J. *The Sole Survivor*. Emu Park, Qld: Alan J. Morris, 1992.

Mudrooroo. *Us Mob: History, Culture, Struggle: An Introduction to Indigenous Australia*. Sydney: Angus & Robertson, 1995.

Mulvaney, Derek John. *A Good Foundation: Reflections on the Heritage of the First Government House*. Canberra: Australian Government Publishing Service, 1985.

Nakata, Martin. *Savaging the Disciplines: Disciplining the Savages*. Canberra: Aboriginal Studies Press, 2007.

Newton, John and William Cowper. *Olney Hymns in Three Books*. London: W. Oliver, 1779.

Norton, Judith and Horace Norton. *Dear William: The Suttors of Brucedale—Principally the Life and Times of William Henry Suttor Senior*. Sydney: The Suttor Publishing Committee, 1994.

Nugent, Maria. *Captain Cook Was Here*. Cambridge: Cambridge University Press, 2009.

O'Malley, Seamus. *Making History New: Modernism and Historical Narrative*. Oxford: Oxford University Press, 2015.

Oxley, John. *Journal of the Two Expeditions into the Interior of New South Wales, 1817–1818,* vol. 1 (Australiana Facsimile Editions no. 6). Adelaide: Libraries Board of South Australia, 1964.

Palmer, Edward. *Early Days in North Queensland*. Sydney: Angus & Robertson, 1983. First published 1903.

Perkins, Rachel and Marcia Langton. *First Australians: An Illustrated History*. Carlton, Vic: Melbourne University Publishing, 2008.

Phillips, Richard. *Mapping Men and Empire: A Geography of Adventure*. London: Routledge, 1997.

Phipson, Joan. *Bennelong*. Sydney: Collins, 1975.

Plomley, N. J. B. *The Tasmanian Aborigines*. Launceston, Tas: N.J.B. Plomley in Association with the Adult Education Division, Tasmania, 1977.

Rapier, L. A. and Nellie Watson. *The Townsville Story: They Fashioned a City Beam by Beam*. Townsville: Willmetts Print, 1952.

Read, Peter. *A Hundred Years War: The Wiradjuri People and the State*. Sydney: The Australian National University Press, 1988.

Read, Peter. *A Rape of the Soul So Profound*. Sydney: Allen & Unwin, 1999.

Read, Peter. *Charles Perkins: A Biography*. Ringwood: Penguin, 2001.

Reid, Frank. *The Romance of the Great Barrier Reef*. Sydney: Angus & Robertson, 1954.

Reynolds, Henry. *Frontier*. Sydney: Allen & Unwin, 1987.

Reynolds, Henry. *Why Weren't We Told?: A Personal Search for the Truth about Our History*. Ringwood, Vic: Penguin, 2000.

Reynolds, Henry. *Nowhere People*. Camberwell, Vic: Penguin, 2005.

Reynolds, Henry. *The Other Side of the Frontier: Aboriginal Resistance to The European Invasion of Australia*. Sydney: University of New South Wales Press, 2006.

Robertson, William. *Coo-ee Talks: A Collection of Lecturettes upon Early Experiences among the Aborigines of Australia Delivered from a Wireless Broadcasting Station*. Sydney: Angus & Robertson, 1928.

Rowley, C. D. *The Destruction of Aboriginal Society*. Harmondsworth, UK: Penguin Books, 1980. First published 1970.

Russell, Penny. *Savage or Civilised: Manners in Colonial Australia*. Sydney: University of New South Wales Press, 2010.

Russell, William (Werriberrie). *My Recollections*. Camden, NSW: The Oaks Historical Society for the Wollondilly Heritage Centre, 1991. First published 1914.

Rutherford, Jennifer. *The Gauche Intruder: Freud, Lacan and the White Australian Fantasy*. Carlton, Vic: Melbourne University Press, 2000.

Sadleir, Richard. *Aborigines of Australia*. Sydney: Thomas Richards, Government Printer, 1883.

Salisbury, T. and P. J. Gresser. *Windradyne of the Wiradjuri: Martial Law at Bathurst in 1824*. Sydney: Wentworth Books, 1971.

Sayre, Gordon M. *The Indian Chief as Tragic Hero: Native Resistance and the Literatures of America, from Moctezuma to Tecumseh*. Chapel Hill: The University of North Carolina Press, 2005.

Schaffer, Kay. *In the Wake of First Contact: The Eliza Fraser Stories*. Cambridge: Cambridge University Press, 1995.

Schama, Simon. *Dead Certainties (Unwarranted Speculations)*. New York: Alfred A. Knopf, 1991.

Sheppard, Barrie. *The Life of Bennelong: Living in Two Cultures*. Carlton, Vic: Echidna Books, 2005.

Smith, Keith Vincent. *King Bungaree: A Sydney Aborigine Meets the Great South Pacific Explorers, 1799–1830*. Kenthurst, NSW: Kangaroo Press, 1992.

Smith, Keith Vincent. *Bennelong: The Coming in of the Eora*. Sydney Cove 1788–1792. East Roseville, NSW: Kangaroo Press, 2001.

Smith, Keith Vincent. *Wallumedegal: An Aboriginal History of Ryde*. North Ryde, NSW: Community Services Unit, City of Ryde, 2005.

Smith, Ollie and Diana Plater. *Raging Partners: Two Worlds, One Friendship*. Broome, WA: Magabala Books, 2000.

Spence, Percy and Frank Fox. *Australia*. Cheltenham, Victoria: Vantage House, 1982.

Starck, Nigel. *Life after Death: The Art of the Obituary*. Carlton, Vic: Melbourne University Publishing, 2006.

Stephensen, P. R. *The History and Description of Sydney Harbour*. Sydney: Rigby Ltd, 1966.

Stern, Alexandra. *Eugenic Nation: Faults and Frontiers of Better Breeding in Modern America*. Berkeley: University of California Press, 2005.

Suttor, George. *Memoirs of George Suttor F.L.S. Banksian Collector (1774–1859)*, edited by George Mackaness. Australian Historical Monographs 13. Sydney: D. S. Ford Printers, 1977. First published 1948.

Suttor, H. M. *Australian Milestones and Stories of the Past, 1770–1914*. Sydney: John Andrew & Co., 1925.

Suttor, W. H. *Australian Stories Retold and Sketches of Country Life*. Bathurst, NSW: Glyndwyr Whalan, 1887.

Swift, Graeme. *Waterland*. London: Heinemann, 1983.

Swift, Jonathan. *Gulliver's Travels*. Adelaide University. Accessed 4 March 2009, ebooks.adelaide.edu.au/s/swift/jonathan/s97g/.

Tench, Watkin. *A Narrative of the Expedition to Botany Bay and A Complete Account of the Settlement at Port Jackson*. In *Watkin Tench's 1788*, edited by Tim Flannery. Melbourne: Text Publishing, 2009.

*The Annual Biography and Obituary for the Year 1829*, vol. 13. London: Longman, Rees, Orme, Brown and Green, 1829.

Wallace, Jennifer. *The Cambridge Introduction to Tragedy*. Cambridge: Cambridge University Press, 2007.

Watson, Frederick, ed. *Historical Records of Australia*, series 1, vol. 11. Sydney: The Library Committee of the Commonwealth Parliament, 1917.

Weaver, Jace. *Other Words: American Indian Literature, Law, and Culture*. Norman, Oklahoma: University of Oklahoma Press, 2001.

Weaver-Hightower, Rebecca. *Empire Islands: Castaways, Cannibals, and Fantasies of Conquest*. Minneapolis: University of Minnesota Press, 2007.

Welch, David. *17 Years Wandering among the Aboriginals, James Morrill 1864 and Eric Mjoberg 1918*. Virginia, NT: D Welch, 2006.

White, Hayden. *Tropics of Discourse: Essays in Cultural Criticism*. Baltimore: The Johns Hopkins University Press, 1978.

White, Richard. *Inventing Australia: Images and Identity*. Sydney: Allen & Unwin, 1981.

Willey, Keith. *When the Sky Fell Down: The Destruction of the Tribes of the Sydney Region 1788–1850s*. Sydney: Collins, 1979.

Willmot, Eric. *Pemulwuy: The Rainbow Warrior*. Sydney: Bantam Books, 1987.

Wilton, Elizabeth M. *The Unknown Land: A Story of Captain Phillip and Bennelong*. Adelaide: Rigby Limited, 1969.

Wyndham, Marivic. *A World Proof Life: Eleanor Dark, a Writer in Her Times, 1901–1985*. Sydney: UTSePress, 2007.

Ziegler, Oswald L. *Sydney Has an Opera House*. Artarmon, NSW: Ambascol Press, 1974.

# Film, Television and Theatre

Bangarra Dance Theatre. *Bennelong*. Choreographed by Stephen Page with Alana Valentine (dramaturg), premiered at the Sydney Opera House, June–July 2017.

Enoch, Wesley and Anita Heiss. *I am Eora*. CarriageWorks Theatre, Redfern, 8–14 January 2012.

McDonald, Malcolm. *The Extraordinary Tale of William Buckley*, presented by Michael Cathcart and David Tournier. Broadcast 11 April 2010. ABC television. December Films.

Nowra, Louis and Rachel Perkins. 'Episode 1: They Have Come to Stay'. *First Australians*. Broadcast 12 October 2008. Blackfella Films and Special Broadcasting Service Corporation.

Pearson, Wayne. *Windradyne: Wiradjuri Resistance, the Beginning*. Sydney: Aboriginal Education Unit, NSW Department of School Education, 1993.

*The Timeless Land: The Early Days of British Settlement in Australia*. Australian Broadcasting Commission: Roadshow Entertainment, c. 2006. First broadcast c. 1980.

## Speeches and Lectures

Burney, Linda. 'Speech To Teachers Federation Conference'. 1 July 2007. AIATSIS and NSW Teachers Federation, Canberra, 2007.

Calma, Tom. 'Essentials for Social Justice: Reform'. Australian Human Rights Commission. Speech delivered on 20 February 2008. Accessed 15 June 2018, www.hreoc.gov.au/about/media/speeches/social_justice/2008/essentials_reform20080220.html.

Jones, Victor Bernard. 'The Saga of James Morrill: The First Known White Resident of North Queensland'. Heatley Memorial Lecture, Townsville, 1979, transcript held by the Bowen Historical Society.

Loos, Noel. 'The History of North Queensland in Black and White: A Personal Retrospective'. Lecture presented at Thuringowa, 7 July 2008, Sir Robert Philp Lecture Series. Accessed 14 April 2012, www.townsville.qld.gov.au/facilities/libraries/resources/Documents/L2%20Loos%20Transcript.pdf (site discontinued).

McKew, The Hon. Maxine, Member for Bennelong (NSW). First Speech to Parliament. 14 February 2008. Accessed 4 December 2008, www.maxinemckew.com.au/2008/02/14/first-speech-to-parliament (site discontinued).

Rudd, Kevin. 'Speech by Prime Minister Kevin Rudd to the Parliament', 13 February 2008. Australian Government, Department of Foreign Affairs and Trade. Accessed 27 March 2012, www.dfat.gov.au/indigenous/apology-to-stolen-generations/rudd_speech.html.

Smith, Bernard. 'The Spectre of Truganini'. Boyer Lectures series. Sydney: Australian Broadcasting Commission, 1980.

Stanner, W. E. H. 'After the Dreaming'. Boyer Lectures series. Sydney: Australian Broadcasting Commission, 1968.

## Published or Broadcast Interviews

Comrie-Thompson, Paul, with Gary Johns and Warren Mundine. 'Nugget Coombs Revisited'. Counterpoint, ABC Radio National. Broadcast 23 April 2007. Accessed 8 April 2012, www.abc.net.au/radionational/programs/counterpoint/nugget-coombs-revisited/3233406.

Gotera, Vicente F. '"Lines of Tempered Steel": An Interview with Yusef Komunyakaa, *Callaloo* 13, no. 2 (Spring, 1990): 215–29.

Watson, Irene. 'The Aboriginal Tent Embassy 28 Years after it Was Established: Interview with Isobel Coe'. *Indigenous Law Bulletin* 5, no. 1 (2000): 17–18.

## Archival Sources

Bill Murray, Private Collection, Ayr.

Community Based Conservation. Voluntary Conservation Agreements. Brucedale–Suttor, Bathurst District, VCA075, Department of Environment, Climate Change and Water File: F/2030.

Copy of a statement made by James (Jimmy) Morrell before one of Her Majesty's justices of the peace for Queensland in the Court House, Bowen, 23 February 1863. State Library of Queensland. Heritage Collections. James Morrell Papers, Box 8923, Reference Code OM74-92 (courtesy of Phillip Murray, Townsville).

Murray-Prior, Thomas Lodge. Private Letter Book ('Journal of Tour of Inspection' [1863]). Mitchell Library, MS 3117, CY Reel 495.

NSW State Archives: Colonial Secretary, NRS 897, main series of letters received, 1788–1825.

Papers of P. J. Gresser. Australian Institute of Aboriginal and Torres Strait Islander Studies, MS21.

Phillip Murray, Private Collection, Townsville.

Suttor Family Papers 1774–1929. Mitchell Library Manuscripts Collection, MSS 2417.

Suttor Family Papers. Mitchell Library, MSS 1520/2, Diary of Charlotte Augusta Anne Suttor.

Townsville Museum and Historical Society Inc., files relating to James Morrill.

## Newspapers and Periodicals

*ABC Central West* (2017)

*Aboriginal Information Service Newsletter* (1976)

*The Age* (2008)

*The Argus* (1863)

*The Australian* (1822–1836, 1971)

*Ayr Advocate* (1981)

*The Benelong Bugle* (Sydney: J. Parks, Sydney Opera House Site) (1962)

*Bowen Independent* (1937, 1964)

*The Brisbane Courier* (1865–1929)

*Bush Matters* (National Parks and Wildlife Service NSW) (2002)

*The Canberra Times* (2000, 2008)

*Central Western Daily* (2015)

*The Courier* (Brisbane) (1863)

*The Courier Mail* (Brisbane) (2001)

*Cummings and Campbell's Monthly Magazine* (1931)

*Daily Mirror* (1956)

*The Daily Telegraph* (1922, 1977)

*Education Views* (2007)

*Empire* (1863)

*Geelong Advertiser* (1864)

*The Guardian* (2017)

*Illustrated Sydney News* (1871)

*Living Australia* (1985)

*National Aboriginal Day Magazine* (Department of Training and Workforce Development, Western Australia) (1981)

*Newcastle Herald* (2015)

*NSW Government Gazette* (2008)

*Parade* (1957)

*Pemulwy Newsletter* (Sydney: NSW Aboriginal Education Consultative Group) (1987–88)

*Port Denison Times* (1865, 1902)

*Queensland Guardian* (1863)

*The South Australian Advertiser* (1863)

*The Sun Herald* (2011)

*Sunday Mail* (2002)

*The Sunday Telegraph* (1973)

*The Sydney Gazette* (1805–36)

*The Sydney Monitor* (1822–36)

*The Sydney Morning Herald* (1863–2012)

*Townsville Daily Bulletin* (1907, 1929)

*Townsville Evening Star* (1893, 1927)

*Truth* (Brisbane) (1916)

*Western Advocate* (2001, 2016)

*The Western Times* (1954, 1962)

*The World's News* (1923)

## Theses

Fullagar, Kate. 'Savages and Moderns: The New World in Britain, 1710–c.1800'. PhD thesis, University of California, Berkeley, 2004.

Long, J. P. M. 'Bathurst 1813–1840: A Study of the Foundation and Development of the First Settlement on the Western Side of the Great Dividing Range'. BA honours thesis, University of Sydney, 1953.

Loos, Noel. 'Frontier Conflict in the Bowen District, 1861–1874'. MA thesis, James Cook University, Townsville, 1970.

## Miscellaneous

*Bowen Historical Society Bulletin*, 1964–2003. Issues 1–34 (1964–92) are held in the Mitchell Library, subsequent issues courtesy of the Bowen Historical Society.

'Caring for Place, Caring For Country' (education kit). Darlinghurst, NSW: Aboriginal Education and Training Directorate, NSW Department of Education and Training, c. 2005.

Koories in Theatre. 'Moobbajia: Speak an Unknown Language: The English Language Through Koori Eyes' (flyer). Sydney: Museum of Sydney, 1995. Held at the AIATSIS Library.

Macquarie Rivercare interpretive panels, Macquarie River Bicentennial Park, Bathurst, c. 2000.

NSW National Parks and Wildlife Service (Bathurst), interpretation materials for Windradyne's Grave, Brucedale, 2010.

www.ingramcontent.com/pod-product-compliance
Lightning Source LLC
Chambersburg PA
CBHW042336230426
43664CB00045B/2928